THE FALKLANDS WAR

Also by David Monaghan

JANE AUSTEN: Structure and Social Vision

JANE AUSTEN IN A SOCIAL CONTEXT

THE NOVELS OF JOHN LE CARRÉ

SMILEY'S CIRCUS: A Guide to the Secret World of John Le Carré

'EMMA': Contemporary Critical Essays

The Falklands War

Myth and Countermyth

David Monaghan

First published in Great Britain 1998 by
MACMILLAN PRESS LTD
Houndmills, Basingstoke, Hampshire RG21 6XS and London
Companies and representatives throughout the world

A catalogue record for this book is available from the British Library.

ISBN 0–333–65581–8

First published in the United States of America 1998 by
ST. MARTIN'S PRESS, INC.,
Scholarly and Reference Division,
175 Fifth Avenue, New York, N.Y. 10010

ISBN 0–312–21331–X

Library of Congress Cataloging-in-Publication Data
Monaghan, David.
The Falklands War : myth and countermyth / David Monaghan.
p.   cm.
Includes bibliographical references (p.   –   ) and index.
ISBN 0–312–21331–X (cloth)
1. Falkland Islands War, 1982—Public opinion—History.
2. Thatcher, Margaret—Public opinion—History.   3. Falkland Islands
War, 1982—Art and the war.   4. Falkland Islands War, 1982-
-Literature and the war.   5. Falkland Islands War, 1982—Motion
pictures and the war.   6. War in the press—Great Britain—History.
7. Myth.   8. Dissenters—Great Britain—Attitudes.   9. Public
opinion—Great Britain—History.   I. Title.
F3031.5.M643   1998
997'.110241—dc21   98–12681
                                                                              CIP

This book is printed on paper suitable for recycling and made from fully managed and
sustained forest sources.

10   9   8   7   6   5   4   3   2   1
07   06   05   04   03   02   01   00   99   98

Printed and bound in Great Britain by
Antony Rowe Ltd, Chippenham, Wiltshire

In memory of my mother

Contents

Acknowledgements

Many people and institutions have helped in the preparation of this book. I am particularly indebted to the Social Sciences and Humanities Research Council of Canada and to Mount Saint Vincent University for research grants. I also owe a debt of gratitude for the help that I have received from the staff of the British Film Institute, the British Library, the British Library Newspaper Division and the Imperial War Museum. Further thanks are due to Valerie Adams for good advice at an early stage in the preparation of this book, to Jim Aulich for sharing with me his collection of Falklands War material and for providing me with a proof copy of his book, *Framing the Falklands*, and to Greg Philo who was extremely helpful both during and after my visit to the Glasgow University Media Group.

Earlier versions of chapters 4 and 5 were published in Norman Page and Peter Preston, ed. *The Literature of Place* (London: Macmillan, 1993) and *Works and Days* 11 (1993): 79–100. I am grateful to Macmillan and to the editors of *Works and Days* for permission to reprint this material.

Introduction

For the most part, we know about war only as it is represented in words and images. Compared to other major life events such as birth, sex and death, relatively few people are ever directly involved in war, especially in the narrow sense of combat. Even a vicarious experience of any but the most sanitized versions of what an individual goes through in combat is most often denied to the civilian, because those who serve on the front line are usually either unable or unwilling to communicate a personal understanding of battlefield horrors that so drastically contradict the comfortable space accorded to war within peacetime constructions of reality.

Samuel Johnson, writing in 1771, offers some particularly acute observations about the attitudes instilled in civilians by their merely mediated understanding of war. He remarks, for example, on the 'coolness and indifference' with which people who will not be called upon to fight respond to the outbreak of war and goes on to note how 'those that hear of [war] at a distance, or read of it in books, but have never presented its evils to their minds, consider it little more than a splendid game; a proclamation, an army, a battle, and a triumph' (p. 370). Siegfried Sassoon's famous denunciation of the First World War, 'A Soldier's Declaration' (1917), includes similar comments on the inability of noncombatants to understand what happens on the battlefield. He writes scornfully, for example, about the 'callous complacence with which the majority of those at home regard the continuance of agonies which they do not share, and which they do not have sufficient imagination to realize' (quoted in Barker, p. 3).

We can also turn to Samuel Johnson for an insightful assessment of the perceptual and linguistic problems encountered by the soldier as he tries to bridge the gap between what 'heroic fiction' (p. 370) has taught him about war and the 'hopeless misery' (p. 371) that is its reality. A further example of the inadequacy of language learnt during peacetime in communicating the soldier's experience of combat is provided by a scene from Pat Barker's *Regeneration* (1991) in which the psychologist W. H. R. Rivers comes across a traumatized veteran whose psychosomatic

muteness so completely expresses the horror of 'Mons . . . , Ypres
. . . , the Somme . . . , Arras' (p. 224) and other First World War
battles that he is paradoxically 'silenced' (p. 238) when an electric
shock treatment restores his voice. Ken Lukowiak similarly comments on the way in which the linguistic resources at his disposal
failed him when he tried to write to his wife about his part in
the battle for Goose Green: 'I could not write. I was searching
for the words to describe the events of the past few days but I
could not find them. They had been stolen from me, along with
a part of my soul, on the battlefield of Goose Green' (p. 97).

Those who take on the task of giving meaning to particular
wars and to war in general thus have tremendous freedom but
also, whether or not they acknowledge it, a huge burden of responsibility. At one end of the spectrum are propagandists and
sensationalizers and at the other those with ambitions to uncover
what war has to tell us about the human condition. From an
ideological perspective, however, it is the sum total of all interpretative acts that is finally crucial because of the important part
played by the meanings that cluster around a country's wars in
reinforcing, supplementing or subverting official formulations of
national identity.

Although they occupy a privileged position amongst interpreters
of war, power elites have not been very successful in making
the major wars of this century carry meanings that serve their
ideological ends. For example, establishment ideas about war as
a glorious and honourable crusade destined to end in national
purification and revitalization that were dominant at the beginning of the First World War had been largely discredited by the
time a peace settlement was achieved in 1918. As Hynes argues
in *A War Imagined*, such ideas became increasingly untenable as
an apparently endless conflict developed involving battles of
unprecedented bloodiness fought not by knights on noble steeds
but by the millions of common soldiers who lived and all too
frequently died in the 'troglodyte world' (Fussell, p. 36) of the
trenches. Therefore, they were gradually forced to yield the interpretive field to an understanding of war shaped by the antiheroic
writings of the unusually large number of 'articulate men' (Hynes,
p. 114) who served on the front line. As a result of the efforts of
Owen, Sassoon, Graves and others, the First World War finally
yielded up a myth structured around embitterment and mistrust
that, in Hynes' view, 'altered the ways in which people thought

not only about war, but about the world' (p. xi).

The experience of the United States during the Vietnam War was similar. Stubborn resistance on the part of a supposedly inferior enemy combined with antiwar protest at home and unrelenting media coverage of the ever-increasing number of American casualties eventually resulted in a widespread loss of faith in what Englehardt calls 'victory culture'. Originally scripted as a glorious expression of the American Dream in which capitalist efficiency and technological know-how triumphs over the dark forces of communism, the military incursion into South East Asia ended up as the 'nightmare' (Englehardt, p. 194) story of a victimized United States sucked down into the 'quagmire' (pp. 198–9) of 'war without end' (p. 195).

In sharp contrast, few dissenting voices were heard in Britain during the Second World War. Nevertheless, this war also finally generated a set of meanings that was, if anything, even more destabilizing than the more obviously subversive interpretative processes at work during the Great and Vietnam Wars. Thus, in his book, *The Myth of the Blitz*, Angus Calder explains how, as a result of the Dunkirk and Blitz experiences, the traditional and essentially upper class myth of an ancient nation standing alone in defence of 'humane values' (p. 18) was first supplemented by and then made subordinate to a new narrative strand that emphasized the role of ordinary people and 'communitarianism' (p. 204) in shaping the country's destiny. This new understanding of the British class system had gained such wide acceptance by the end of the war that the voters chose as their first peacetime Government a Labour Party committed to making a reality of the egalitarian principles embedded in the myth of the Blitz.

However, in the case of the Falklands War, which is the main subject of this book, the British establishment was much more successful in creating an interpretive framework that served its own ideological agenda than it had been during either of the two World Wars. The Falklands War was relatively brief, beginning with the Argentinian invasion on 2 April 1982 and ending with the recapture of Port Stanley on 14 June 1982. Nevertheless, it lasted long enough for Margaret Thatcher to transform the struggle for the Falklands into a myth of national rebirth in which feats of arms would open up the way for a simultaneous retrieval of pre-Welfare State verities and radical change along monetarist economic lines.

Alternatives to a reading of the situation designed to lend credibility to the Conservative Party's contradictory and previously
faltering political agenda were offered by Labour MPs such as
Tony Benn and left of centre newspapers such as the *Guardian*,
the *Observer* and the *Daily Mirror*. However, few people were
willing to listen to the voice of dissent partly because Thatcher's
Falklands myth struck a deep chord with a population desperate for some good news about the future of a country apparently locked into an irreversible postcolonial decline and partly
because of the convergence of a number of factors helpful to the
Prime Minister's cause. These included the widespread support
Thatcher received amongst the British tabloid press; the failure
of most Labour MPs to challenge a myth of nation intended to
discredit the Party's achievements in the period following its
election in 1945; the logistical problems inherent in a war fought
in a remote location 8000 miles from home as a result of which
it became impossible for newspapers and, more important, television to communicate disillusioning images of death and wounding; and, most significant of all, the speedy and conclusive manner
in which the task force overcame the challenges facing it on the
way to total victory over Argentina.

There was huge public support for Thatcher's version of events
by the time the war in the South Atlantic reached its triumphant
conclusion. Nevertheless, the Falklands myth did not achieve its
final shape with the recapture of Port Stanley. On the contrary,
in the years since the end of the war subversive retellings of the
Falklands story have proven to be amongst the most effective
tactics employed by critics of the Conservative hegemony that
Thatcher secured by seizing the interpretive initiative in 1982.
The dissident voices to which I am referring are not, of course,
those of intellectuals intent upon subjecting Margaret Thatcher's
absurdly hyperreal scenarios to cool-headed rational analysis,[1]
as Christopher Norris would have wanted (1990, 1992), but those
of artists in command of a variety of techniques capable of generating narratives with as much visceral appeal as Thatcher's.

Reworkings of the Falklands myth are thus to be found across
a broad generic spectrum including works for children (John
Branfield's novel, *The Falklands Summer* [1987]); cartoons (*Further Down on Maggie's Farm* [1982] and *The 'If...' Chronicles* [1983]
by Steve Bell; *The Tin-Pot Foreign General and the Old Iron Lady*
[1984] by Raymond Briggs; *Father Kissmass and Mother Claws* [1985]

by Bel Mooney and Gerald Scarfe); stage plays (*Sink the Belgrano!* [1986] by Steven Berkoff; *Restoration* [1988] by Edward Bond; *Woundings* [1986] by Jeff Noon; *Arrivederci Millwall* [1987] by Nick Perry); films (*Resurrected* [1989], written by Martin Allen and directed by Paul Greengrass; *The Ploughman's Lunch* [1983], written by Ian McEwan and directed by Richard Eyre; *For Queen and Country* [1988] written by Martin Stellman and Trix Worrell and directed by Martin Stellman); television plays (*The Falklands Factor* [1983] written by Don Shaw and directed by Colin Bucksey); television films (Nick Perry's adaption of *Arrivederci Millwall* [1990], directed by Charles MacDougall; *An Ungentlemanly Act* [1992], written and directed by Stuart Urban; *Tumbledown* [1988], written by Charles Wood and directed by Richard Eyre); television documentaries (Yorkshire television's *The Falklands War: The Untold Story* [1987]); ITN/Granada; *Battle for the Falklands* [1982]; BBC 1's *The Price of Victory* [1983] and *Task Force South: The Battle for the Falklands* [1982]; Channel 4's *The Falklands War* [1992]; art works (Manchester City Art Gallery's *The Falklands Factor* exhibition [1988–9]); a poem ('Elegy for the Welsh Dead in the Falkland Islands, 1982' [1988] by Tony Conran); a novel (*Swansong* [1986] by Richard Francis); travel books (*Coasting* [1986] by Jonathan Raban; *The Kingdom by the Sea* [1983] by Paul Theroux); soldiers' memoirs (*When the Fighting is Over* [1988] by John and Robert Lawrence; *A Soldier's Song* [1993] by Ken Lukowiak; *A Message from the Falklands* [1983] by David Tinker; *Summer Soldier* [1990] by Philip Williams).

The most effective of these countermythic works, as I will be demonstrating later in this book, reframe the official Falklands myth as a network of lies constructed by a self-interested politician willing to distort language and history in order to advance her own political agenda. Thus reshaped, the official myth is made to function as a metaphor for a neoconservative Britain utterly lacking in the integrity fundamental to the fulfillment of Thatcher's promises of national rebirth. Understood in this way Britain is no longer a country infused with a spirit of new hope but one where power and wealth are concentrated in the hands of a small, corrupt élite, leaving the rest of the population to seek escape from their unsatisfactory lives in nostalgia or violence.

Because of the attention paid to Thatcher, her construction of reality and to the type of society she claimed to be shaping, events in the South Atlantic only intermittently take centre stage in the alternative Falklands myth. Nevertheless, the people of the

Falklands, the islands themselves and the war that was fought there have proven to be fruitful sources of further metaphors for a Britain very different from the one postulated by Margaret Thatcher. According to the official myth, the Falkland Islands is a rural paradise inhabited by a racially and culturally homogeneous population content to live under the benevolent rule of a British colonial administration and is therefore a model for the Britain Thatcher is seeking to liberate from the choking grip of socialist corporatism. The task force, in its turn, embodies the sense of purpose, commitment to the national good and even the entrepreneurial spirit that will characterize a British people freed from the shackles of the Welfare State. In the countermyth, however, these metaphorical attributions are turned on their heads with the result that the Falklands, their inhabitants and the service personnel who fought the war with Argentina now mirror a nation whose terminal decline, far from being reversed, is actually being accelerated as a result of the socially divisive and crassly materialistic policies of the Thatcher Government.

In the chapters that follow I will be examining the rhetorical strategies employed first by politicians and journalists in constructing the Falklands myth and then by a number of playwrights, film makers, cartoonists and travel writers intent upon displacing this myth with alternative understandings of the Falklands War and its significance for British society. Inevitably, my starting point is the narrative constructed by Margaret Thatcher, her parliamentary supporters and the tabloid press in order to make events in the South Atlantic lend credibility to a Conservative ideological agenda that was finding little public support in the months immediately prior to the outbreak of hostilities.

Thus, much of Chapter 1 is devoted to an analysis of some important texts that demonstrate how politicians and journalists worked together throughout the war with Argentina to establish a connection between the recovery of the Falklands and the retrieval of the authentic Britain long submerged beneath the debilitating Welfare State policies pursued by successive Labour and Conservative Governments since 1945. The later parts of the chapter focus on two key texts from the period immediately following the Argentinian surrender in which Thatcher, now employing a matter of fact style rather than the inflated rhetoric characteristic of her wartime utterances, turns her attention away from the regressive and towards the radical parts of the

Conservative Party's Janus-faced hegemonic project by identifying entrepreneurial themes in the Falklands War.

The Falklands War was very much a personal triumph for Margaret Thatcher and attempts to impose an alternative framework of meaning upon it are hardly likely to have been successful without a reassessment of her role as maker and hero of the official Falklands myth. Chapter 2 deals with three works that have taken on this task. The first is Don Shaw and Colin Bucksey's television play, *The Falklands Factor*. Overtly about Samuel Johnson's role in the Falklands crisis of 1770–1, *The Falklands Factor* is ultimately concerned with identifying similarities between Thatcher and Lords North and Chatham as ruthless politicians prepared to sacrifice all their obligations to humanity in order to advance personal political goals. The other two works discussed in this chapter, Steven Berkoff's play, *Sink the Belgrano!* and Steve Bell's *If...* cartoon strip offer a very similar view of Thatcher. However, their methods are much more direct than Shaw's and in retelling the Falklands story they substitute an almost bestial demagogue for the regal figure at the centre of the official myth.

Thatcher also makes an appearances in *The Ploughman's Lunch*, *Arrivederci Millwall*, *The Kingdom by the Sea* and *Coasting*, the works under examination in the next two chapters. However, all four are ultimately more concerned with challenging the idyllic image of Britain under Conservative rule that emerges from Thatcher's Falklands narrative than with Thatcher herself. Ian McEwan and Richard Eyre's film, *The Ploughman's Lunch* and Nick Perry's play/ film *Arrivederci Millwall* are brought together in Chapter 3 because each approaches its subject by offering alternatives to the heroic, patriotic soldier-entrepreneur who functions as the representative Englishman in the official Falklands myth. For McEwan, the true standard bearer for the spirit of Thatcherism is James Penfield, a would-be classless man on the make with no loyalties to anyone but himself and no regard for British institutions or history beyond the possibilities they provide for exercises in cynical self promotion. Perry, on the other hand, structures his critique of Thatcherite Britain around the activities of Billy Jarvis, a violent, xenophobic and deeply materialistic football hooligan.

There are also striking similarities in the approach that Paul Theroux and Jonathan Raban take to their subject matter in *The Kingdom by the Sea* and *Coasting*, the two travel books that are the focus of Chapter 4. Not only are both books records of journeys that Theroux and Raban took around Britain during the Falklands War but, more important, both are written from a postmodern perspective that allows their authors to challenge the authority of the archetypal patterns upon which their own and Thatcher's narratives are based before moving on to develop national stories of a very different character to the one embedded within the official Falklands myth. Thus, the revitalized Britain envisioned by Thatcher is transformed by Theroux and Raban into a decaying place where the past serves not as repository of the national essence but as a nostalgic bolt hole for a despairing petit bourgeoisie and the future, far from promising a monetarist nirvana, is likely to be even more violent and repressive than the present.

My attention shifts in Chapter 5 from the Falklands myth to the language in which it is embodied. The two films around which this chapter is organized, *Tumbledown*, written for television by Charles Wood and directed by Richard Eyre, and *Resurrected*, written by Martin Allen and directed by Paul Greengrass, share a concern with teasing out some of the moral issues obscured by the chivalric language that was so effective in helping Thatcher and her supporters make the Falklands War function as myth rather than as history. *Tumbledown* is the story of Robert Lawrence, a lieutenant in the Scots Guards who suffers a terrible head wound during the assault on Mount Tumbledown, while the plot of *Resurrected* develops out of the ironic situation created when the very ordinary Kevin Deakin reappears six weeks after his supposed hero's death in the same battle. In dramatizing the torment experienced by the crippled Lawrence and the psychically wounded Deakin as they try to bridge the gap between what actually happened to them in combat and the heroic conception of wartime death and wounding, the authors and directors of the two films make the point that Thatcher's exploitation of the political potential of chivalric rhetoric caused her to lose sight of her obligations to those members of the armed forces whose bodies and minds were co-opted to the service of disembodied ideals.

The book ends with an analysis of Stuart Urban's television film, *An Ungentlemanly Act*, the most significant work to emerge from the tenth anniversary of the Falklands War. The homage that Urban pays to aspects of the official Falklands myth is testimony to its continuing appeal. However, in finally offering a

critical assessment of the symbolic role played by an idealized
Falkland Islands in the official myth and more broadly of the
very concept of war, Urban also reflects the considerable degree
of scepticism that had developed about the value of Thatcher's
South Atlantic adventure in the ten years since the end of the
Falklands War.

It would be unwise to overrate the political importance of the
body of work with which I am dealing in this book. Certainly it
can claim some credit for the failure of the British public and
media to react with much enthusiasm to the tenth anniversary
of a war about which they had once been so enthusiastic. At the
same time, though, the ideological agenda that Thatcher promoted
through the medium of the Falklands War continues to flourish.
As I write towards the end of 1996, the Conservative Government, now led by John Major, seems to be on its last legs. However,
the likely victor in the next election is not the Labour Party of
Jim Callaghan, Michael Foot or Neil Kinnock, who between them
suffered four defeats at the hands of the Conservatives, but the
New Labour Party of Tony Blair, a man who has expressed
admiration for Thatcher, who seems embarrassed by the term
socialism and who appears to have little respect for the trade
union movement.

However, what I will be arguing in the main body of this book
is that there are two important reasons why the literature and
films of the Falklands War deserve consideration. First of all, as
I will demonstrate through close readings of the interplay between
theme and generic convention, the best of these works, amongst
which I would include all of the films, plays, cartoon strips and
travel books examined in the chapters that follow, are complex
works of art that rise well above the level of counter propaganda.
Second, the body of literature and film that has developed in
response to the official Falklands myth offers a complex and
sympathetic view of the human condition. In so doing, it serves
to remind us that there are alternatives to the reductive and
savagely dehumanizing monetarist and entrepreneurial agenda
that was given credibility by Thatcher's skillful manipulation of
her war with Argentina and that continues to this day to dominate
the political and social landscape in Britain and other countries.

Notes

1. I have in mind the work of a number of left wing commentators who have written incisively about the Falklands myth but to a very limited audience. These include Barnett, Chambers, Hall, Hobsbawm, Nairn, Samuel, and Wright.

1

Margaret Thatcher and the Making of the Falklands Myth

The Argentinian invasion of the Falkland Islands on 2 April 1982 presented Margaret Thatcher and her Conservative Government with a crucial challenge. Should the Argentinians succeed in retaining control of the islands, Thatcher's already shaky image as a strong political leader would be destroyed, making electoral defeat inevitable. Should the invaders be ousted, however, either through diplomacy or, preferably, through a military counter attack, Conservative supremacy would be greatly reinforced. As things turned out, the Argentinian forces were routed by a task force dispatched to the South Atlantic on 5 April and sovereignty over the Falklands was restored to Britain on 14 June. It was therefore the Argentinian Junta that fell from power while Thatcher and her Party scaled unprecedented heights of popularity.

Military assessments of the Falklands campaign suggest that there was a high level of risk inherent in the decision to send a task force 8000 miles into a South Atlantic winter to face an enemy well entrenched on the ground and capable of fighting an effective air war and that, regardless of Thatcher's assertions to the contrary, defeat was a distinct possibility on a number of occasions (Thompson, J., pp. xvii–xix). Nevertheless, while she may have been the child of good fortune, Margaret Thatcher, aided by her political allies and a friendly media, most notably the *Sun* newspaper, mounted an extremely effective campaign in the war of words that raged on the home front. As a result she ensured that the maximum benefit would accrue to herself and the Conservative Party in the event that her bold gambit in seeking a military solution to the Falklands crisis paid off. In this chapter, I will analyze some of the ways in which Thatcher used the

situation created by Galtieri's invasion not simply to increase
support for the Government but also to consolidate her previously stuttering campaign to establish a new hegemony based
on a wedding together of radical monetarist economic policies
and a regressive vision of British society.

THATCHER'S VISION OF BRITAIN

Once she had taken over the leadership of the Conservative Party
from Edward Heath, Margaret Thatcher wasted no time in
announcing that she was a new type of 'conviction' politician
(Barnett, p. 69) who rejected the consensus politics that had dominated the postwar era. 'Socialism', she stated baldly at the 1975
Party Conference, her first as leader, is 'bad for Britain', not only
because it leads to poor economic management, in the form of
'high inflation, high unemployment, low productivity and record
taxation', but also because it is spiritually stultifying and has
caused a 'loss of confidence' and 'a sense of hopelessness' (1989,
p. 20) in the British public. The Welfare State did not, therefore,
feature prominently in Thatcher's vision of the future. Instead,
she pledged herself to a capitalist system capable, in her view,
of producing 'a higher standard' of both 'prosperity and happiness' (1989, p. 21).

Thatcher's version of capitalism was heavily influenced by new
right or neoconservative thinking in general and the economic
theories of Milton Friedman in particular.[1] Its main features were
a commitment to sound money, less government, privatization,
lower taxes and sharply reduced public spending, and deregu-
lation aimed at allowing the logic of the marketplace to assert
itself. Odd as it might seem, however, this obviously radical
economic-social programme was not presented as something new
but as a turning back of the clock in order to make 'the Britain
you have known . . ., the Britain your children will know' (1989,
p. 22). Only by setting such a direction, Thatcher argued, could
she hope to rescue her country from the ever-increasing threat
posed by socialism's 'deliberate attack on our values – on merit,
excellence, our heritage and our great past' (1989, p. 22). Thus,
as Raphael Samuel puts it, 'a Government ruthlessly intent on
modernizing (and Americanizing) British society nevertheless
call[ed] for a return to traditional ways' (1: lvii). Iain Chambers

similarly comments that the 'Thatcher vision [was] indebted to a backwards-looking sense of national heritage despite its stress on profit and the enterprise culture' (p. 17).

As Thatcher moved from talk of money supply growth, PSBR (Public Sector Borrowing Requirement) and minimum lending rate to a discourse constructed around phrases such as 'our heritage' and 'our great past', so the real world gave way to myth, the secular to the sacred and history to essence or timelessness. What Thatcher hoped to achieve by a shift in both idiom and relationship to time and space was to locate herself within a well-established nostalgic tradition, broadly Conservative but profoundly appealing to all sectors of the British population. When viewed from the perspective provided by this tradition, the contemporary state, Great Britain, dissolves into the 'ancient nation', England, a rural paradise, structured around the patriarchal family and a well-defined social hierarchy, and inhabited by an inward-looking, racially homogeneous 'island race'.

Although this idealized nation transcends actual time and space, it nevertheless takes on tangible form through its association in the popular imagination with some of the more heavily mythologized eras, events, people, places and institutions in British history. Thus, by simply speaking of 'our heritage' or 'great past', Thatcher could rely on conjuring up a network of images including the Monarchy, Parliament, the Church of England, the Golden Age of Queen Elizabeth I, Shakespeare's history plays, the eighteenth-century country house, the Empire, the long afternoon of Edwardian England, and the 1930s version of 'Deep England', an idealized landscape of 'exquisite moderation' (J. B. Priestley, quoted by Calder, p. 185) stretching 'from Hardy's Wessex to Tennyson's Lincolnshire' (Calder p. 182).

Furthermore, despite being in one sense forever frozen in immutable perfection, 'England' can most profitably be understood as part of a narrative structure. According to this narrative, the real England is constantly under threat from enemies within and without, not of destruction, because that would be impossible, but of becoming submerged, lost or forgotten. However, so the story goes, at such times the forces of good, usually through military action taken in defence of the weak, reassert the nation's fundamental ideals of freedom, rule of law, family and the Christian faith, thereby restoring a revitalized England its destined position of moral preeminence within the world community.[2] The mythic history of England is not, therefore, either static or linear. On the contrary, it is built around the cyclical repetition of a single narrative in which the 'Absolute Spirit' (Wright, p. 26) of the nation disappears from view under the pressure of specific social or political forces or because of the amnesia of its people only to reappear in its full glory as the result of mighty deeds performed by heroic people.

Thatcher seems to have had two main objectives in proposing that, far from merely setting a new economic course, her pursuit of monetarist and free enterprise policies constituted an act of resistance against socialist tyranny which, if successful, would earn her a place alongside Churchill, Wellington, Wolfe and other heroes in the national myth of endless renewal. First, she was tapping into that huge reservoir of nostalgic longing for faded glories that existed amongst a public finally aware, as a result of the events of the 1970s, that Britain's transition from imperial power to modern liberal democracy had been accompanied not only by the disappearance or radical alteration of many well-established national institutions but by an absolute political and relative economic decline.

Second, and more important to her specific political objectives, by locating herself in a mythic context, Thatcher was moving into a realm where, as Roland Barthes argues, 'contingency' is made to seem 'eternal', 'reality [is] ..., emptied ... of history [and becomes] filled ... with nature', 'and 'speech' is 'depoliticized' (p. 155). As a result she was able to transform a hegemonic project structured around a new right agenda that contested much of what had been taken for granted in Britain's postwar political and economic landscape into a patriotic call for national unity. Because of its supposed origins in a natural bond of shared space and time, this call offered no scope for debate. In other words, Thatcher was proposing a Britain whose 'soul' is 'the perfect naturalization of a [Conservative] hegemonic view of the nation' (Wright, p. 50), with the ultimate goal of transforming an ideological stance into a commonsense fact. Or, as Stuart Hall puts it, Thatcher 'deployed a discourse of "nation" and "people"' in order to identify 'being British' with the 'restoration of competition and profitability; with tight money and sound finance' (pp. 27, 29).

The depoliticized character of the discourse that the adoption of a mythic view of nation made available to Margaret Thatcher

obviously added a great deal of force to her attacks on the Labour
Party, the Welfare State and trade unions by transforming what
was actually no more than one term in a heavily polarized ideological contest into a definitive statement about the irrelevance
and indeed the antipathy of socialism to the 'real' Britain. As a
result, it became possible for Thatcher to state categorically that
'the Conservative Party is an integral part of the British tradition, not to be explained in abstract terms, but as a part of the
living flesh of British life over the generations'. Socialism, on
the other hand, is simply 'one of the blind alleys of history' (1989,
p. 50).

Thatcher thus made socialism vulnerable to attacks on two fronts.
On the one hand, it could be engaged in an ideological debate
in which socialist values and policies were challenged with the
aim of proving the superiority of capitalism. On the other, by
conjuring up a mythic image of the real nation as Tory, Thatcher
was able to create a hierarchy of absolute value in which socialism stands in opposition to everything that is authentically British.
Neither Conservative ideology nor myth gave similar permission, however, for Thatcher to openly promote the racist agenda
that was, according to many of her critics, the second major item
in her new right programme.[3] Consequently, despite the support that she would have won amongst far-right Tories at least,
Thatcher had to eschew overt attacks on Britain's racial minorities if she was to avoid sharing the fate of her mentor, Enoch
Powell, who was denied a place in the Heath Cabinet of 1973
following a series of speeches demanding repatriation of black
immigrants and was eventually forced to leave the Conservative
Party.

In practice, though, the requirement that she operate in a covert
fashion did not much hinder Thatcher because of the many opportunities provided by nationalistic discourse, in an era of mass
immigration from the Caribbean and the Indian subcontinent,
for dropping broad hints that the ranks of those enemies who
were supposedly laying seige to the traditional ways, shared values
and old loyalties of the 'island race' included more than socialists.
Once defined in terms provided by this almost messianic language
of national rebirth, black immigrants, like the political left, could
easily be treated as a group whose exclusion was a matter not
of ideological contestation but of self-evident necessity.

Although the Conservatives were victorious in the 1979 election, four years after Thatcher had assumed the leadership of the party, there is little evidence to link this success to the distinctive blend of hard-headed new right economic policies and visionary images of national revitalization out of which, as we have seen, she shaped her political agenda. For all the energy she put into casting herself in the role of national saviour, Thatcher was disliked by a broad segment of the public because of her antagonistic and hectoring political style. Neither would her attempts to stigmatize the Labour Party as a socialist enemy within seem to have had much relevance to the defeat of a Callaghan Government brought down by the very unions with which Thatcher accused it of forming an unholy alliance against the real interests of the nation. Despite the increased access to the public ear that she enjoyed as Prime Minister, Thatcher was no more successful in capturing the imagination of the public during her first three years in power. Indeed, by the end of 1981, the popularity of the Conservatives had fallen to the lowest level ever recorded by a British Government and Thatcher herself became briefly the most unpopular postwar Prime Minister (Gamble, p. 108).

There are several obvious reasons why Thatcher's ideological programme failed to win widespread acceptance. First, while many British people were certainly gripped by a nostalgic longing for the nation's lost glories, especially as Labour's economic crisis lengthened into the Conservatives' recession, it must have been almost immediately evident that there was little of a practical nature that Thatcher or her ministers could do to make a reality out of their particular vision of the authentic nation, so remote was it from the actual circumstances that prevailed in contemporary Britain. Only a few fragments of Empire remained, life in Britain was primarily urban, class relations were characterized by conflict rather than by authority and deference, multiracialism had become an established feature of the social landscape, most people no longer accepted the precepts of Christianity, and even such basic principles as the rule of law no longer enjoyed universal consent. The few measures the Government did take during the Thatcher years – the white-first policy, attacks on the power of trade unions, and the introduction of a more nationalistic school curriculum, for instance – simply underlined the size of the gap between present reality and Thatcher's conception of Britain.

Second, a blatant contradiction existed between the type of

society envisaged in the idea of a return to the national heritage and the kind likely to emerge from economic reform along new right lines. Most obviously, a creed of pure entrepreneurship, under which it becomes 'more stylish to consume rather than to care' (Young, p. 537), is irreconcilable with Christian values, a commitment to the protection of the weak, a sense of duty and even, in the case of someone like Robert Maxwell, a regard for the rule of law. Similar contradictions are to be found in the roles assigned to the working class in Thatcher's two models of British society. As participants in a traditional social hierarchy, they would be expected to accept their lot in life and defer to their betters. As members of 'a property owning democracy', on the other hand, they would be free to enjoy the fruits and suffer the risks that go along with participation in an 'enterprise culture'.

Third, and most important in our present context, there was a major problem with Thatcher's attempts to subsume her myth of national revival within a neoconservative discourse. Even a people such as the British, who longed for something to satisfy their deep-rooted nostalgia, were scarcely desperate enough to take a set of monetarist policies and a group of new right ideologues as adequate objective correlatives for the acts of heroism and great heroes required to recover England's 'lost inheritance', 'the essential stuff of [its] history' (Wright, pp. 178, 176).

THE FALKLANDS WAR AND THATCHERITE IDEOLOGY

Viewed in the context of Thatcher's struggles to smooth over the gaps, contradictions and rough spots in her 'Janus'-faced (Nairn, p. 348) vision of the nation moving simultaneously into the past and the future, the Falklands War begins to look less a problem for the Conservative Government than a golden opportunity to repackage its ideological project into a more acceptable form. There can be few situations, for example, so well suited to Thatcher's oppositional style of rhetoric than that created in wartime, when all official discourse is inevitably rooted in the positioning of the two sides around the rigid polarities of such moral absolutes as good and evil. Furthermore, war provides much more fertile territory than economic policy for the working up of these polarities into a mythic discourse. Indeed, the situation created by the Argentinian invasion of the Falkland Islands was so rich as to allow Thatcher, aided by her fellow Conservatives and the media, to develop a two-tiered mythic narrative that succeeded in enhancing the popularity of both the Prime Minister and her Party and in finally advancing at least parts of the hegemonic project that had been so badly stalled up to this point.

The first tier of the Thatcherite narrative is based on the archetype of the heroic quest and serves to raise the war above its immediate circumstances, thereby disarming opposition and replacing debate with an appeal to deeply atavistic urges. The second more specific tier comprises the familiar story in which England, having been aroused from a deep slumber in response to the needs of a helpless victim deprived of liberty and democracy by an act of villainy, once again dons the mantle of greatness and regains its destined position of moral preeminence amongst the nations of the world. A version of this story had, of course, already played a part in Thatcher's attempts to claim a role for the Conservatives as the natural Party of Government. Now, though, the hero, who is variously Thatcher herself, as warrior queen, the British task force and individual soldiers, most notably Colonel 'H' Jones, takes on a more familiar martial guise, thus allowing attempts to postulate the gurus of monetarism as a new model of heroism to be abandoned, at least until the war had run its course.

Other aspects of Thatcher's ideological agenda were advanced by the transformation of the British troops and, more significantly, the Falkland Islands and its inhabitants into symbols of the essential England. This transformational process gave concrete form to the Prime Minister's previously implausible claims to be involved in a process of national retrieval; it also provided a platform for the further development of her prewar programme to exclude racial minorities and the political left since their role as enemies within acquired a sharper edge by being placed in a wartime context. A final stage in the mythologizing of the Falklands War occurred when, relying on the enormous prestige accruing to her in the days following military victory, Thatcher twice offered reworkings of the Falklands myth in which she shifted the source of national revival from military heroism back to free enterprise.

THATCHER'S USE OF WARTIME DISCOURSE

Throughout the Falklands War, the conventions of traditional wartime discourse proved to be particularly compatible with Thatcher's customary rhetorical style, especially in the context of parliamentary debate with its ritualized structure of antagonistic polarities. Thus, as early as the emergency session in the House of Commons on 3 April, the day after the Argentinian invasion, we find discussion of the Falklands War organized almost exclusively around the kind of simple assertions and binary oppositions so well suited to Thatcher's style of argumentation. The tone of the debate is set by the Prime Minister's opening comments about sovereignty in which she eschews all reference to the muddled history of claims and counterclaims that had long bedevilled Britain's dispute with Argentina over the Falklands in favour of a series of categorical statements intended to reduce the issue to a simple matter of self-evident right and wrong. According to Thatcher, then, there can be 'no doubt about our sovereignty which has been continuous since 1833' (Morgan, p. 5). There is a similar certainty in her assertion that, by 'usurp[ing]' 'the lawful British Government of the islands', the Argentinians acted without 'a shred of justification and not a scrap of legality' and made themselves guilty of 'unprovoked aggression' (p. 4). Both Edward DuCann, who states that 'our sovereignty is unimpeachable' (Morgan, p. 10) and Donald Stewart, for whom Argentinian claims to sovereignty over the Falklands have always been 'totally unfounded' (Morgan, p. 15), echo their leader's dogmatism.

By thus erasing the messy reality that existed prior to 2 April, Thatcher laid the groundwork for a reading of the crisis as a simple conflict between two sharply contrasting opponents. On the one side is Argentina, which Thatcher invariably speaks of as 'the aggressor' (Langdon, p. 1); on the other is Britain, always assigned the role of the 'aggrieved' or the 'victim' (Thatcher, 1986, p. 74) in Thatcherite discourse. In similar vein, Thatcher takes every opportunity to emphasize the differences that exist between 'a military junta and a democratic government of free people' (Morgan, p. 74). Building on these essential distinctions, Thatcher is able to construct a lengthy list of contrasts between the virtues and vices of the two sides, most notably in the series of binary oppositions around which her address to the Conservative

Women's Conference is organized. Thus, she sets off 'the rule of law' against 'the rule of force'; 'peace – with freedom, with justice, with democracy' against 'armed aggression' and 'illegal seizure'; active seeking of 'a peaceful solution' against 'playing for time'; 'principle' against 'expediency'; 'self-determination' against 'colonialism'; 'the cause of freedom and the rule of law' in 'support of 'the weak' against 'aggression by the strong'; and 'justice' against 'jingoism' (Thatcher, 1986, pp. 73–6).

Thatcher's efforts received support during the Falklands debates from Parliamentary colleagues such as Arthur Palmer and David Stoddard who contrast Britain, 'a democracy . . ., unequalled in the world' with Argentina, 'an evil regime', 'a squalid military dictatorship', ruled by 'a trigger-happy junta' (Morgan, pp. 255–6); John Nott, who promises that, while the Argentinians 'put out' 'propaganda and misinformation', the British will 'publish nothing but facts' (Morgan, p. 199); and Winston Churchill, for whom the Falklands War is a struggle between 'honest, decent English gentlemen' and Argentinian 'crooks' (Morgan, pp. 56–7). The stigmatization of the Argentinians as the antithesis of the democratic, freedom loving, peaceable and honest British is further reinforced by John Peyton's characterization of their 'regime' as 'odious' (Morgan, p. 33) and by W. R. Rees-Davies's use of a metaphor in which they become savage dogs that must be brought 'to heel' (Morgan, p. 261).

Taking its lead from the Government, the popular press consistently emphasizes the heroism and humanity of 'our boys' while casting the Argentinians as the villains of the piece. Once war has broken out they are usually referred to with the demeaning epiphet 'Argies'; subjected to sneering headlines such as 'STICK IT UP YOUR JUNTA!' (*Sun*, 1 May 1982, p. 2) and the infamous 'GOTCHA!' (4 May 1982, p. 1); depicted in Franklin's cartoons as unshaven and imbecilic gauchos in over-sized sombreros (12 May 1982, p. 6); and accused of such dirty tricks as the use of napalm (3 June 1982, p. 1) and the treacherous deployment of white flags (1 June 1982, p. 5). Given the tabloids' endorsement of Thatcher's Churchillian pose, it is inevitable that the role vacated by Adolf Hitler in 1945 should be assigned to the Argentinian leader, General Galtieri (1 May 1982, p. 2).

There is no better testament to Thatcher's success in defining the style of wartime debate than in the adoption of this confrontational and absolutist rhetoric by members of the Official Opposition. Apparently forgetting their own experiences during the prewar period when they had been lampooned as Soviet fellow travellers in contrast to the true patriots of the Conservative Party, several prominent Labour politicians added their voices to the chorus of anti-Argentinian hysteria that echoed through the House of Commons in the days following the invasion of the Falkland Islands. Thus, the Argentinian leadership is, according to the former Solicitor General, John Silkin, 'a tinpot Fascist junta' (Morgan, p. 1) and 'a bunch of hangmen' (p. 64) while Jim Callaghan, Prime Minister in the last Labour Government, describes the Junta's 'regime' as 'odious and corrupt' (Morgan, p. 153).

THE FALKLANDS WAR AS ARCHETYPAL NARRATIVE

The reduction of a complex situation to self-evident truths and the polarization of the combatants into unyielding postures of good and evil, right and wrong, opened up the way in the Falklands War, as it does in all wars, for the construction of a simple narrative that takes its content from mythic archetypes rather than actual events. Thus, as early as 15 April, during an ITV interview, Margaret Thatcher is able to tell the complete story of a war that has, as yet, barely begun: 'Failure? The possibilities do not exist . . . We are assembling the biggest fleet that has ever sailed in peacetime – an excellent fleet, excellent equipment, superb soldiers and sailors . . . We must go out calmly and quietly to succeed . . . We have to recover those islands' (Webster, 1982A, p. 2). That her opening words loosely paraphrase what Queen Victoria said to A. J. Balfour during Black Week in 1899, shortly after the British had suffered three successive defeats at the hands of the Boers, underlines the fact that her narrative is grounded in mythic archetypes rather than a rational analysis of the situation.

Thatcher's mythic approach to the war is equally well illustrated by her persistence in constraining it within the parameters of heroic narrative even after the British task force had completed the brutal, confused and often ugly business that constituted the actual retaking of the Falklands. Thus, in her interview with George Gale in the *Daily Express* on 26 July, Thatcher continues to talk about the war as if it were a simple tale in which the hero, who is a composite figure created by collapsing all distinctions between herself and the task force, performs great deeds and endures terrible trials before achieving the goal of his/her quest. The retaking of South Georgia becomes 'a wonderful operation', while 'the worrying times one lived with were when we lost our ships'. Similarly, the achievement of establishing a beachhead on the Falklands is set against 'the depressing time' when the Argentinian airforce came to 'bomb, bomb, bomb'. At the end of all these triumphs and tests is, inevitably, the moment of victory: 'When the call came from out of the blue, we were not found wanting' (1982, pp. 16–17).

Thatcher's mythic conception of the Falklands War is nowhere more in evidence, however, than in the almost certainly unconscious emphasis that she puts on the magic number seven while recounting how dreary negotiations finally yielded to the enchanting alternative of war: 'For seven weeks we sought a peaceful solution by diplomatic means. . . . We studied seven sets of proposals' until 'seven weeks to the day after the invasion, we moved to recover by force what was taken from us by force' (1986, p. 74).

There were two major factors specific to the Falklands War that assisted Thatcher in superimposing a mythic framework on actual events. One of them is to be found in the obvious parallels that exist between the task force's 8000 mile journey into the wintry seas of the South Atlantic and the great voyages of Homeric and Virgilian epic. Thus, for G. M. Dillon 'the passage of the British Task Force to the South Atlantic became a rite of passage to war' that helped transform the dispute over the Falkland Islands into 'a classic socio-political drama' (p. 101). Similarly, Ian Holm, the narrator of the ITN-Granada television documentary, *Battle for the Falklands* (1982), speaking over footage of the *Canberra* returning to port, offers a gloss of the war as an initiation tale in which 'we took out boys and brought back men'.

The mythic possibilities inherent in the voyage south were greatly enhanced by the careful stage management of the embarkation of the first 36 ships from Portsmouth on 5 April, with its particular emphasis on the two aircraft carriers *Hermes* and *Invincible*. The impact on the thousands who gathered to see the fleet off and the millions more who watched on television of a grand and colourful pageant made up of huge warships, their decks lined with troops, and of military bands, playing 'A Life on the Ocean Wave', 'Rule, Britannia!' and the modern pop anthem, 'Sailing', is summed up by a *Times* article headlined, 'The Royal

Navy in Action: The Great Ships Sail Off to War': 'For older watchers the sight of the British ships going to war was an evocation of times past; for their children and grandchildren the stuff of fireside yarns' (Tendler, p. 12).

The ability of these stirring pictures and sounds to transform the complex network of events and personalities that constitutes the messy reality of the Falklands War into a simple heroic journey was reinforced by the absence, in the weeks that followed, of vivid visual representations of the war itself. Thus, while delayed black and white photographs and still further delayed film footage of the *Sheffield* sinking or the *Antelope* blowing up cannot help but have called into question the epical image of war created on 5 April, they lacked immediacy and were thus deprived of the emotional force required to seriously undermine it.[4]

That Thatcher herself was keenly aware of the mythic possibilities inherent within the task force's 8000 mile voyage is made obvious by the vocabulary she employs to describe what the British public has just seen in person or on their television screens: 'We are assembling the biggest fleet that has ever sailed in peacetime – an excellent fleet, excellent equipment, superb soldiers and sailors . . ., the most honourable and brave members of her Majesty's services' (Webster, 1982A, p. 2).

Further, and perhaps more striking, whenever Thatcher wanted to evoke a physical space weighty enough to accommodate great deeds and to provide tests worthy of the true hero, she ignored the ugly Falklands terrain where the war's climactic battles took place in favour of the majestic ocean. Thus, it is concern about the dangers posed for the task force in winter by a marine landscape of 'very terrible weather, gales and freezing' (Webster 1982B, p. 4) upon which she focuses during her *Panorama* interview. Similarly, in addressing the Scottish Conservatives, she summons up a frightening picture of the British fleet being 'tossed about the Atlantic on those intemperate seas' (Langdon, p. 1).

The last feature of the Falklands War of use to Thatcher in her myth-making efforts derives from the air of unreality that surrounded the islands and their inhabitants. As Anthony Barnett puts it, the Falklands were 'a cipher' whose 'nothingness . . . gave Thatcher perfect scope for action' (pp. 69, 134). Major factors in depriving the Falklands of a sense of presence were widespread ignorance in Britain about the history or even the location of the islands and the shape like a Rorschach blot that faced anyone who took the trouble to look them up on a map. The sparsity and lateness of both still and moving pictures ensured that a certain feeling of intangibility lingered even after the British troops had established a physical presence on the Falklands.

The actual topography of the Falklands, with their stunted mountains, boggy lowlands, rugged coastlines and constant rainfall, is scarcely the stuff of high romance. However, because they remained less than fully visible throughout a period when the eyes of the world were focused on them, the Falkland Islands could be made to function as the kind of ephemeral fairytale landscape needed for a story of maidenly virtue enthralled. The same blurred perspective made the inhabitants of the islands, in reality a rugged and mostly male group of people engaged in the hard labour of sheep farming, suitable candidates for the part of damsel in distress. Speaking during the emergency debate of 3 April, Thatcher herself reports that the islanders were reduced to 'tears' (Morgan, p. 5) as their British champion, Sir Rex Hunt, went into exile, leaving them at the mercy of the Argentinian invaders. Michael Ancram later adds flesh to this characterization with his rather melodramatic claim that the Falklanders are 'prisoners in their own homes' and that 'their property and land have been raped' (Morgan, p. 57). Almost all subsequent references to the islanders seek to embellish their mythic role as damsel in distress by dwelling on their dependence, helplessness, weakness and smallness. In her *Panorama* interview, for example, Thatcher depicts them as diminutive victims who, having been brought 'under [the] heel' of the savage Argentinian tyrant through 'a totally unprovoked act of aggression', now look to the British hero to do his 'duty' by 'stand[ing] up for them' (Webster, 1982B, p. 4).

THE FALKLANDS WAR AND THE MYTH OF NATIONAL REBIRTH

The quest narrative, around which official discourse was broadly structured during the Falklands War, thus served Thatcher and her supporters well because it possessed an atavistic appeal that was invaluable not only in stimulating public enthusiasm for the Government's South Atlantic adventure but also in deflecting attention away from the gross mismanagement that had precipitated the Argentinian invasion. Mythic patterns also served the more specific function of advancing the Prime Minister's hegemonic project.

As we have already seen, Thatcher's attempts to present her programme of economic reform as the latest manifestation of the British myth of cyclical rebirth through acts of heroism enjoyed little success in the three years following the election of a Conservative Government in 1979. With the outbreak of the Falklands War, however, Thatcher was able to offer the public a more familiar version of the myth in which military rather than economic heroism provides the spark for national revitalization. Thus, as early as 14 May, Thatcher employs the archetype of water, with its powerful connotations of death and rebirth, in making the claim that, as a consequence of the task force's efforts in the South Atlantic, she feels 'this ancient country rising as one nation. . . . Too long submerged, too often denigrated, too easily forgotten, the springs of pride in Britain flow again' (Barnett, p. 65). While such a change of emphasis could do little in any immediate sense to enhance the credibility of Thatcher's monetarist project, it did serve her broader goals by suggesting to the British public that the Conservatives, as the Party in power during one of Britain's great mythical moments, were the nation's natural rulers.

Thatcher and her supporters employed two main tactics to encourage a view of the Falklands War as a key moment in the British national myth. First, they repeatedly made connections between the current war and earlier wars that already enjoyed mythic status and, second, in talking about the Falklands War, they frequently made use of the chivalric language that has been, since the nineteenth century, the accepted medium for mythomilitary discourse.

The British tradition of great military triumphs was most frequently evoked during the Falklands War through references to the Second World War, a conflict in which Britain was also faced by a fascist enemy and the most recent occasion when actual events were submerged beneath a mythic vision of the nation. Margaret Thatcher herself, as the *Sun* notes approvingly, rarely missed a chance to show 'the Churchill touch' (24 May 1982, p. 6). Her speeches also make frequent use of the vocabulary and slogans of the Second World War. She tells the Conservative Women's Conference, for instance, that 'we, of all people, have learnt the lesson of history: that to appease an aggression is to invite aggression elsewhere' (1986, p. 75) and reminds Parliament of the 'wartime ... phrase "Careless talk costs lives"' (Morgan, p. 326). Thatcher further alludes to the Second World War while speaking in a radio interview with Jimmy Young about the Falkland Islanders' probable feelings towards the Argentinians following their experience of invasion: 'It's just like the Channel Islands during the last war. They wouldn't easily have invited the Germans back' ('Prime Minister's', p. 6).

During debates in the House of Commons, Thatcher found considerable support for her attempts to connect the Falklands and Second World Wars from both sides of the House. Thus, Labour's Douglas Jay twice echoes her reference to the dangers of appeasement (Morgan, pp. 16, 288) and his fellow socialist, John Silkin, refers to Galtieri as 'a bargain basement Mussolini' (Morgan, p. 19). Jim Callaghan similarly seeks to lend weight to his comments about the courage of the British forces in the Falklands by claiming that 'the sons of those who ran the convoys to Murmansk and Iceland in the last war can do as well as their fathers' (Morgan, p. 155).

However, the extension of this tradition of military glory back beyond the Second World War was a task undertaken almost entirely by right wing politicians. Edward DuCann alludes to Wellington at Torres Vedras (Morgan, p. 10) and Enoch Powell, besides urging Thatcher to live up to her Iron Lady soubriquet (Morgan, p. 11), seeks to encourage the Government and the nation to face up to the challenge of the land battle about to commence in the Falklands by quoting the Iron Duke himself on the Battle of Waterloo: 'Hard pounding this, gentlemen; let's see who will pound hardest' (p. 320). Other references to the Napoleanic Wars include John Page's 'We know that it will do its duty. The Fleet expects us, this day, to do ours' (Morgan, p. 168) and Thatcher's retrospective suggestion that, in considering the dangers posed by the South Atlantic winter, her thoughts turned to Napoleon's Russian campaign: 'I had the winter at the back of my mind. . . . It beat Napoleon at Moscow' (1982, p. 16). Going even further back into history in search of momentous victories, Hugh Fraser offers a rather strained reference to the defeat of the Spanish fleet in 1588 by describing the task force as 'a remarkable armada' (Morgan, p. 39) and Lord Hailsham, speaking on television, quotes Henry V after his victory at Agincourt (ITN, 14 June 1982).

A number of comparisons between the Falklands and earlier British wars can also be found in the pages of both the tabloid and broadsheet press. The *Sun*, for instance, uses the headline 'BLITZED' (8 May 1982, p. 1) in a report of the bombing of Stanley airport; refers to the British Harrier pilots as 'THE FABULOUS FEW' (10 June 1982, pp. 14–15), an analogy reinforced by the headline 'SCRAMBLE' (8 April 1982, p. 1); makes reference to 'MAGGIE'S LONGEST DAY' (12 April 1982, pp. 2–3); and argues that, like Malta in the Second World War, the Falkland Islands should be awarded the George Cross (24 May 1982, p. 6). References to other wars include a quotation from Rupert Brooke's 'The Soldier' (1 June 1982, p. 6) and a description of the Argentinian fleet (of five ships) as 'an Armada' (13 April 1982, p. 2).

The Times, in its editorial of 5 April, likens the defence of the Falklands to Britain's defence of Poland against Hitler's unwarranted aggression in 1939 ('We Are', p. 9)). A later story on the American reaction to the Falklands War draws analogies not only with the Second World War but with Sir Roger Keyes at Zeebrugge and calls on Margaret Thatcher to find the voice of Elizabeth I addressing her army at Tilbury (Fairlie, p. 10).

An awareness of the Battle of Britain, Waterloo, Trafalgar and other great moments in the nation's heavily mythologized military past has been so thoroughly instilled in the consciousness of the British public by the education system and popular culture that, in moments of national crisis, the barest reference is sufficient to arouse a surge of patriotic feeling. However, such references are all the more effective when couched in the quasi-chivalric language developed in the nineteenth century to elevate British militarism above the realm of rational debate.

Although more usually inclined to the resounding cliché than to lofty rhetoric,[5] Margaret Thatcher nevertheless facilitated the introduction of chivalric conventions into Falklands War discourse by her use of diction drawn from the reformed public school ethos that provided the nineteenth-century cult of supposedly medieval knightly virtues with much of its actual moral underpinning. She thus speaks of Britain as if it were modelled on Dr Arnold's 'robust' and 'sound' (Morgan, p. 232) sixth former who refuses to 'flinch' (BBC News, 2 June 1982) in the face of a challenge. A similar tone of muscular Christian enthusiasm can be heard when she offers her unwillingness to negotiate with the defeated Argentinians as a 'fervent belief' (Morgan, p. 355)

and when she calls on reporters to 'Rejoice!' at the recapture of
South Georgia (Haviland 1982, p. 1).

In similar moralistic vein, Thatcher repeatedly defined Britain's
wartime goals in terms of the great abstractions upon which the
nineteenth-century knightly code was built.[6] Thus, concerns for
the right way, justice, loyalty, fair play, courtesy and fidelity are
all expressed in the conclusion to her address to the Conservative Women's Conference: 'Our cause is just. It is the cause of
freedom and the rule of law. It is the support for the weak against
the aggression of the strong' (Thatcher, 1986, p. 76). Other knightly
qualities invoked by Thatcher include 'honour', 'discipline'
(Thatcher, 1982, p. 16), 'courage and resolution' (Morgan, p. 275).

Finally, there are also at least two occasions upon which Thatcher
makes use of the archaic vocabulary typical of chivalric discourse
in order to dignify her own pronouncements. In a television news
interview, she refers to our 'forefathers' (BBC1 News, 2 June 1982)
and concludes her address to the Conservative Women's Conference with a quotation from Shakespeare's *King John* that not
only includes medievalisms such as 'nought' and 'rue' but also
allows her to substitute 'England' for 'Britain' (1986, p. 76). This
usage with its connotations of an ancient kingdom populated by
gallant knights and loyal serfs is, of course, fundamental to the
construction of a chivalric frame of reference. We should not,
therefore, be surprised that Thatcher was unwilling to admit the
unsuitability of her terminology even when chastised by Gordon
Wilson in the House of Commons for excluding the Scots, Welsh
and Irish from her definition of nation (Morgan, p. 327).

Thatcher's attempts to lend gravitas to the Falklands War by
speaking of it in chivalric terms found support from a number
of other speakers during debates in the House of Commons. John
Nott, for instance, strikes a noble pose by proclaiming, 'We are
in earnest and no one should doubt our resolve' (Morgan, p. 69),
as does Julian Amery when he talks of Britain as 'a proud and
ancient nation' (Morgan, p. 286). Christopher Murphy achieves
a similar tone by substituting the poetic, archaic and militaristic
term 'banner' (Morgan, p. 312) for the more mundane 'flag'. Both
Peter Viggers, who describes the war in the South Atlantic as 'a
crusade for freedom' (Morgan, p. 331), and Richard Crashaw,
who asks 'should we not steel ourselves to carry through our
resolve in what we believe to be a righteous cause?' (Morgan,

p. 339), exploit the ability of chivalric rhetoric to invest war with a sense of divine purpose.

This aspect of chivalric discourse is nowhere more pronounced, however, than when the subject is death in battle and both MPs and journalists took full advantage of the rhetorical opportunities provided by British casualties in the Falklands. Stephen Hastings is, for example, echoing the language of remembrance services as he argues that, 'if the Government should be prevailed upon to surrender now on any essential principle when victory is within our grasp . . ., it would mean that those who have died have died in vain' (Morgan, p. 264). His parliamentary colleague, Peter Griffiths, makes similar use of the chivalric convention that completion of an armed struggle is a sacred trust owed to the memories of those who have been killed in battle when he responds to calls for a negotiated settlement by arguing that 'the most appropriate memorial to the brave young men who lost their lives in HMS "Sheffield", . . . would be to carry through the enterprise for which they gave their lives as quickly as possible' (Morgan, p. 209).

The suggestion, implicit in Griffith's use of the conventional euphemism 'gave their lives', that the dead soldier, like Christ before him, has made what Peter Temple-Morris calls 'the supreme sacrifice' (Morgan, p. 320) is fleshed out by John Nott when he states that those who died in the Falklands did so 'for the freedom of other British people' (Morgan, p. 320). The deeply spiritual significance ascribed to death in battle by Griffiths, Temple-Morris and Nott through their use of the language and conventions of chivalry is further emphasized by the echo of the Lord's Prayer to be heard in Alan Clark's claim that 'those who sacrificed their lives in these battles . . . made that sacrifice' so 'that British families shall be delivered from oppression' (Morgan, p. 357).

The sanctification of the dead soldier provides those seeking to dignify war with such a powerful tool that, following the sinking of the *Sheffield*, even the *Sun* frequently adopted an uncharacteristically elevated style and expressed unusually lofty sentiments in its accounts of British deaths. For example, a story about the casualties incurred in the taking of Goose Green runs under the headline, 'THEY GAVE THEIR LIVES FOR FREEDOM', and is illustrated with photographic portraits intended to serve as a

'roll of honour carved with pride' for the dead 'British hero[es]
(25 May 1982, pp. 4–5). The most significant of all these deaths,
in the *Sun*'s version of events, is that of Colonel 'H' Jones and
in its issue of 31 May prominence is given, in a story headlined,
'GLORY AT GOOSE GREEN', to an eye witness account by the
BBC's Robert Fox in which Jones is treated as the type of the
crucified Christ: 'In the evening they brought his body down
from the hillside' (31 May, pp. 2–3). It is not until the next day,
however, that the *Sun* enters full remembrance mode with an
inset photograph of Jones on page one accompanied by Rupert
Brooke's lines, 'some corner of a foreign field/ That is for ever
England', three pages about the Goose Green burials, and a page
six editorial in which Brooke is quoted at length. Each paragraph
of the editorial concludes with a capitalized, 'WE SHALL
REMEMBER THEM' (1 June, 1982, pp. 1–6).

As the traditional party of the upper classes, the Conservatives generally had little difficulty in associating themselves and
their involvement in the Falklands War with what is essentially
an establishment myth of national rebirth through acts of military heroism (Wright, pp. 45–7). Consequently, they could claim
to be the natural Party of Government, thereby diminishing the
credibility of the Labour Party's ambitions to return to office.
However, each of the two World Wars of the twentieth century
threatened, in quite different ways, to undermine Thatcher's
attempts to connect the Conservative Party and its political pred-
ecessors to a seamless tradition of great military victories stretching
back from the defeat of the Argentinians in the Falklands to
Henry V's triumph over the French at Agincourt.

The problem with the Great War is, as Samuel Hynes demonstrates, that it generated a myth not of rebirth but of disillusion-
ment that undermined the establishment and was therefore a
potential embarrassment to anyone seeking to locate themselves
within the history of British militarism. The First World War did
not in the end, though, much trouble Thatcher and her supporters since, with the exception of the *Sun*'s occasional reference to
Rupert Brooke, they simply erased it from their version of the
nation's military past. In doing this they were on fairly safe ground
in that there was little likelihood that any other faction could
benefit from association with what has always been generally
considered a national fiasco. What few references there are to
the First World War in the House of Commons arise out of

attempts by members of the opposition such as Stuart Holland, who predicts that the British landing on the Falklands will be 'a minor Gallipoli' (Morgan, p. 296), to associate the Falklands War and thus the Conservative Party with an alternative tradition of war as senseless slaughter.

The Second World War, however, posed a rather different problem. In this case, the Thatcherite forces were extremely eager to claim what is for many British people the greatest of all their country's military triumphs as their own. Unfortunately for them, though, the Second World War much less obviously belongs to the establishment than do British wars in general. There are certainly some important aspects of the myth that sustained the British people during the struggle with Hitler that are, as Angus Calder points out, compatible with Thatcher's concept of what constitutes the authentic nation. These include a cluster of associated ideas in which Britain, 'an Old Country' (Calder, p. 15), 'standing alone' (p. 52) 'rediscover[s]' (p. 7) the 'Absolute Spirit of "England"' (p. 14) and a vision of 'deep England' (p. 182). However, as Calder goes on to demonstrate, there are several features at the very heart of Second World War mythology that strongly contradict Thatcher's attempt to postulate a single Tory tradition of war. The most notable of these derive from the lesson taught by the Blitz that, faced with a military challenge, 'Britain had all been in it Together . . ., and had Taken it . . ., and had Carried On' (p. 230). The lesson of the Blitz, according to Calder's argument, not only strengthened Britain's commitment to democratic values currently under threat from a fascist enemy (p. 58) but laid the foundation for a new national ideal of 'communitarianism' (p. 204) and 'egalitarian[ism]' (p. 272). Out of this ideal sprang demands for a political programme based on 'consensus and commitment to social amelioration under state direction' rather than on the 'selfishness' and 'greed' (pp. 271–2) fostered by the ideology of free enterprise. These demands were satisfied, of course, by the election in 1945 of a Labour Government with a mandate to create the Welfare State, an idealogical concept of such hegemonic force that it was largely accepted by both Conservative and Labour Government's until the election of Thatcher in 1979.

The Second World War was for Thatcher, then, something of a two-edged sword. By drawing attention to the war, as she could hardly avoid doing, she was likely to remind the British public that uniquely in the national tradition of military endeavour this was the 'People's War' (Calder, p. 266). She was thus in danger not only of lending credibility to Labour, the People's Party, but also to Welfare State policies. Viewed from the vantage point provided by Second World War mythology, such policies can much more readily be understood as the product of a great moment of national revival than, as Thatcher was trying to convince the electorate, the cause of postwar national decline. However, should she succeed, despite these problems, in accommodating the Second World War within her own vision of 'the national past – "our" common heritage – ... as the historized image of an instinctively conservative establishment' (Wright, p. 47), Thatcher stood not only to gain from association with a prestigious war but to greatly advance her project of excluding Labour and its policies from any conception of the authentic nation.

In order to ensure that the Second World War served rather than frustrated her hegemonic ends, Thatcher not only remained silent about the egalitarian elements of Second World War mythology while playing up the more traditional ones but also annexed for herself any characteristics peculiar to this myth that could be separated from their socialist associations. The emphasis in the myth of the Blitz, for instance, on Britain as a peaceable nation might carry with it an implicit criticism of establishment militarism but it does not offer any very concrete endorsement of socialism. Therefore, Thatcher is on fairly safe ground on the numerous occasions when she emphasizes Britain's commitment as 'a mild, quiet people' (Morgan, p. 271) to 'a peaceful settlement' through negotiations in preference to the 'use [of] force' (Webster, 1982B, p. 4) or when she asserts that nothing is more important than 'peace' except 'liberty and justice' (Morgan, p. 143). Much bolder, though, is the attempt implicit in Thatcher's postvictory comment, 'It's been everyone together' (*Task Force South*), to co-opt the Blitz ideal of 'Britain had all been in it Together' for the Falklands War and therefore her own Party.

However, the most risky of all these appropriations of Second World War mythology, but also the most important to Thatcher's own ideological programme, was her attempt to include democracy amongst the major values being upheld in the war against the Argentinian Junta. Democracy and socialism are certainly not synonymous in general but came close to being so during the Second World War in that the fight to preserve democracy from an enemy outside was at the same time regarded as a struggle to create a more egalitarian society at home. This connection was reinforced by the fact that the 'People's War' was the first occasion on which democracy assumed primacy amongst the values for which the British are prepared to take up arms.

Thatcher's strategy for breaking the connection between democracy and socialism involved always speaking of democracy as one of Britain's eternal verities. Thus, in her speech to the Conservative Women's Association Thatcher moves without any sense of strain from talking about the Falklands War as a campaign waged in the defence of 'democracy' to situating it within the great tradition of British militarism: 'As always we came to military action reluctantly. But . . . when not only British land, but British citizens are in the power of an aggressor, then we have to restore our rights and the rights of the Falkland Islanders'. There is, of course, no historical basis for Thatcher's claiming of democracy as a traditional British value. However, she avoids close scrutiny on this occasion as on others by employing vague but charged moral generalizations such as 'rights' and, more frequently, 'freedom' – which, as she says, has long been considered part of the British 'birthright' (1986, pp. 73–5) – as synonyms for democracy. That the two words would have meant something very different in, for example, the eighteenth century – when a vigorous concern for freedom in the sense of legal rights and the right to free speech was rarely accompanied by a desire for the universal franchise or the rule of the people – is not something Thatcher invites either her immediate audience or the wider British public to contemplate.

A second strategy employed by Thatcher to reinforce the suggestion that, like all British wars, the Second World War was Tory involved consistently identifying it with one person: Winston Churchill. Churchill was invaluable to Thatcher not only because he was a Conservative but because she had sought throughout her career to present herself as his successor. Her first address to the Conservative Party Conference as leader, for instance, began with the assertion that she was following in Churchill's footsteps (1989, p. 19). Therefore, it became easy for her to claim that, as two wars conducted against similar fascist enemies by closely identified Prime Ministers, the Second World War and the Falklands War did not simply belong to the same tradition but were virtually the same war. This suggestion is made with particular force at the point in her memoirs when Thatcher draws attention to the role played by Chequers in both her war and Churchill's, thereby creating the impression that in literally covering the same ground as Churchill she was also repeating his conduct of national affairs (1993, p. 193).

As a result of her concerted efforts at merging the two wars Thatcher succeeded in increasing the prestige of the Falklands War through association with the much more significant conflict of 1939–45; even more important, she lent weight to her efforts to convince the public that the Second World War and the obviously Tory Falklands War were conducted in pursuit of the same ideological goals.

SOME IDEOLOGICAL DIMENSIONS OF THE FALKLANDS MYTH

As this discussion has progressed, it has become increasingly evident that the various strategies employed by Thatcher to shift the Falklands War out of the arena of history and into the realm of national mythology were intended not only to insulate her Government from reasoned criticism of its conduct with respect to Argentina's claim to sovereignty over the Malvinas but to advance her broader ideological goals. In order to achieve a fuller understanding of the ideological dimensions of the Falklands myth, it is necessary to consider some important aspects of the roles of the islands, their inhabitants and the British troops in this myth.

Earlier I suggested that in 1982 the Falklands Islands were enveloped in an aura of unreality that made it easy for Thatcher to accommodate them within a reading in which the war with Argentina is transformed into an heroic quest. However, Thatcher also seems to have been acutely aware that, at another level, the Falklands, far from being a tabula rasa, offered a preexisting text easy to shape into a vivid representation of the anachronistic nation that she had long claimed as the authentic Britain. Thatcher's tactic involved foregrounding some striking similarities between the Falkland Islanders and a heritage industry version of the British people. The islanders, most of whom have origins in Britain, are, for instance, racially homogeneous, are engaged in rural occupations such as sheep farming, live in patriarchal family units and belong to a society structured along semifeudal lines. If, in addition, one is prepared to overlook significant differences between the rugged landscape of the Falklands and the lush, rolling Southern countryside of 'Deep England', it then becomes quite easy to transform the Falklands and their people into a living embodiment of the lost ideal of Thatcherite mythology.[7]

This identification served Thatcher's ideological ends in several ways. It made possible, for example, the suggestion that by setting out to reclaim the Falklands from the Argentinians, Thatcher was not just engaging in a war that connected militarily to the nation's glorious past but was seeking a quite literal retrieval of that past. What had prior to the war been a nebulous and indeed implausible commitment to resurrect the long-lost authentic nation, therefore came to assume a much more tangible and imaginatively, if not logically, credible form. The development of this aspect of her Falklands myth involved Thatcher in a textualizing exercise that made 'Falklanders' stand not just for British, as was the case throughout the war, but for some of the more nostalgic connotations of the term. In her *Panorama* interview, for instance, Thatcher describes the islanders as being 'of British stock' (Webster, 1982B, p. 4) and, in the House of Commons, as 'British in stock and tradition' (Morgan, p. 5), terms that suggest a lineage deeply rooted in the past and even the very soil of the nation. Elsewhere, Thatcher employs equally regressive synonyms for British such as 'an island race' (Barnett, p. 28) and 'the Queen's subjects' (Thatcher, 1993, p. 181) when speaking of the Falklanders and draws on a defensively nostalgic 'little Englander' vocabulary in claiming the 'defence of our way of life' (Morgan, p. 35) as the purpose of the war to liberate the Falklands.

The identification established between the Falkland Islands and the authentic Britain served a second and equally important ideological function by providing a platform for the continuation of Thatcher's peacetime struggle with groups she considered 'enemies within'. Throughout the war and in its immediate aftermath, Thatcher generally adopted a Churchillian stance by posing as a leader who, in a time of crisis, is capable of putting the interests of the nation ahead of party politics. Thus, in her interview with George Gale, she denies any thoughts of calling a snap election in the wake of victory because 'the Falklands thing was a matter of national pride, and I would not use it to further political purposes' (1982, p. 17). Useful as this statesmanlike pose was in enhancing Thatcher's personal prestige, it did of course force her to refrain from making the kind of vigorous attacks on the enemies of her hegemonic project she usually relished. Offered an easy ball to smash, for instance, when Winston Churchill asks if she is aware of the contrast between 'her leadership and resolve' and the cowardice of 'those who run for cover at the first whiff of grapeshot', Thatcher eschews savaging the peace wing of the Labour Party in favour of the conciliatory comment, 'I think that the vast majority of our people, whatever their political views, are firmly behind the action the Government are taking' (Morgan, p. 145).

The limitations that Thatcher imposed on herself during the Falklands War were, however, more apparent than real; a simple reference to the Falkland Islands, with their absence of left wing politics, trade unions and black inhabitants, was all that was now needed to re-mark the boundaries established in the prewar period between those included in the idea of the nation developed by Thatcher and her supporters and those excluded from it. Besides allowing her to maintain the fiction that she had risen above the hurly burly of party politics, at least for the duration of the war, there are two ways in which this method of attack by exclusion was particularly valuable to Thatcher.

First, while the type of frontal assaults favoured by Thatcher before the war helped to demonize her enemies, they were also somewhat self defeating because their very vigour served to acknowledge that these enemies posed a real threat. Indeed, the more violently Thatcher excoriated her foes, the larger proportions they assumed or, in some instances, the greater sympathy they attracted. The presentation of the Falklands Islands as the authentic Britain, on the other hand, contained within it the implicit suggestion that the process of renewal was now complete and that the Labour Party, trade unions and black immigrants were no longer forces with which to be reckoned. The effectiveness of this matter of fact strategy can perhaps be gauged by comparing it with the *Sun's* tactic of identifying hysterically exaggerated and sometimes ludicrous parallels between the Argentinian Junta and various enemies of Thatcherism, all of whom it lumped together as 'our domestic fellow travellers' (27 May 1982, p. 6).

Second, the implicit exclusion of ethnic minorities from the image of the authentic Britain embodied in the Falkland Islands considerably extended the range of opportunities available to Thatcher and her supporters for the delivery of coded racist messages. Thatcher's reference to the Falklanders as 'not strangers' but 'our own people' (1986, p. 75), for instance, draws an obvious distinction between these true Britons and those who are strangers in British society, namely, black immigrants. Similar distinctions between the Falklanders, considered British despite living 8000 miles away, and ethnic minorities, resident in Britain but nevertheless regarded as aliens, can just as easily be identified in the descriptions of the islanders as 'sixth generation British subjects' (Morgan, p. 84), as 'British people who speak only one language' (p. 118), and as 'not foreign to us. They are of us' (p. 57) offered by Conservative MPs Michael Shersby, Frederick Bundren and Michael Ancram.

This coded racist agenda occasionally became even more sharp edged through the exploitation of the metonymic relationship that existed, as Paul Gilroy points out (p. 51), in the minds of many British people between black immigrants and swarthy Argentinians as invaders of the homeland. When Thatcher describes the Argentinians as 'an alien creed' (Barnett, p. 26), for instance, she clearly intends her audience to recall not only the legal status of unnaturalized immigrants but the strange religious and social customs with which they, as surely as the military invaders of the Falkland Islands, threaten the British way of life. More pointed still is her reference to the Junta's intention 'to flood' the Falklands 'with their own nationals' (Morgan, p. 279). The imagery employed here of an island race threatened with submersion would have been instantly recognizable to most British people as having its origins in a tradition of racist discourse reaching back through Thatcher's own unguarded use of the term 'swamping' during a speech on immigration to Enoch Powell's infamous 'rivers of blood' speech (Holmes, pp. 97–8; Nairn, p. 256).[8]

The image of the Falkland Islands as the authentic Britain further served the Thatcherite agenda by disentangling her racist and imperialist themes. It was, of course, essential to the promotion of her regressive vision of nation that Thatcher dwell on the colonial possessions upon which Britain's reputation as a great country was built. However, in a period when the dark-skinned people who inhabited the hot, dry places that made up a significant part of Britain's overseas possessions had become engaged in a process of 'colonization in reverse' (Brennan, p. 47–8) by emigrating to the motherland in large numbers, there was an obvious danger in drawing attention to the imperial past.

For Thatcher to remind the British public, for example, that the roots of black immigration could be traced back to a period of national glory was to take the risk of giving racial minorities the very legitimacy that it was her goal to deny them. Conversely, because it provides such reminders of the origins of the thousands of Asian and Caribbean immigrants who, according to the proponents of the new racism, pose an ever-increasing threat to Britain's traditions and customs, talk of Empire, rather than stirring up anticipated patriotic sentiments, might simply have served to dishearten and anger the more right wing of Thatcher's supporters. However, when the occasion for imperial rhetoric is provided by the Falkland Islands – as it was in Thatcher's postvictory claim that Britain is still 'the nation that had built an Empire and ruled a quarter of the world' (Barnett, p. 150) – the Empire assumes a new shape as a cold, wet and green place inhabited by white people. The Falklands thus provided Thatcher with an image of Empire, not as what Homi K. Bhabha terms 'a daemonic double' (p. 319) but as a comforting mirror image of the motherland, with the result that it became possible to develop racist and imperialist discourses simultaneously without any danger of the one tainting the other.

The role of the Falkland Islands and their inhabitants in giving tangible form to Thatcher's idea of the 'real Britain' and in advancing her racist agenda was supplemented by some of the functions assigned to the British troops in Falklands War mythology. In addition to the obvious part they played as national heroes setting out on a quest to liberate the Falklands, army, navy and airforce personnel performed an important role in integrating an image of the traditional family into the broader fabric of Thatcher's authentic nation. Throughout the war Thatcher referred to the armed forces as 'my boys', thus locating them within a national family. The patriarchal nature of this family is defined, as Seidel and Gunther demonstrate, by the traditional gender roles assigned by the popular press to the men of the task force and their mothers, wives and fiancées (pp. 120–3). Thus, there are few issues of the *Sun* published during the Falklands War that fail to include at least one story stressing the gap between the active man embarking on a quest for death or glory and the passive woman who serves the national cause by waiting for and worrying about him while carrying on with the everyday business of domestic life, whether it be giving birth (19 May 1982, p. 2) or merely having a birthday party (14 May 1982, p. 1). The assumed naturalness of this patriarchal image of the family is never more evident than in the humour the *Sun* finds in a story of dockside parting in which 'Nurse Wendy Marshall says a loving farewell to her boyfriend Glen Bucknell . . . but SHE is the one going off to war' (10 May 1982, p. 2). The sheepish looks on the couple's faces in the accompanying photograph suggests an acute awareness of how ludicrous they have made themselves by abrogating their proper roles.

Once they had been identified as part of what constitutes Thatcher's definition of the real Britain, the armed forces, who were overwhelmingly white, almost automatically became another medium for the promotion of the idea that the authentic nation is racially homogeneous. Anyone watching the seven-part BBC documentary *Task Force South: The Battle for the Falklands*, which brings together almost all the film footage shot during the Falklands War, would, for instance, see no more than three or four black faces amongst the many shots of 'our boys'. The only significant nonwhite presence in the task force was provided by the Nepalese Gurkhas. However, because of their image as panga-wielding jungle fighters, they simply reinforced the sense of returning to an older order of things when blacks were content to remain a separate breed even while serving their imperialist masters.

THE FALKLANDS MYTH AND MONETARIST ECONOMICS

In spite of her carefully cultivated posture as a Churchillian leader prepared to sacrifice partisan interests for the sake of national unity, Thatcher was thus able to embody within her mythic reading of the Falklands War some major aspects of her own hegemonic project. What the logic of the mytho-military version of British history that she promoted to good effect throughout the war never allowed her do, though, was to tie national rebirth to entrepreneurial values and monetarist economics. No sooner was the fighting over, however, than Thatcher offered a revised interpretation of the meaning of the Falklands War intended to restore the progressive part of her ideological programme to its prewar position as the engine of British revitalization. This dramatic shift is evident in both her address to the Party faithful on Cheltenham racecourse on 3 July and in her *Daily Express* interview of 26 July.

The most striking thing about these texts for the reader who comes to them after reading Thatcher's wartime speeches and interviews is their tone. Apart from the brief burst of enthusiasm for 'the great victory' 'our country has won' with which she opens her Cheltenham speech and some talk of the war as heroic quest during the interview with George Gale, Thatcher makes remarkably little attempt to aggrandize Britain's recent military achievement. Instead, she speaks in a matter of fact and even brisk style as if to suggest that now the war 'is all over' (Barnett, p. 149), it has ceased to engage her. The invasion of 2 April is thus no longer described as a great crisis, a blow to national honour or a threat to world peace. Instead, it is simply a 'problem' with which 'you've got to cope': 'But we got people together and, if I might put it this way, we saw that night that we could in fact get a Task Force on its way by the following Monday. That is what we did' (Thatcher, 1982, p. 16).

This change in tone is, of course, a deliberate choice on Thatcher's part and not the product of any real loss of enthusiasm for her recent achievement. Well as it served her throughout the Falklands War, the Churchillian persona is simply not appropriate for the entrepreneurial reading of recent events that she now wants to offer. In its place, as she makes explicit in the Gale interview, Thatcher has taken on a new role as 'manager and organiser' of a national household that has recently been making some rather large demands on her executive abilities. Thus, in explaining to Gale how her gender helped in dealing with the Falklands crisis, Thatcher states that, 'You might not think of it that way, George, but each woman who runs a house is a manager and organiser. We thought forward each day, and we did it in a routine way, and we were on the job 24 hours a day' (1982, p. 16).

At no point in either speech or interview does Thatcher admit that there has been a change in the significance that she wishes to attach to the Falklands War. Instead, she simply begins to ascribe the 'stirr[ing]' (Barnett, p. 151) and 're-kindl[ling]' of the 'spirit which has fired [Britain] for generations past' (p. 153), now termed 'the Falklands Factor' (p. 150), to entrepreneurial values and ceases speaking about acts of military heroism performed in a noble cause. Thus, the first example Thatcher offers during her Cheltenham speech of the 'competen[ce], courage and resolut[ion]' demonstrated by the British during the Falklands War is drawn not from the achievements of the task force but from those of the commercial shipyards that 'adapt[ed] ships way ahead of time' (Barnett, p. 150). Later, she asks her audience to wonder not at some daring deed performed on the high seas or during the recapture of Port Stanley but at 'what British Aerospace workers did when their Nimrod aeroplane needed major modifications', an achievement that could, if repeated 'in peacetime, establish us as aeroplane makers to the world' (p. 151).

Any credit that is granted to the armed services for generating 'the spirit of the South Atlantic' (Barnett, p. 150) derives from their ability to model the type of social organization where entrepreneurship can flourish. The heroic feats of the task force are, as a consequence, reduced to 'an object lesson' in what can be achieved when everyone works together for 'the success of the whole' (p. 150). The 'brilliant leadership' of the officers is worthy of mention only to the extent that it mirrors similar achievements in 'our factories at home' (p. 151) and points up the need for more 'self-starters . . ., princes of industry, people who have a fantastic ability to build things and create jobs' (Thatcher, 1982, p. 17). Similarly, the lower ranks are to be praised not because of their success on the field of battle but because the unquestioning obedience required of them by their position in the military hierarchy serves as an example to British workers who must recognize that 'true solidarity' involves loyalty to their 'country' (Barnett, p. 152) not to their union. 'Professionalism' (Barnett, p. 150; Thatcher, 1982, p. 16), which was only one of a number of qualities attributed to the armed forces during the Falklands War, now occupies a privileged position in both speech and interview to the almost total exclusion of more heroic virtues.

Thatcher completes her reassessment of what the Falklands War means with the suggestion that, far from sparking a national revival, the war simply fanned a flame already kindled by prewar Conservative economic policies: 'We have ceased to be a nation in retreat. We have instead a new-found confidence – born in the economic battles at home and tested and found true 8000 miles away' (Barnett, pp. 152–3). Thus, credit for the flourishing of a new national spirit during the challenging period that followed

the invasion of the Falkland Islands is due, not to the unique
demands of wartime, but to that same politics of conviction with
which Thatcher set out in 1979 to destroy the postwar consensus: 'It was principles, conviction and persistence that did it.
Not consensus, compromise, but conviction, action, persistence,
until the job was done' (Thatcher, 1982, p. 17). The enduring
reward for such an effective conduct of the war is, according to
Thatcher, to instill in the British people the 'confiden[ce]' and
'new mood of realism' needed in order for them to be able to
accept the necessity of monetarist policies: 'That disreputable
method [of printing money in order to pay out of higher inflation what we dare not tax and cannot borrow] is no longer open
to us . . . Our people are now confident enough to face the facts
of life' (Barnett, p. 152). With this last bold revisionist gesture
on Thatcher's part, the reshaping of the mythic frame that she
had placed around the Falklands War is completed with the result
that it can now accommodate both the radical and the regressive aspects of her ideological package.

DISSENTING VOICES

The logic behind this astounding shift from military to entrepreneurial explanation for the national revival supposedly achieved
during the Falklands War cannot, of course, stand up to any but
the most cursory scrutiny. The connection Thatcher establishes
between the demands of wartime and the realities of peace is
clearly spurious. The rigid hierarchical structures and codes of
discipline characteristic of military life, for instance, are not a
practical model for peacetime industrial relations. Neither is there
any but the most superficial similarity between the efficiency
and professionalism of a task force trained to maim and kill and
the skills required of a businessman seeking to make a profit.
Equally disingenuous is Thatcher's expectation that workers who
put the war effort ahead of their personal interests will be similarly self-sacrificing when asked to help fatten their employers'
peacetime profits.

There is a similar lack of rational basis for most other parts of
the interpretative structure in which Thatcher enveloped the
Falklands War. To read the war as myth, as she does, may satisfy
some deep-felt need in the public consciousness and may create

the impression that significant change has been achieved but in reality it does nothing to alter or eradicate either the immediate circumstances surrounding the war or the broader historical and social forces at work in contemporary Britain. The Britain of myth may, for instance, always stand alone in its battle against tyranny but the real Britain that went to war with Argentina was just as dependent on American permission and support as it had been throughout its period of postwar decline.

Neither are there any grounds, other than in rhetorical flourish and fanciful metaphor, for positing the Falkland Islands as the living embodiment of the authentic Britain, even assuming that such a place ever did or could exist. Far from being a rural idyll, the Falklands are cold and bleak and their inhabitants eke out grim lives of near poverty, totally dependent not on some benevolent squire but on the Falklands Islands Company, a subsidiary of the asset stripping, multinational Coalite Company. Furthermore, this group of what were presented as quintessentially British people did not at the time of the war with Argentina even enjoy full citizenship or any but the crudest approximation of democratic rights.

These and other objections to the Thatcherite interpretation can be found in a number of newspaper articles written by opponents of the decision to take up arms against Argentina and in the parliamentary speeches of some Labour MPs. E. P. Thompson, for instance, offers an alternative mythic reading of the war in which 'what will be descending shortly on our task force in those wintry seas will be a squadron of furies', armed with 'a compendium of the arsenal of the free world' and 'under the command of Admiral Nemesis' (p. 12). Several speakers in the House of Commons, including Nigel Fisher (Morgan, p. 11) and Willy Hamilton (Morgan, p. 93) also propose revised endings to Thatcher's quest myth in which the civilian population of the Falklands is wiped out in a climactic land battle or, in Dennis Canavan's version, the British troops become involved in 'a full-scale blood bath, which no one will win' (Morgan, p. 213). Other speakers counter the positioning of the Falklands War within a glorious history of British military triumphs by comparing it to fiascos such as the Duke of Buckingham's expedition to New Rochelle in 1627 (Morgan, p. 298), the charge of the Light Brigade (pp. 13, 291), Gallipoli (p. 296) and Vietnam (p. 338).

The mythic status of the Falkland Islands as a place worthy of the attentions of a huge task force was also challenged on a number of occasions. In the House of Commons, Frank Hooley speaks dismissively of the Falklands as 'a few wind-swept islands in the South Atlantic' (Morgan, p. 54) and Andrew Faulds describes them as 'an outcrop of rocks' (Morgan, p. 291). The potentially deconstructive force of this introduction of commonplace reality into the shining world of myth is nowhere better illustrated, however, than when, in responding to Thatcher's aggrandizing talk of 'British sovereign territory', Edward Rowlands describes South Thule as 'a piece of rock . . ., which is totally uninhabited and which smells of large accumulations of penguin and other bird droppings' (Morgan, p. 6).

Further questioning of official versions of the Falklands War focused on the noble motives claimed by the Conservatives to justify taking up arms against Argentina. MPs Nigel Spearing and Stan Thorne both suggest, for instance, that the task force was dispatched to save the reputation of the Government and its leader and to preserve commercial interests rather than to restore the independence of the Falkland Islanders (Morgan, pp. 61, 161–2). Thatcher's often repeated assertion that her Government was acting out of a concern for the integrity of British sovereign territory is similarly undermined when Tony Benn points out that there were no protests from the Conservative benches when Ian Smith challenged British sovereignty in Rhodesia (Morgan, p. 163). And, finally, a *Guardian* editorial accuses the Government of pursuing 'gun-boat diplomacy' in the cause of 'the politics of national pride' (19 April 1982, p. 12).

Opposition politicians also attacked the Government by characterizing the tone of utterances issuing from the Conservative benches as 'gung ho' (Morgan, p. 46) and 'jingoistic' (p. 89) rather than fervently patriotic. The *Financial Times* picked up on this theme by offering a critique of Thatcher's 'melodramatic attempts to strike a hushed Churchillian tone' (Davidson, p. 17). Support for these debunkings of the style of Thatcherite discourse is provided by a number of cartoons that mock the Prime Minister's belligerent and grandiose posturing. Thus Gerald Scarfe depicts her as a boxer, clad in singlet, shorts and high-heeled shoes, squaring up to Galtieri (*Sunday Times*, 11 April 1982; reprinted in Aulich, p. 86) and Gibbard as the Lord Nelson figurehead of an aircraft carrier whose prow is inscribed with the slogan, 'Argies Here We Come' (*Guardian*, 19 May 1982, p. 1).

A final challenge to official versions of the Falklands War developed out of questions about the competence of Thatcher and her Government. Willy Hamilton, for instance, blamed the war, not on the Junta, but on Thatcher's 'ineptitude' while Leo Abse and Andrew Faulds reacted to the sinking of the *Sheffield* by describing the Falklands campaign as 'a massive folly' and as 'a lunatic exercise' (Morgan, pp. 93, 201, 203).

Witty, insightful and eloquent as many of them were, these attempts to demolish the framework of meaning that Thatcher and her supporters had erected around the Falklands War enjoyed little success. Public support for the Government's willingness to risk thousands of lives and spend millions of pounds in the defence of 1800 Falklanders increased the closer the task force drew to the war zone and was overwhelming by the time the invasion was launched.[9] To some extent the failure of oppositional voices can be attributed to the tendency of the mainstream media to ignore or denigrate them. The *Sun*, for example, gave considerable space to Thatcher's various utterances but referred rarely and always pejoratively to her critics in the House of Commons and elsewhere. The issue of 23 April is fairly typical in that it gives front page coverage, under the headline 'DEADLINE MIDNIGHT', to some belligerent comments made by Thatcher in the House of Commons about the slow progress of peace talks and on page two places an article by Winston Churchill advocating the bombing of Argentina in a much more prominent position than a companion piece by Tony Benn on the need to bring the fleet home. In order to make the *Sun*'s position absolutely clear, the editorial on page six is devoted to an attack on Benn.

Ultimately, though, Thatcher's interpretation of the situation prevailed because the war turned out much closer to the way she said it would than to any of the disastrous scenarios offered by her opponents and because, like all successful ideologues, she aimed her message at people's emotions rather than their minds. The public chose to listen to Thatcher rather than to those who presented the war as a cynical exercise in vote winning, an anachronistic piece of gunboat diplomacy or, as Borges put it, 'two bald men fighting over a comb' (quoted by Theroux, p. 47), because she spoke in terms that alleviated their deepest fears about their country, validated their prejudices and allowed them to feel pride in self and nation. Having bonded at such a primeval level with the British public, Thatcher had little difficulty in persuading large numbers of them to accept the ideological agenda concealed beneath her patriotic outpourings.

For all the help that she received from her parliamentary colleagues and from a friendly media in convincing the British public that events in the South Atlantic had revived 'the real spirit ' (Barnett, p. 150) of the nation and that this authentic nation modelled her own partly traditionalist, partly new right vision of the state, the Falklands War was ultimately a personal triumph for Margaret Thatcher. So much was this the case that for many people she became synonymous with the nation whose greatness she had proclaimed. Thus, cartoonists and commentators repeatedly identified Thatcher with national icons such as Wellington, Nelson, Churchill, Elizabeth I and Boedicea or with the nation itself in the shape of Britannia.[10] The revival in popularity of James Thomson's 'Rule, Britannia!' during the Falklands War noted by Eric Hobsbawm (p. 269) might even be attributed to the need to provide the regal Thatcher with an anthem of her own.

However, no sooner had Thatcher's wartime discourse gained her complete ascendency over her opponents than it seems to have run out of steam. Thatcher herself, as we have already seen, began to modify the framework of meaning that she had erected around the Falklands War immediately the fighting had ended by privileging the disciplines of monetarist economics over thrilling military achievements and there have been few significant attempts in the postwar period to supplement or expand the Thatcherite myth. Ian Curteis's *The Falklands Play* (1987), a hagiographical portrait of Thatcher as war leader written for the BBC, was never produced, and combat novels such as Adam Hardy's *Strike Force Falklands* (1983–5) series and Jack Higgins's *Exocet* (1983), which glorify Britain's military achievement in the Falklands, seem to have had little appeal for any but readers of military fiction. John Boorman's film, *Hope and Glory* (1987), an autobiographical evocation of the spirit of the Blitz, probably owes something to the mood of national euphoria stirred up by the Falklands War as, according to Susanne Collier, does Kenneth Branagh's 'stirring and self-consciously patriotic' (p. 144) film version of *Henry V* (1989), but in each case the line of connection is fairly blurred and circuitous.

There would seem to be at least two reasons for this paucity of attempts to extend official discourse about the Falklands War beyond its immediate context. First, the deep rootedness of

Thatcher's Falklands narrative in the inflexible patterns of heroic myth closes off the play of signification and leaves little scope for further development. Second, the Thatcherite myth of the Falklands War is so inextricably bound up with the giddy mood that swept across Britain during the spring of 1982 that any retelling is likely to seem at best hollow and worst ludicrously inflated. In the postwar period, therefore, the Falklands myth has been more or less relegated to some dusty shelf where the Conservatives store their ideological baggage, never really forgotten but only occasionally brought out, until her fall from power at least, to remind the public of the Party's achievements under Margaret Thatcher.

This is not to say, however, that the Falklands War fell into imaginative limbo with the retaking of Port Stanley. While the official myth might have been frozen into immobility, an alternative myth began to flourish as the fading of patriotic fervour created an audience receptive to more oppositional or subversive assessments of the Falklands War and its meaning. Responsibility for the development of this counter myth has fallen into the hands of creative artists able to advance their claims to truth not just through reasoned argument, which is doomed to failure when set against myth, but through the same devices employed to such good effect by Thatcher and her supporters: compelling narrative, powerful rhetoric, vivid metaphor and the creation of intense feeling. It is the task of the rest of this book to examine some of the most effective of these counter myths which have, despite their darker faces and lack of access to the mass audience made available to Thatcher by a compliant media, nevertheless gradually eroded the monolith of the official understanding of the Falklands War.[11]

Notes

1. For discussions of Thatcherite economic principles see Bleaney, pp. 132–47; Gamble, pp. 83–127; Hall, pp. 19–34.
2. For discussions of this mythic view of English history see Cottrell, pp. 264–71; Wright, p. 176–85.
3. For discussions of the racist dimensions of Thatcherite ideology see Gilroy, pp. 43–69; Solomos, pp. 123–39. For the broader historical context of British racism also see Holmes, *passim*.
4. For discussions of the difficult circumstances facing reporters in the

Falklands during the war see Mercer, pp. 144–50 and Morrison, pp. 164–87. Adams and Harris also offer excellent accounts of the role of the media during the Falklands War.

5. For a devastating analysis of Thatcher's dependence on the cliché see Raban, 1989, particularly p. 4.

6. For discussions of nineteenth-century chivalric codes, see Fussell, pp. 21–28, 135–9 and Girouard, passim.

7. Even the problem of landscape is partly erased if one takes into account the success of the television series *All Creatures Great and Small* in creating a space for the Yorkshire Dales within the imaginary landscape known as 'deep England'. In this context, it is worth noting Rex Hunt's description of the Falklands landscape as 'James Herriot country' (p. 21).

8. Powell's exact words spoken in Birmingham on 20 April 1968 were 'As I look ahead, I am filled with foreboding. Like the Roman, I seem to see "the River Tiber foaming with blood"'.

9. The MORI poll of 26 May 1982 reported an increase in satisfaction with Thatcher's leadership from 53 per cent on 8 May to 84 per cent. See Femenia, p. 195.

10. See Dresser for a full account of Britannia's role as a British national icon.

11. Nora Femenia's study of the relationship between Thatcher and Galtieri's wartime 'scripts' was published too late to have much impact on this chapter. However, Femenia's findings seem largely consistent with my own. Readers interested in further pursuing the question of political discourse during the Falklands/Malvinas War should consult her book.

2

Confronting the Icon: Portrayals of Margaret Thatcher in *The Falklands Factor, Sink the Belgrano!* and *If...*

By the end of the Falklands War, as we saw in the previous chapter, Margaret Thatcher had not only manufactured a vision of the nation that perfectly matched the Conservative Party's political agenda but, by taking on a role comprising part warrior queen, part Winston Churchill and part mother of the people, had put herself in an almost unassailable position. Challenges to the Thatcherite interpretation of the Falklands War were not likely to have much success, therefore, without a radical reassessment of Thatcher's dual function as maker and hero of the Falklands myth. In this chapter I will look at three works – Don Shaw and Colin Bucksey's television play, *The Falklands Factor* (broadcast on BBC 1 in 1983), Steven Berkoff's stage play, *Sink the Belgrano!* (performed in 1986 and published in 1987), and Steve Bell's cartoon strip, *If...* (published in the *Guardian*, April–June 1982 and in book form in 1982 and 1983) – that have taken on this daunting task. Although their revisionist views of Thatcher are remarkably similar in broad outline, in that they all locate a deceitful and self-interested politician in the space previously occupied by an honourable and inspirational national leader, each work approaches its subject from a very different direction.

At one extreme is Shaw's television play which stands well back from the events of 1982 and views Thatcher from the perspective provided by Samuel Johnson's experience of and thoughts about the immediate and broader issues at stake in the

Falklands crisis of 1770–1. At the other is Berkoff's agitprop stage play which, in a thinly fictionalized account of the political events leading up to the sinking of the Argentinian cruiser *The General Belgrano*, confronts Thatcher head on by substituting a grotesque and deliberately offensive caricature for the almost regal figure familiar to the British public during the Falklands War.

The ground occupied by Bell's cartoon strips lies somewhere between these two extremes. Although they appeared on a daily basis in the *Guardian* while the Falklands War was in progress, and therefore reflect their author's spontaneous reaction to unfolding political and military events, the *If* . . . cartoons manage to maintain a greater detachment from their subject matter than does *Sink the Belgrano!*. This detachment derives from the repeated shifts in perspective that Bell achieves by blending real and fictional characters and by moving back and forth between good-humoured comedy and more savage satire. No one approach is definitive. Rather, the power of the three works is a combined one because, by coming at Thatcher from a variety of angles, they are able to trim down the almost iconic status she enjoyed during the Falklands War to more fallible human or, in Berkoff's case, subhuman proportions.

THE FALKLAND, FACTOR: THATCHER FROM A JOHNSONIAN PERSPECTIVE

The Falklands Factor, which was broadcast in April of 1983, is on the face of it a piece of literary archaeology inspired by the current interest in all things Falklands. The general subject of the play is the crisis experienced by the Ministry of Lord North following the expulsion of the small British garrison from Fort Egmont in the Falkland Islands by a Spanish fleet in 1770. More specifically, it deals with the ways in which Samuel Johnson responded to North's demands that he write in defence of the unpopular peace settlement achieved in 1771. Shaw's interests, however, as should be obvious to anyone who notes the source of his title in Thatcher's Cheltenham speech, are rather more contemporary than his immediate topic might suggest.

In choosing as the basis of his plot an incident from the eighteenth century, Shaw is not seeking disengagement from the events of 1982 but a strategic vantage point from which to examine and judge the political performance of Margaret Thatcher and her supporters. The point that Shaw wants to make about the war with Argentina is that the public was manipulated by a language of national crisis into accepting a clever politician's self-serving agenda. However, such an argument, baldly stated, would have met with considerable resistance from an audience cast in the role of dupes. Therefore, Shaw employs a two-hundred-years old political debate as a kind of stalking horse under cover of which he is able to advance cautiously on his real target. Shaw's strategy is to win consent for a highly critical view of the discursive practices of prowar politicians from an earlier period of little concern to the vast majority of his audience while simultaneously dropping hints about the relevance of this view to the rhetorical practices of the Thatcherite forces in 1982. If successful in persuading his audience to take a fresh and cooler look at the ways in which meaning was manufactured just 12 months prior to the broadcast of this play, Shaw stands to make significant inroads into the apparently monolithic myth of the Falklands War by calling into question the probity of the figure at the centre of that myth.

Shaw's overt subject matter has the further and equally important advantage of providing him with a point of access into *Thoughts on the Late Transactions Respecting Falkland's Islands* (1771), the pamphlet that Samuel Johnson wrote in response to North's demands. *Thoughts* is most obviously of use to Shaw because of the contribution it makes to a play that is not only about discourse but also embraces within its 50 minutes running time a wide range of ways of speaking and writing. Thus, Johnson's essay is able to add history, invective, heroic fiction and negotiations to the parliamentary speeches, journalism, satirical verse, combative conversation and narrative commentary already woven into the fabric of *The Falklands Factor*. More important, though, because of its superior moral, intellectual and literary qualities, *Thoughts* functions in Shaw's play as a credible alternative to the mainstream political discourse practised by North and his political opponent William Pitt, the Earl of Chatham, in the eighteenth century and by Margaret Thatcher in the twentieth. Additionally, Johnson's running commentary on the irrationality, pettiness, self-interestedness, materialism and lack of humanity that characterize the speeches and journalistic writing of the prowar faction in 1770–1 carries the main burden of Shaw's case against Thatcher.

Ultimately, though, the relationship between Johnson's *Thoughts* and Shaw's *The Falklands Factor* is even more profound than I have so far suggested. The main subject matter of the play is the sequence of events that culminates in the production of Johnson's pamphlet and its antithetical structure is based on Johnson's. Most notable of all, though, excerpts from *Thoughts* several times provide Shaw with the text of *The Falklands Factor*. Thus, rather than relating to each other as text and source, *The Falklands Factor* and *Thoughts* become something close to a single hybrid text functioning with sometimes devastating effect as a critique of the linguistic practices of both eighteenth and twentieth-century politicians. Shaw must, of course, have been well aware that few members of his audience would ever bother to explore the full possibilities of this intertextual relationship by going from the play to the pamphlet. Indeed, he caters to the incurious majority by developing a deeply sympathetic portrait of Samuel Johnson designed to bolster the authority of the evocative but relatively brief excerpts from *Thoughts* included in the text of *The Falklands Factor*. In my analysis, however, without exploring all the ways in which the play and the pamphlet intersect, I will try to do some justice to the rich possibilities inherent in considering Johnson's complete text alongside Shaw's by making reference to *Thoughts* whenever such a procedure seems likely to significantly enhance an understanding of *The Falklands Factor*.

Johnson organizes *Thoughts* around a series of binary oppositions, the most important being moral principles/self interest, good/evil, human/inhuman, regard for facts/fanciful imaginings, experience/speculation, emotion/hysteria. The first term is in each case a characteristic of the type of discourse favoured by Johnson himself, one that ultimately moves from specific issues to larger questions of truth; the second set of terms are attributes, in Johnson's view, of the discourse that develops out of the short-term thinking of those, particularly politicians, whose only concern is to gain an advantage over their opponents.

However, in dealing with the Falklands crisis of 1770–1, Johnson does not maintain a rigid distinction between himself and all politicians but allows that, in taking steps to avoid war, North's Ministry was motivated by a fundamentally disinterested and moral regard for 'equity', 'humanity' and the 'safety of their fellow citizens' (p. 315) that contrasts strongly with the narrowly political motives of the prowar faction led by Chatham. As a result, Johnson is in some danger of making the uncharacteristically naive suggestion that broader moral principles can be reliably deduced from an individual's position on a specific issue. In structuring *The Falklands Factor* around a similar set of oppositions, Shaw, who clearly takes the position that Johnson was forced to be excessively generous to North by threats to his pension, is careful to reaffirm that there are fundamental differences between truth-seeking and politically motivated discursive practices even when they have an immediate goal in common. Thus, some of the most important parts of Shaw's Johnsonian analysis of the deficiencies of political discourse are developed in scenes that focus, not on Chatham or his chief propagandist, Junius, but on North and the satirical poet, Blanding, both of whom are strong advocates of peace.

North's actual performance as a political speaker receives very little emphasis in *The Falklands Factor* apart from one brief rhetorical outburst in which he tries to convince Johnson of the connection between preparations for war and the securing of peace. Instead, Shaw takes advantage of the opportunities provided by the several encounters between North and Johnson in his play to explore not so much political discourse itself as the motives that underlie such discourse. When Johnson is asked to consider the possibility of taking a seat in the House of Commons, he declares that 'good oratory needs conviction' and that, therefore, he could not lie for his party. Values such as these are not, however, what motivate North in his capacity as a politician. His attempts to secure a peaceful solution to the Falklands crisis were not, for instance, based on a principled opposition to war but, as he freely admits, the pragmatic 'real world' consideration that 'we cannot afford a war'. Neither does he disagree when Johnson adds as a further motive that 'war serves [your political opponents'] interests as peace serves yours'. Instead, by asking, 'Who serves Dr Johnson's interests?', North demonstrates his assumption of a universality of self-interest, thus lending credence to Johnson's later assessment that he does not give 'a fig for the Falklands' but is merely concerned to advance his career.

A further illustration of the narrowly instrumental terms within which political discourse operates is provided by the way in which North responds to Johnson's assessment that the scathing journalistic attack on the peace settlement written by Junius is of 'minor literary merit'. For North, aesthetic considerations, which

arise out of a broad concern with the function of writing in a
civilized society, are irrelevant; what matters is that Junius has
achieved his immediate goal of increasing support for the prowar
forces. This highly reductive view of speech and writing, inevitable in one who views the world from an exclusively political
perspective, is even more clearly evident in the tactics employed
by North to enlist Samuel Johnson's assistance in countering the
influence of Junius. At no point does he enquire whether Johnson
has the conviction to write in support of the recently negotiated
peace. Instead, he first tries to bribe him with the offer of a seat
in the House of Commons; then, in response to Johnson's objections to serving as another's voice, he threatens him with the
loss of his pension. Finally, North resorts to flattery by arguing
that Johnson has a responsibility to use his literary gift in order
to influence public opinion.

As presented by Don Shaw, politicians clearly have an extremely
limited understanding of the function of writing. We should not,
therefore, be surprised to learn that North withdraws *Thoughts*
from sale once it has helped secure his Ministry's position simply
because it includes some critical comments about his ally, Sir
George Greville. As a result he suppresses a passionate, morally
sound and rational work that far transcends its immediate purpose. For North, the pamphlet's moral and literary qualities are
important only in so far as they provide him with a warning
about the dangers of keeping his promise to find Johnson a seat
in Parliament. Were a man like Johnson, who possesses 'independent convictions' and whose writing has 'a disturbing power',
to become a politician, he would, in North's view, behave 'like
an elephant' and 'trample his friends as well as his enemies'.

Blanding's opposition to the forces urging Britain into a war
with Spain is completely free of the self-interestedness that moti-
vates North, as he reveals when he takes the risk of arousing
popular anger by reciting his satirical poem to a half-drunken
tavern audience that later cheers Junius's prowar newspaper article.
Furthermore, he expresses a number of sentiments that echo those
to be found in Johnson's pamphlet, the most notable being that
the main purpose of war is to 'line the pockets' of 'contractors
and printers'. Sincerity and clear thinking are not enough, however, to win Samuel Johnson's approval. While Blanding's verse
may be amusing and forceful, from a literary standpoint it is
nothing more than a piece of doggerel littered with clichés such

as 'rule the roost', awkward phrasing introduced to ensure that 'men of muse' supplies a rhyme for 'views', and a number of contrived rhymes including 'Chatham'/'at 'em' and 'pockets'/ 'blockheads'. As a man of high literary standards, Johnson has no choice but to dissent from the general drunken applause that greets the end of the recitation by suggesting that Blanding 'should join the fleet rather than be a writer'. The full severity of this rebuff is obvious to anyone who recalls Johnson's comment that 'being in a ship is being in jail, with the chance of being drowned' (Bate, p. 326).

Through his presentation of North and Blanding, Shaw thus suggests that, even when its immediate object is worthy, there is, from a Johnsonian perspective, something inherently meritricious about a discourse focused so single mindedly on the gaining of immediate political advantage as to ignore broader moral or artistic concerns. His point is starkly reinforced by a series of brief scenes set in the House of Commons as Chatham and his supporters speak in favour of war with Spain. The most striking quality of these scenes is their noisiness, which derives from the strident tones in which speeches are delivered and the raucousness of voices raised to encourage or deride the current speaker. This cacophonous quality is especially marked by its contrast to the calm, collected tone of voice adopted by the narrator, whose account of the eviction of the British garrison from the Falklands in June of 1770 is intercut with scenes of parliamentary debate.

Although the narrative voice, which is supplied by Warren Clarke, is different from that of Samuel Johnson, who is played by Donald Pleasance, the two voices are nevertheless extremely close both in style and in their concern for historical context. Indeed, later in the play, it is the narrator and not Johnson who relays to the viewer the fruits of the latter's research into the history of the Falklands. By thus blurring distinctions between the narrator and Johnson, Shaw makes it clear that he has introduced a contrast of voices into his scene of parliamentary debate in order to give dramatic expression to the gap that exists between the rational and reflective qualities of a Johnsonian discourse founded in facts and dedicated to the pursuit of larger truths and the irrational hysteria inevitable in a political discourse whose only goal is to promote factional interests. A particularly striking illustration of this gap is provided by Shaw and his director, Colin Bucksey's, decision to illustrate the narrator's account of the polite manner in which the Spanish commander dealt with the British garrison at Fort Egmont with cartoons depicting the invasion force as pigs that clearly serve as visual representations of the xenophobically distorted perspective of the prowar faction in the House of Commons.

Although Shaw relies on his director's ability to dramatize rather than Johnson's words to make his point during this and other scenes of parliamentary debate, he is nevertheless directly indebted to *Thoughts* for the connection between noise and irrationality around which his critique of political discourse is constructed. Thus, on one occasion, Johnson speaks about 'that noisy faction' detestable to any 'honest man' 'which has for too long filled the kingdom, sometimes with the roar of empty menace and sometimes with the yell of hypocritical lamentation' (p. 363). On others he refers to the 'feudal gabble' (p. 367) and 'tumultous clamour about honour and rights, injuries and insults' (p. 379) issuing from the ranks of Chatham's supporters before going on to describe them as 'inferior bellowers of sedition' (p. 382). By substituting noise for language and hence for reason and moral perspective, the opposition to North has, in Johnson's view, ceased to be human. Their 'roars' and 'bellows' he regards as the sounds of creatures in a menagerie. Elsewhere in the pamphlet Johnson compares these 'enemies of mankind' (p. 375) to 'phthiriasis' (p. 386) or crab lice, 'animals' (p. 386), and to almost subhuman 'savages' (p. 386). He also likens Chatham's ally Junius to 'a monster' (p. 377).

Like Johnson, then, Shaw is clearly interested in pursuing some of the larger moral questions raised by the narrowly partisan objectives of almost all political discourse. However, again like Johnson, Shaw also has a specific target, the identity of which is initially suggested by the parallels the narrator establishes between the events of 1770–1 and those of 1982 through his frequent repetition of the phrase 'then as now', as in 'then as now the British had no choice but to withdraw' and 'then as now angry questions were asked in Parliament'. Even more pointed are the close similarities between the arguments that Shaw attributes to the Chathamite faction as it presses for war with Spain and those put forward by Margaret Thatcher and her supporters to justify taking up arms against Argentina.

The Earl of Chatham is, for example, anticipating Thatcher's dire warnings about the global consequences of allowing unprovoked aggression to go unchecked when he argues that, even though they 'are devoid of economy', Britain must not 'yield the Falklands' because to do so will encourage the Spanish 'to attack others'. His later impassioned claim that 'England', once 'the terror of Europe' but now 'asleep', is in danger of becoming an 'object of contempt if we do not act as one nation' and engage in a 'war which will be won by British spirit alone' is replete with echoes of Thatcher's attempts to dignify the Falklands War by locating it within a myth of national revitalization achieved through heroic feats of arms. This Thatcherite myth of nation is also brought to mind by Chatham's allusions to British heroes of the past who were driven to perform mighty deeds by 'a point of honour'. These include Woolf, Major Douglas, who 'burned his ship rather than quit her', and 'the gallant Walk, who destroyed the fleet of France'. The background voices singing 'Rule, Britannia!' as Chatham calls for 'war with honour rather than peace without honour' provide yet another link with 1982 when, as I noted in the previous chapter, James Thomson's patriotic song enjoyed an enormous revival in popularity.

In a later scene, also set in the House of Commons, the Chathamite Edmund Burke adopts two positions familiar to anyone who comes to *The Falklands Factor* from the parliamentary debates of 1982. First, his brusque dismissal of the peace settlement achieved by Lord North because it has failed to establish Britain's inalienable sovereignty over the islands recalls the absolutist terms in which Thatcher and her supporters spoke of their country's claims to the Falklands. Second, in arguing that the 'dishonourable peace' is a betrayal of all those who have lost their lives or been injured during the dispute with Spain, Burke takes a position regarding discussions of a negotiated settlement close to that adopted by Stephen Hastings, Peter Griffiths and other Conservative MPs in the period following the sinking of HMS *Sheffield*.

By cutting away at one point from parliamentary attacks on the peace settlement to a montage of newspaper stories that echo the bellicose and nationalistic tones of Chatham and Burke, Shaw establishes yet another point of contact with the Falklands War of 1982 when the *Sun* and other newspapers consistently took their tone from the speeches of the Thatcherite forces in the House of Commons. The connection established here between parliamentary speeches and journalistic writing, and thus between the arenas in which political discourse operated in both Falklands

Wars, is developed further by a later cut that shifts the action
from the noisy House of Commons to a rowdy tavern. Here a
drunken customer raises his voice above the general din in a
style reminiscent of that of his parliamentary counterparts and
reads aloud a newspaper story that closely mimics Chatham's
appeal to the sleeping nation by warning that Britain must 'rouse'
and 'stand up for thine honour' if she is to avoid becoming 'the
scorn of the world'.

Presented, as they are, either in the pages of newspapers catering
to drunkards or in the context of an almost comically riotous
House of Commons concerned with a dispute that has none of
the urgency of the recent war with Argentina, these Thatcherite
sentiments ring out much less impressively than they did in 1982.
Invocations of the country's offended honour and demands for
a national revival that had so recently stirred the British people
cease to have much impact when uttered by the Earl of Chatham
in the context of a long-forgotten skirmish with Spain over what
Johnson called 'a tempest-tossed barrenness' (p. 358) soon to be
abandoned voluntarily by Britain. The fact that it was the same
islands, admittedly with a rather larger and more firmly established population of British loyalists but scarcely less obscure to
most people and not much less barren, that were the subject of
the fervour that swept the country in 1982 further calls into
question the rational basis of Thatcher's nationalistic rhetoric.

Shaw further undermines Thatcher's credibility by creating a
context where the worth of her argument that failure to counter
the Argentinian invasion of the Falklands would endanger world
peace can be judged alongside that of what history has shown
us to be Chatham's hysterical and exaggerated claims about the
dire consequences of yielding the islands to Spain. Similarly, the
further logical sleight of hand inherent in Chatham's attempt to
answer the charge that there is no point in defending the economically worthless Falklands by comparing them to Gibralter,
thereby extending a genuine correspondence between the colonies' economic situations into the groundless implication that
they share an important strategic function, calls to mind the
irrationality of many of the analogies that Thatcher draws between
the Falklands and the authentic Britain.

The inadequacy of the Prime Minister's approach to the Falklands War of 1982 is most decisively exposed, however, when
Shaw tests the validity of both Edmund Burke's assertion that

'the Falklands are ours by right of sovereignty' and, by implication, Thatcher's equally dogmatic rejection of Argentinian claims to the islands against the conclusions Samuel Johnson arrives at as the result of careful research into the topic. These conclusions are stated quite categorically in the pamphlet when Johnson, speaking with the confidence of one who has read all the relevant documents, declares the contention 'that our settlement of Falkland's Island was not only lawful but unquestionable' to be a 'general errour' running 'through the whole argument of the faction' (p. 379).

However, Shaw, or perhaps more accurately director Colin Bucksey, makes the point, which is no less damaging to Thatcher's credibility than it was to that of the prowar forces in 1770–1, somewhat less directly in *The Falklands Factor*. Rather than rely entirely on Johnson's actual words, Bucksey employs simple visual techniques in order to give dramatic expression to the air of uncertainty that emerges as the Falkland's first historian conducts his research. Thus, as the narrator summarizes the numerous early sightings that Johnson comes across in the course of his reading, so the flags of Spain, Britain, Holland and France are pinned to a map of the Falklands. Similarly, each name given to the islands by the 'wandering navigators who passed by them in search of better habitation' (p. 350) is inscribed on the map and then crossed out to be replaced by its successor. The British 'Hawkins' Maidenland' gives way to the Dutch 'Sebald's Island', which is displaced, in its turn, by the French 'Les Malorines' and then by the Spanish 'Malvinas'.

Through this dramatization of Johnson's observation that 'nothing has happened' to the Falklands and that 'these islands have hitherto changed only their name' (p. 350), Bucksey helps Shaw make the point that competing flags and names constitute the entire body of early evidence about the sovereignty of the Falkland Islands and that any arguments to the contrary, such as those made by Burke and Thatcher, simply fly in the face of history. For Shaw, speaking through Nicholas Calvert, the one reasonable voice to be heard during the parliamentary debates dramatized in *The Falklands Factor*, politicians who demonstrate this kind of cavalier disregard for facts are 'the foolishest men'.

The willingness of politicians, whether they be North and Chatham in the eighteenth century or Thatcher in the twentieth, to subordinate all other considerations to immediate party

advantage and to disregard facts and what might reasonably be
deduced from them brings Johnson and, in turn, Shaw to the
conclusion that conventional political discourse is both immoral
and irrational to the point of madness. Thus, Johnson, in his
pamphlet, likens Chatham's prowar faction to 'Milton's prince
of hell' and ascribes to them emotions, such as 'fretfulness', 'rage'
(p. 384) and 'paroxisms of fury' (p. 385), more usually associated with the seriously disturbed. In his play, Shaw offers as his
definitive comment on political morality Johnson's judgement that
'my being so good is no reason why you [North] should be so
ill'. Director Bucksey points up the insanity of political discourse
by means of a dissolve from Johnson describing madness as
occuring 'when fancy controls reason and leads to ungovernable
speech' to a flashback of Chatham making his appeal to the spirit
of the nation.

In order to further underline the inadequacies of the usual run
of political discourse, Shaw foregrounds within his play two
sections from Samuel Johnson's *Thoughts*. In sharp contrast to
the speeches and writing of Chatham, North, Junius and, by
implication, Thatcher,[1] these are carefully crafted pieces of prose
that seek to convince through a complex interplay between facts,
rational arguments, occasional displays of deeply felt emotion,
firm moral convictions, and a concern with universal truths. The
first extract, taken from the early historical sections of *Thoughts*,
provides Shaw with opportunities to demonstrate the important
part played by facts and reason in Johnsonian discourse. The
second, drawn mostly from Johnson's lengthy meditation on the
evils of war, allows him to draw attention to the broader and
deeply felt moral concerns that ultimately displace the pamphlet's
immediate political purpose.

Johnson's ability to draw rational conclusions from a bedrock
of fact is effectively illustrated by the scene in which he begins
work on his pamphlet in defence of North's peace settlement.
At this early stage in his project, Johnson is intent, as Shaw reveals
through the device of interior monologue, on judging the validity of the prowar faction's demands. His method for achieving
this goal is to balance the benefits to be gained from fighting for
possession of the Falklands against the evils inherent in giving
up the 'pleasures' of peace, the greatest of which is 'happiness'
(p. 350; quoted by Shaw). A respect for hard facts means that
Johnson has little difficulty in 'proportion[ing] the eagerness of

the contest to its importance' (p. 349). The Falklands, as he has discovered by accepting the challenge to be their first 'historian', are 'a few spots on earth which . . . had almost escaped human notice' (p. 350; quoted by Shaw) and a 'tempest-tossed barrenness' (p. 358; quoted by Shaw). Even now that they are settled, they remain 'a bleak and gloomy solitude . . . where a garrison must be kept in a state that contemplates with envy the exiles of Siberia; of which the expence will be perpetual and the use only occasional' (p. 369; quoted by Shaw). Therefore, since Spain has already agreed that the British can return to Fort Egmont, albeit without dropping what the informed historian has already recognized are its legitimate claims to sovereignty, Johnson can only conclude that it is 'madness' (p. 370; quoted by Shaw) to press for war over such a useless place.

The disinterested spirit in which Johnson approaches his analytical task is revealed by the double-edged nature of his conclusions. On the one hand, they clearly serve his patron's interests by labelling the supporters of war as insane and by stressing how clever North has been in gaining effective control of the Falklands despite strong evidence that they rightfully belong to Spain. On the other, by constantly emphasizing the worthlessness of the Falklands, Johnson is also implicitly taking away much of the credit he has granted to North for securing, as a term of the negotiated peace, the garrison's unhindered return to Fort Egmont. While sufficiently partisan to avoid explicit comment, Johnson is hinting here that it is scarcely less insane to seek possession of the Falklands through peaceful means than it is to fight for them.

Brief as it is, this interior monologue, beautifully spoken by Donald Pleasance, also serves to demonstrate that it is not just the quality of the author's analytical skills that distinguishes Johnson's writing from the usual run of political discourse but also his ability, as an artist, to employ fine writing towards serious moral ends. Johnson states early in his pamphlet that the story of these islands provides the historian with 'few opportunities for descriptive splendour, or narrative elegance' (p. 350). Instead, he must perform the much more difficult task of evoking the sense of absence that is the most striking characteristic of a place lacking any of the qualities normally associated with pleasant and habitable human space. That Johnson is well up to the challenge is evidenced by his success in developing a bleak description of the islands that captures their essential vacuity while at the same time serving as the basis for a disquisition on the moral significance of solitude.

Johnson's literary skills and moral concerns both inform his use of the phrase, 'a few spots of earth', which carries with it the suggestion that, besides being so tiny as to barely exist, the Falklands have a diseased quality that makes them inhospitable to the development of human society. Johnson elaborates on his portrayal of the islands' inhospitable character through the use of the phrase 'tempest beaten barrenness', in which a trochaic rhythm and alliteration/assonance combine to communicate a sense of harshness, coldness and sterility. The adjectives 'bleak' and 'gloomy' in the phrase 'bleak and gloomy solitude' perform a similar function. The noun 'solitude' more sharply focuses the moral concerns hinted at in the earlier metaphor of disease by establishing the Falklands as the antithesis of the ideal of community and friendship that had long been the focus of Johnson's hopes of achieving the elusive goal of happiness. The moral significance assigned to the Falklands by Johnson is further reinforced by a final powerful image in which, by likening them to 'exiles in Siberia', he transforms the troops garrisoned there into pariahs and outcasts, poor unfortunates deprived by their masters' obsession with gaining sovereignty over a geographical cipher of any chance of experiencing the happiness to which all humans have the right to aspire.

In the final minutes of *The Falklands Factor*, which are given over to a lengthy interior monologue taken almost verbatim from *Thoughts*, Shaw not only provides an even better example of his main character's ability to extend what begins as an analysis of a specific situation into a well-written moral treatise but also demonstrates the part that powerful emotions sometimes play in advancing his argument. Although he does in passing score some points on behalf of Lord North for achieving 'by quiet negotiations all the real good that victory could have brought us' (p. 372; quoted by Shaw), Johnson's real concern during this monologue is with war, not as a matter of immediate policy but as a larger moral issue rooted in fundamental questions of good and evil. Having firmly located war in the category of evil, Johnson then explores the mixture of irrational and immoral reasons that persuade countries to continue fighting with each other. His ultimate goal in doing this is not simply to avert war with

Spain over the Falklands but to put an end to all war.

Viewed from a policy perspective, as it was in 1770–1 and 1982, war can be a complex subject involving careful assessment of the appropriate weight to be given to possible and probable gains and losses. However, from the particular moral point of view adopted by Johnson, whose definition of good is that which advances human welfare, it is a very simple subject. Since happiness, the prime object of human life and therefore the ultimate good, is, as he suggests in the extract from *Thoughts* discussed earlier, a characteristic of peace, then war, the antithesis of peace, must be considered 'the extremity of evil' (p. 370; quoted by Shaw). By standing back in this way from the messy and emotional circumstances that surrounded the events of 1770–1, much as they did in 1982, in order to gain a broad, conceptual view of war Johnson is able to cast a new light on the subject and to offer as the main responsibility of politicians or, as he puts it, 'those whose station intrusts them with the care of nations' (p. 370; quoted by Shaw), the preservation of peace. The target of his pamphlet therefore becomes not just Chatham and his supporters but all politicians who are willing to take their country into a war without first exploring every possible alternative.

As a supremely practical man, however, Johnson is well aware that behaviour with respect to war is not usually influenced by this kind of thinking. Therefore, as a first step towards effecting change, Johnson goes on to investigate why almost all nations have continued to wage wars rather than look after their citizens' best interests by taking whatever steps are necessary to preserve the peace. His conclusion is that irrationality lies at the root of ordinary people's willingness to let their leaders involve them in a war while there are usually immoral reasons why those in positions of power and authority choose war over peace.

In examining how the 'greater part of mankind' respond to the outbreak of war, Johnson notes a 'coolness and indifference'. This response has its origins, he argues, in the fact that, rather than being aware of what really happens in war, most people 'hear of it at a distance, or read of it in books' and therefore regard what happens on the battlefield as 'little more than a splendid game' (p. 370; quoted by Shaw) that their side is bound to win. Even soldiers, he goes on to say, fail to understand that what they will experience in war 'is ill represented by heroic fiction' (p. 370; quoted by Shaw). This latter point about the ability of written representation not only to conceal reality from the civilian but to construct a version of experience so powerful that it continues to function in the face of contradictory evidence is reinforced by Shaw's introduction into his play of a scene in which a crippled beggar speaks enthusiastically to Johnson about the very war that has robbed him of his legs and his ability to make a decent living.

Cold reason is inevitably one of the weapons that Johnson employs in seeking to disabuse people of their irrational attitude to war. By simply stating, 'it is evident that of contradictory opinions one must be wrong', he is able, for example, to point out the illogicality of the 'mutual confidence' in victory that typically discourages both sets of citizens from urging their governments in the days 'before the sword is drawn' to avoid 'that wantonness of bloodshed that has so often desolated the world' (p. 372; quoted by Shaw). However, Johnson is acutely aware of the limited usefulness of logic in the face of vivid literary representation and, therefore, he also brings to bear all his own considerable artistic skills into the creation of an alternative fact-based depiction of war intended to dispel the romantic aura that has previously obscured its reality.

Recognizing that simply to emphasize that many deaths occur on the battlefield is hardly likely to deter a public deeply imbued in the idea that those killed in combat 'die on a bed of honour' (p. 370), Johnson dwells instead on 'means of destruction more formidable than the cannon and the sword' (p. 371; quoted by Shaw). These include diseases spread by 'incommodious encampments and unwholesome stations' that make 'courage' and 'enterprise', virtues sufficient to all situations in heroic fiction, 'useless' and 'impracticable' (p. 371; quoted by Shaw). In a passage not quoted by Shaw, Johnson conjures up a brief but powerful scene of men languishing 'in tents and ships, amidst damps and putrefaction, pale, torpid, spiritless, and helpless, gasping and groaning' until they die and are 'at last whelmed in pits, or heaved into the ocean, without notice or remembrance' (p. 371). His account reaches its chilling climax in an image, which Shaw includes in *The Falklands Factor* as a brief demonstration of Johnson at his most effective, not of the thrilling noise of death in battle so familiar to the readers of heroic fiction but of the awful quiet that falls as 'fleets are silently dispeopled, and armies sluggishly melt away' (p. 371).

The regretful tone that characterizes Johnson's analysis of the perceptual failings of ordinary people is displaced by one of scornful indignation when he turns his attention to the powerful figures who embrace war, not because of any lack of understanding but because they can make a profit from it. Thus, in this instance at least, Johnson seems to be on operating on the assumption that, while there is some possibility of enlightening those who act irrationally, he can only hope to discredit those who behave immorally.

Politicians attract his scorn because, focused as ever on their own short-term interests, they often find 'a foreign war' useful in 'withdraw[ing] the attention of the publick from domestick grievances' (p. 372; quoted by Shaw). Even worse, beneficiaries of political patronage, such as 'paymasters and agents, contractors and commissaries', people he characterizes as being 'without virtue', promote war because they grow 'rich from it as their country is impoverished' and 'rejoice when obstinacy or ambition adds another year to the slaughter and devastation' (p. 371; quoted by Shaw).

The morally purposeful anger that these kind of offences against the sanctity of human life stir up in Johnson is nowhere better illustrated than by the mocking hyperbole that he employs in his description of 'the sudden glories' earned through wartime profits by financiers and suppliers 'whose equipages shine like meteors and whose palaces rise like exhalations' (p. 371; quoted by Shaw). His final simile's allusion to the creation of Pandemonium in *Paradise Lost* (1, 710–11) allows Johnson to firmly group such people with politicians who, as we have already seen, he compares to 'Milton's prince of hell' (p. 384).[2] Equally expressive of Johnson's deeply felt and morally rooted indignation is the brief but evocative sketch in which he creates a picture of these same calculating and immoral financiers and suppliers 'laugh[ing] from their desks at bravery and science, while they are adding figure to figure, and cipher to cipher, hoping for a new contract from a new armament, and computing the profits of a siege or tempest (p. 371; quoted by Shaw).

Shaw's extensive borrowings from Johnson's *Thoughts* point up a gap between two types of political discourse, the one being a product of expediency and the other of serious moral reflection, that serves to discredit the usual run of politician and therefore helps in a general way to advance his case against Margaret

Thatcher. In order to make Johnson into a critic more specifically of Thatcher, Shaw has interpolated two passages from other
parts of *Thoughts* into the excerpts from Johnson's reflections on
war and war mongers upon which the interior monologue
currently under discussion is largely based.

The comment that Johnson makes in Shaw's play about the
tendency of governments to regard a foreign war as a useful
distraction from domestic difficulties is not, for example, included
in his general analysis of the motives underlying war in the original
pamphlet. Rather, it has been lifted from a later section of *Thoughts*,
where Johnson is actually writing about the situation in France,
and placed in a position of prominence near to the beginning of
the interior monologue that completes the action of *The Falklands
Factor*. Shaw manipulates Johnson's text in this way to remind
his audience of a more recent occasion when, as Thatcher's critics claim, a crisis in the South Atlantic came to the aid of a Government weighed down with problems on the home front. Towards
the end of his interior monologue in *The Falklands Factor* Johnson
launches an attack on those 'enemies of mankind' who 'snatch
by violence and bloodshed, what gentler means can equally obtain'
(p. 375) that has similarly been transposed from its original context in *Thoughts* because of its obvious application to a Prime
Minister frequently accused in the Spring of 1982 of failing to
take sufficient advantage of the opportunities for peace provided
by Haig's exercise in shuttle diplomacy.

The applicability of Johnson's reflections on war to Margaret
Thatcher and her war is made most obvious, however, in the
original cut of *The Falklands Factor* at least,[3] by the dissolving of
a montage of images from the Falklands War into the close ups
of Johnson that accompany his interior monologue. Footage of
Thatcher waving and smiling outside 10 Downing Street after
the recapture of South Georgia is introduced at the appropriate
moment, for example, to ensure that she is identified, not as the
saviour of her people, but as a political leader who has failed in
her duty as one of 'those whose station intrusts them with the
care of nations, to avert [the evil of war] from their charge'
(p. 370; quoted by Shaw). The cost of Thatcher's 'eagerness' to
seize the 'first opportunity of rushing into the field' instead of
seeking what 'quiet negotiation' (p. 372; quoted by Shaw) might
achieve is similarly underlined by cueing in Johnson's words to
shots of the mass burials at Goose Green.

Earlier in the scene, the continued relevance of Johnson's analysis of the blindness of both the general public and the ordinary soldier to the realities of war is established by shots of crowds cheering and troops enthusiastically singing 'Rule, Britannia!' as the fleet embarks for the Falklands. The realities that distance and heroic fiction serve to conceal are communicated by successive images of HMS *Galahad* burning, the *Belgrano* sinking, the wounded being removed from the *Galahad*, and of disconsolate Argentinian prisoners. Finally, Johnson's contrasting of the soldiers who bear the brunt of war and the entrepreneurs who reap its financial benefits is made applicable to the contemporary situation by the juxtaposition of a shot of a severely wounded Welsh Guardsman, his leg blown off at the knee, and a number of images of the expensive and sophisticated military hardware employed and destroyed during the fighting over the Falklands Islands.

Johnson's *Thoughts* thus plays a crucial role in *The Falklands Factor* by providing both a benchmark against which to judge the inadequacies of political discourse in general and the material out of which Shaw constructs his specific critique of Margaret Thatcher. However, brief extracts, skilfully chosen though they may be, cannot capture the full complexity of Johnson's masterful work. Therefore, although he implicitly invites his viewers to overcome this limitation by supplementing their experience of his play with a reading the complete pamphlet, Shaw is realistic enough to try to bolster the authoritative role he has assigned to *Thoughts* from within *The Falklands Factor*. To this end, and taking full advantage of the dramatic possibilities inherent in the form of the television play, Shaw offers a portrait of the pamphlet's author designed to enhance the credibility of the work for which he is responsible.

The Samuel Johnson created by Don Shaw in *The Falklands Factor* is almost entirely consistent with Jackson Bates' portrayal of him in the standard biography. The most notable features of this Johnson are to be found the sharp contrasts that exist between him and representative political figures such as North and Thatcher. Whereas North in the play, like Thatcher in the Falklands War, employs a polished personal style and glib, controlled speech in order to create a persona that conceals the real self, Johnson is all too obviously a fallible, multi-faceted human being. Thus, rather than present a dignified public face appropriate to his status as a famous writer, Johnson is inattentive to his appearance, frequents noisy taverns, keeps irregular hours, and speaks frankly in all situations, whether the subject be Blanding's verse or Lord North's moral failings. Johnson's eccentric individuality is made even more evident by his inability or unwillingness to mask his emotions. Examples of this personality trait occur at various points in Shaw's play as Johnson expresses outrage at the sacrifice of a beggar's legs in the cause of war, glories in being mentioned by Horace Walpole, and almost bursts with pleasure at achieving victory in arguments.

Johnson is made extremely vulnerable by his lack of social armour. His transparent delight in receiving praise, for instance, allows him to be used as the butt of a rather cruel joke in which he is first puffed up with pride by Blanding's reference to 'our greatest writer' before being deflated by the revelation that his tormentor is speaking of Shakespeare. This inability to put on a public face also works against Johnson's self-interest. Thus, even though his pension and a possible political career are at stake, Johnson falls asleep during his meeting with North and, on waking, offers a highly critical assessment of the Ministry's motives for seeking a peaceful settlement to the Falklands crisis.

At the same time, though, were he not so completely open, it is unlikely that Johnson would have achieved greatness either as a man or as a writer because it is this very intimacy with the inner self that provides the raw experiental material needed for the development of his moral vision. As Bate puts it, Johnson the moralist is a man who lives so 'close to the edge of human experience in so many different ways' that his pronouncements about the human condition have 'the ring of authority' of one who 'has gone through it himself at genuine risk or peril' (p. 297).

The process by means of which Johnson moves from personal experience to moral stance is repeatedly dramatized in *The Falklands Factor* in order to emphasize its importance to an understanding of the man and his work. Johnson's ability to write so convincingly in his pamphlet about the relationship between madness and other human faculties is shown, for instance, to owe a great deal to a personal struggle precipitated by nightmares in which his reason finds it difficult to ward off the ever-increasing threat of insanity. The content of these nightmares, in which his beloved ward cum servant, Frank Barber, is pressed into naval service before dying a hideous death in battle, also suggests a close connection between Johnson's exploration of the subject of friendship in *Thoughts* and his personal experience of such a relationship.

Similarly, the power of Johnson's description of the Falklands as 'a bleak and gloomy solitude ... where a garrison must be kept in a state that contemplates with envy the exiles of Siberia' (p. 369; quoted in Shaw), without which, as we have seen, his larger moral point would be seriously diminished, derives not from any first-hand knowledge of the islands but from the feelings of imprisonment that often accompany his own bouts of depression and loneliness. Bucksey provides a vivid visual image of the ability of depression to cut Johnson off from human companionship in a scene where he sits silent and withdrawn amidst a crowd of drunken revellers.

Shaw also reveals that, far from being mere philosophical abstractions, charity and compassion, the virtues that reside at the centre of Johnson's moral system, are precisely the principles by which his own conduct is guided. His reaction to the legless beggar and his response to the news that his rival, Blanding, has fallen prey to a press gang are both, for example, characterized by a deep empathy for the suffering of his fellow human beings. An even more telling example of the personal origins of Johnson's altruistic view of human relations is provided by his dream about Frank Barber.

Shaw introduces this dream in part to demonstrate the compassion that Johnson feels for all young men snatched away by brutal press gangs to die in their nation's wars. Of greater importance, though, the fact that it is the boy of ten whose care Johnson undertook in 1756 rather than the man of 25, as Frank was in 1771, who appears in the dream serves to remind the viewer of an act of charity remarkable even in a life filled with such acts. The particular circumstance that explains why Johnson's unconscious chooses Frank rather than the recently press ganged Blanding as the subject of the dream offers particularly telling evidence of the caring spirit in which he discharged his obligations as a guardian. While never in fact the target of a press gang, Frank Barber did run away to sea in 1758, thus abandoning a position as assistant to an apothecary arranged by Johnson in accordance with the boy's own wishes. However, rather than leave his ungrateful ward to suffer the consequences of his impetuous decision, as he might well have felt inclined to do, 'the worried Johnson, at the cost of some embarrassment, tried to get Frank released from the navy ... by getting the notorious John Wilkes to use his influence at the Admiralty' (Bate, p. 326).

Shaw completes his affirmative portrayal of Samuel Johnson and, by addressing the circumstances surrounding the composition of *Thoughts*, his efforts to reinforce the authority of a work that carries the main burden of his indirect assault on Margaret Thatcher with several scenes in which Johnson's personal and artistic integrity are challenged by Lord North. Issues other than those of immediate self-interest and political advantage are, as we have already seen, irrelevant to North. Therefore, he has no compunction about using a combination of bribes and threats in order to convince Johnson that he should help his political patron out of a difficult situation by writing in defence of the recently negotiated peace with Spain. What North has to offer appeals to Johnson, who looks forward to the chance to practice good oratory as a Member of the House of Commons, and what he threatens has serious implications for a man heavily dependent on the income from his pension.

Nevertheless, at no point in the scenes between Johnson and North is there the slightest indication that Johnson's decision to write the pamphlet is influenced by North's appeal to his self-interest. On the contrary, as Johnson makes clear when he tells North that he would be no better than the monkey he believes Junius to be if he were to write at another's command, the cost of agreeing to such a proposal involves a loss of personal integrity that far outweighs anything that North can do to or for him. Thus, when Johnson does finally turn his attention to defending the peace settlement, it is mainly because he has found in war a theme 'mighty' enough to provide him with opportunities to continue his life-long commitment to the pursuit of truth.

At the end of the titles, Shaw adds as a brief coda to *The Falklands Factor* a few lines from a letter written by David Tinker RN, shortly before his death in the Falklands. Both Tinker's letter and Shaw's play are exercises in intertextuality that employ earlier meditations on the relationship between a particular war and war in general as the basis for their own examinations of the specific and universal issues at stake in the Falklands War of 1982. Thus, Tinker, who wants to challenge the validity of national pride as a motive for war, be it in the Falklands or elsewhere, cites what Wilfrid Owen learned from his experiences in the First World War trenches about the futility of fighting 'men – for flags' rather than 'death – for life' (p. 180). Shaw, in turn, uses excerpts from Samuel Johnson's brilliant analysis of the immediate and broader issues at stake in the Falklands crisis of 1770–1, buttressed by an affirmative portrayal of the pamphlet's author, as the foundation for his critique of the more recent war in the Falklands. As a result, he is able not only to redirect the bitter invective that Johnson unleashes against Chatham and his supporters into an attack on Thatcher's behaviour during the war of 1982 but, through his use of Johnson's more general and reflective comments on war, to damn her even more decisively as the type of the war-mongering politician. Shaw's final point, then, is not simply that Thatcher is responsible for one unnecessary war but that, by continuing to function within the parameters of a type of discourse that Johnson recognized as well established by 1770, she is also guilty of passing on for use by future generations an irrational and immoral construction of reality in which war becomes an acceptable means of settling disputes between nations.

SINK THE BELGRANO!: INVERTING THE FALKLANDS MYTH

In *Sink the Belgrano!*, Steven Berkoff covers much the same territory as Don Shaw does in *The Falklands Factor*. However, in contrast to the subtle and complex approach adopted by Shaw, Berkoff relies on simple, direct and often crude techniques. His intention is to mirror the kind of closed narrative employed by Margaret Thatcher in which the play of signifiers is always subordinated to the search for a final definitive signified. However, Berkoff's mirror offers only inverted images, with the result that in every aspect of his play, including narrative structure, the interpretation of specific historical events, character and language, he makes use of Thatcher's own techniques to turn her reading of the Falklands War on its head. Thus, in *Sink the Belgrano!*, heroism is reflected as villainy, good as evil, moral purpose as dishonesty, the spiritual either as the demonic or the material, altruism as crass self-interest, the more than human as the subhuman, mythic archetype as cartoon grotesque, and high diction as low vernacular. In case this plethora of inversions is insufficient to communicate his loathing for Thatcher's management of the Falklands War, or more specifically the *Belgrano* incident, Berkoff also introduces a number of characters into *Sink the Belgrano!* whose major or even sole function is to give voice to his dissenting position.

At the heart of *Sink the Belgrano!* is an intermittent narrative delivered by a chorus and closely modelled on Thatcher's mythic interpretation of the Falklands War in which a slumbering nation finds itself by taking up arms, crossing an ocean and winning a great military victory, in this case, not the recapture of Port Stanley but the sinking of the Argentinian cruiser, *The General Belgrano*. The very different ends to which Berkoff employs the Thatcherite myth are indicated, however, by the almost immediate shift in style from heroic to low vernacular of the choric recitation with which the play opens. The passage begins as a dignified apostrophe in praise of the noble and freedom loving English: 'Oh you most brave and valiant Englishmen/Who never shall, no never bear the yoke' (p. 3). However, it soon begins to reverberate with a violent hooligan slang. The Argentinian enemy is, for example, referred to as 'a greasy foreign bloke' and as 'foreign, greasy, dark unholy scum'; Britain's great history is invoked in terms more usually associated with a street brawl: 'The Boers we kicked to kingdom come'; and the revival of the nation's spirit is expressed in ugly, brutalizing images: 'But once aroused, oh ho! old Albion snorts/ The Bulldog, start-eyed, drools for Argy blood' (p. 3). The effect of this dramatic change in style is to reformulate the Falklands War so that it becomes an expression not of chivalric values, as Thatcher and her supporters tried to argue, but of xenophobic and violent urges of the type associated with National Front extremists.

Subsequent choric recitations are less replete with skinhead diction and sentiments. Nevertheless, they continue to eschew a transcendent Thatcherite reading of the Falklands War in favour of one that emphasizes the murderous brutality that is the existential reality of armed conflict. Consequently, whatever elements there are of panegyric in the play's choric utterances are reserved for the military hardware that is so much more effective in creating mayhem than any knightly hero, however lofty the motives that take him onto the battlefield. In the chorus's version of the Falklands myth, therefore, it is not a Colonel 'H' Jones who achieves apotheosis but 'a brace of Exocet missiles/ That would ascend the brightest heaven of invention' (p. 20) and 'A score of Harriers now unleashed/. . . ./ Then sweeping into the sky/ Dissolving in a womb of cloud' (p. 31).

Berkoff's antimythic narrative, like Thatcher's more conventional heroic tale, ends in a British victory when the nuclear submarine, HMS *Conqueror*, torpedoes the *Belgrano*. The emphasis in *Sink the Belgrano!* is not, however, on the accomplishment of the kind of lofty goals claimed by Thatcher but on the suffering and loss of life caused by British military aggression: 'Three hundred and thirty sailors died at once . . ./ The others dragged their shredded flesh/ To rafts to face the icy sea' (p. 38).

A full explanation of Berkoff's reasons for inverting Thatcher's affirmative use of archetypes is provided by the more historically specific story and characters that add flesh to the mythic framework underpinning *Sink the Belgrano!*. However, in moving from myth to history in order to offer his version of the events leading up to the sinking of the *Belgrano*, Berkoff, again following the example set by Thatcher, does not exchange the stark clarity of archetypes for the complexities of real life. Instead he shuns the mass of confusing and often contradictory evidence that surrounds the *Belgrano* incident in favour of an analysis that inversely mirrors the simplistic official explanation. In the Government's version of events, as presented in the House of Commons by the Minister of Defence, John Nott, on 4 May, the sinking of the Belgrano was a simple matter of military necessity. Thus, while admitting that the *Belgrano* was outside the 200 mile Total Exclusion Zone, Nott claimed that the well-armed cruiser, escorted by two destroyers, was 'closing on elements of our task force, which was hours away' (Morgan, p. 194). Berkoff, by way of contrast, asserts that the War Cabinet was well aware that the *Belgrano* was 'heading back home' (p. 34) and persuaded Nott (thinly disguised as Nitt in *Sink the Belgrano!*) to lie to Parliament in order to conceal the real reasons for what was, from a military perspective, a gratuitous act of mass slaughter. According to Berkoff, Thatcher's motives (or Maggot Scratcher's in the play) for sinking the *Belgrano* were entirely political and arose out of a need to sabotage peace negotiations that were on the verge of averting a war essential to her future electoral prospects.

While a number of studies of the political and diplomatic dimensions of the Falklands War have suggested that there was a degree of disingenuousness and even deceit in official explanations for the sinking of the *Belgrano* as well as a lack of total commitment to the peace process, there are very few that provide much support for Berkoff's thesis.[4] Indeed, Berkoff's case is built upon at least two significant factual errors. First, armed hostilities did not start on 2 May when the *Belgrano* was sunk but on the previous day with an aerial assault on the runway at Port Stanley. Thus, while the torpedoing of the *Belgrano* resulted in the war's first, and indeed most significant casualties, it is difficult to view it as the product of a radical shift in British military strategy prompted by Thatcher's sudden need to sabotage peace talks. Second, although the intervention into the peace process of Peruvian President Fernando Belaunde Terry on 30 April and 1 May was a promising development, he had not brought the two sides to the brink of a truce, as Pimp, Berkoff's version of Foreign Secretary Francis Pym, tells Scratcher in *Sink the Belgrano!*.

Taken at face value such blatant deviations from the historical record would seem to call into question the validity of Berkoff's entire project. However, they can be defended as a necessary part of his technique of inversion. For if, as Berkoff believes, Thatcher frequently rewrote history in order to create an idealized picture of her Government's conduct of the Falklands War, then it is essential that Berkoff similarly simplify reality in order to convey the obverse impression. Thus, whereas Thatcher's self image as the heroic leader of an essentially moral crusade emerged unscathed from the official story of the *Belgrano* incident, Berkoff's subversive version presents the Prime Minister as an extreme example of the 'armoured' personality that is 'dead to all real human response except what concerns them personally' (p. 1).

The emergence out of Berkoff's reworkings of history of this Thatcher doppleganger, a figure so monstrous as to have condemned hundreds of young men to death in order to secure her own political future, brings us close to the heart of the play for, in spite of the significant role played by narrative, it is character that finally carries the main satirical burden in *Sink the Belgrano!*. By renaming Thatcher, Maggot Scratcher, and by calling John Nott and Francis Pym, Nit and Pimp, Berkoff immediately announces his intention to approach character, as he does plot, through stark inversions of the heroic stereotypes that populate the official Falklands myth. Thus, whereas Thatcher and to a lesser extent her colleagues emerge as somewhat more than merely mortal in the version of events in which the Falklands War becomes a rite of passage for a nation rediscovering its heroic potential, they are relegated, as their new names suggest, to a level considerably less than human in Berkoff's revisionist narrative.

To caricature the Foreign Secretary as a man who exploits human sexuality for financial gain is lowering enough but Berkoff does in fact locate Pimp, who has occasional twinges of conscience, considerably higher on the moral chain of being than Nit and Maggot; as the egg of a louse and the legless larva of a housefly, they have not yet even realized their potential as fully developed insects.

Despicable as he is, though, Nit does not sink down as far as Maggot's greater intelligence and domineering personality take her. Berkoff confirms her status as the most grotesque of the three comic book villains by assigning her several monstrous roles. At various points in *Sink the Belgrano!* she is a Lady Macbeth who will 'bring forth men soldiers only' (p. 8); a witch who plans to win over public opinion by cooking up in her 'cauldron' a 'foul stew' comprised of such ingredients as 'hate', 'lies', 'slander' and 'one thousand dead' (p. 16) for consumption by the British press; and 'a dame of iron' (p. 8), 'rigid, hard, inflexible' and with 'a steely heart' (p. 34), whose 'undaunted metal should compose nothing but wars' (p. 8). Taken together these three roles suggest that Maggot is the inversion of all the traditional womanly and motherly virtues so often claimed for herself by Thatcher. Thus, whereas we might expect that as a woman she would be caring towards others and display a deep regard for the sanctity of human life, Maggot in fact openly despises friend and foe alike and is either unconcerned about or openly revels in the prospect that people might die in the advancement of her selfish goals.

The width of Maggot's circle of scorn can be gauged by the fact that it includes not only enemies such as the Argentinian Junta, whose members she describes as 'creeps' (p. 20), and the 'filthy dogs' (p. 7) of the political left but also allies such as Ronald Reagan, mockingly referred to as 'Old Geriatric Joe' (p. 13), and, most striking of all, her own political colleagues. For Maggot, Nit is a 'silly prat' (p. 8), Pimp a 'rotten little turnip' (p. 22) and a 'stupid simpering silly pontz' (p. 27). Her colleagues collectively are 'foul male turds' (p. 12), 'scum' (p. 13) and 'leaking drips' (p. 28). Even the Falkland Islanders, 'adopted babe[s]' (p. 4) according to official rhetoric, are dismissed as 'rotten' and as 'eighteen hundred Bills and Ben [the foolish Flower Pot Men of early BBC children's television]' (p. 27).

Maggot's contempt for her colleagues is revealed not only by

name calling but by her cynical expectation that they will always
to be ready to degrade themselves in her service. She is willing,
for example, to put Pimp, whom she describes as 'a well-paid
politician . . ./ . . . who interprets history / Or bends it here and
there if there/ Be need' (pp. 12–13), 'in the shit' (p. 30) by making
him lie to scuttle the Peruvian peace plan. Similarly, the need to
cover up the real reasons for sinking the *Belgrano* translates into
a plan to make Nit lie to 'the press and parliament' (p. 35) about
the cruiser's real course.

This broadly disseminated loathing, from which only her husband, Denis, seems to be exempt, has its origins in a Hobbesian
view of human relations as brutal competition expressed most
forcefully through the excremental and obscene images that litter
Maggot's speech. Formulated in terms provided by such a vocabulary, Maggot's belief is that, in a world of universal self-interest,
people can only relate by fucking, buggering or shitting on each
other. Thus, ever suspicious that, given the slightest chance, her
closest colleagues, Pimp and Nit, will 'plot behind [her] back'
(p. 13), she resolves to 'throw them out but screw them first'
(p. 12). The same kind of thinking informs her belief that a willingness to negotiate, which would involve easing up on the search
for advantage, is a sign of weakness and will end in her being
'shat upon' (p. 22). For Maggot, a more appropriate response to
the Falklands crisis is to threaten to 'shove the junta up [the
Argentinians'] ass' (p. 23) or, as her sailors put it, to 'fuck their
slaggy Argy ships' (p. 17).

Given her dismissive attitude towards human beings and their
relationships, it is not surprising that Maggot is completely casual
about the deaths that will be an inevitable consequence of a war
with Argentina. Indeed, she not only airily dismisses Pimp's
suggestion that 'To save lives surely is the way' as 'bloody bollacks
compromise you mean' (p. 5) but also makes mass slaughter and
extreme suffering essential ingredients of 'the foul stew' she is
concocting for consumption by 'the entire British press':

Then add more than one thousand dead
Tears of children's salty brine
Broken hearts and widows pining
Mothers mourning for their lost boys
. . . .
Soldiers' howls as they lay burning'. (p. 16)

An even more monstrous dimension is added to Berkoff's portrayal of Maggot by the suggestion that, while her decision to go to war with Argentina might have been an act of cold calculation designed to wipe out the Labour Party's 'two per cent' (p. 22) lead in the opinion polls, the prospect of causing death on a grand scale gives her an almost orgasmic thrill. Thus, Maggot responds to her military adviser's graphic description of the consequences of sinking 'a bloody Argy ship/ . . . packed full, well armed with young men/ A thousand maybe more' (p. 32) by exclaiming, 'Oh Tell, I'm thrilled to ecstasy' (p. 33).

This incident suggests that Maggot is a psychopath dependent on acts of violence for emotional arousal, an impression that is reinforced when, on another occasion, she explains how the prospect of war makes her 'feel [her]self again' (p. 7). Viewed in symbolic rather than psychological terms, and bearing in mind that her only other burst of enthusiasm is occasioned by her success in securing the 'last half pound' of 'lean and meaty bacon' (p. 14) for Denis's supper, Thatcher is a savage beast, specifically the British lion, which can be aroused only by the scent of a prey (p. 7).

It might seem that by his use of the dramatic devices of choric recitation, plot and character, Berkoff has done all that is necessary to turn almost every aspect of the official Falklands myth on its head, particularly the role of politicians who are transformed from heroic champions of the weak and oppressed into vile insects scrabbling in the dirt to satisfy their base urges or ferocious beasts devouring everything around them. Nevertheless, Berkoff chooses to reinforce his argument by introducing a number of characters into *Sink the Belgrano!* whose sole function is either to expand and reiterate his critique of the Government's conduct or to offer an alternative code of behaviour.

The first characters to perform this frankly polemical role are a group of Falklands farmers who point up the hypocrisy of a Government that, having 'done sweet FA for all these years', is now granting an almost mantric status within its discourse to the proposition that the islanders' 'wishes must be paramount' (p. 6). Such a concern for their welfare, they go on to suggest, could hardly be genuine because it is totally uncharacteristic both of a heartless Government, whose 'souls couldn't give a fart', and of a Prime Minister incapable of seeing beyond material interests: 'Her eyes are on some distant parts/ Antartica or oil' (p. 6).

Sailor 1, the sole dissenting voice amongst a *Conqueror* crew generally prepared to 'trust our state' and 'believe in England's green/ And pleasant' (p. 10), reiterates the Falkland Islanders' critique of 'big words' (p. 9) by arguing that 'subtle quotes' such as 'self-determination, paramount, law and order' are so devoid of real moral signification that they can be made to serve the most odious of causes. To prove his point he cites Hitler's invasion of 'Sudetenland [which] must have, he said/ Self-determination for those Nazi bores' (p. 10). The Sailor's position is reinforced by his Commander who advises the crew of the *Conqueror* not to 'look for principles in politics/ It's just a game they play' and who points out that considerations of 'size or race' (p. 11) alone are decisive in determining where Britain will take a stand in defence of its colonial heritage. Thus, he reminds them that, 'When [Ian Smith] seized power in '65 . . . , No Task Force/ Then rushed in and said we're here to defend/ Rhodesia's black men' (p. 11). Neither, he predicts, will Britain 'go in there and fight' 'for old Hong Kong' in 1997 because 'China's a bit too big for us' (p. 11).

Alternatives to the armoured approach of Maggot Scratcher and her political colleagues are provided by an unidentified Sailor, perhaps Sailor 1, and by a politician known only as Reason. As the *Conqueror* closes in on the *Belgrano*, the Sailor, speaking out of a compassion that would be unrecogizable to Maggot, insists on defining the cruiser's crew, not as political pawns or demonized enemies, but as 'blokes like us' (p. 37) who should not be fired on without warning. Then, immediately before the order to fire is given, he engages in an act of sympathetic identification by imagining what it will be like for any Argentinian sailor cast into 'the raging, icy sea':

A few more minutes he might live
Dreaming in his icy bed
Until the cold has drained his heart
And death sucks out his last breath'. (p. 37)

Finally, the Sailor prays, 'let them not feel any pain', and appeals to 'Jesus Christ' (p. 37), a figure whose ideal of charity is anathema to a Maggot who acknowledges His existence only through the blasphemous use of His father's name.

Like the Sailor, the politician Reason, who speaks out against

the voices baying for blood during the emergency debate of
3 April, proposes an alternative to mainstream discourse based
on a respect for human life founded in Christian principles:

If you can call yourself Christians
If you believe in Christ our Lord
Then you will seek the bloodless way
Not solve it with a flaming sword'. (p. 25)

However, just as the new perspective introduced by the Sailor
fails to prevent the firing of the torpedo, so Reason is shouted
down with cries of 'Coward, Appeaser' and 'Commie' (p. 25) that
seem aimed as much at Christ as at him.

This confirmation of the inability of Maggot or her supporters
to listen to or understand a point of view that gives the individual
suffering human being priority over self-interest or material gain
prepares the way for the final moments of *Sink the Belgrano!* when
Margaret Thatcher's assertion that 'I would do it again' is projected
onto a screen. Thus, Berkoff closes the always small gap that, in
his opinion, exists between the grotesque figure who dominates
his play and the real woman who, in direct contradiction of
Christian teaching, sent hundreds of Argentinians to their deaths
without, it would seem, a moment's regret.

IF . . . : THE FALKLANDS WAR AS CARTOON

In his *If. . .* cartoon strip, first published in the *Guardian*, Steve
Bell adopts a position regarding Margaret Thatcher's conduct of
the Falklands War that is fairly close to that of Don Shaw and
Steven Berkoff. Like them, he proposes that an inflated rhetoric
of national purpose and moral principle was employed to conceal
much less noble party-political goals. His approach is closer to
Berkoff's than Shaw's in that the narrative he develops is based
on a deconstruction of heroic quest motifs, his subject matter is
overtly the Falklands War and his chosen medium calls for the
exaggeration of cartoon rather than the subtly indirect techniques
employed by Shaw. However, Bell differs from Berkoff in often
making his satirical targets ridiculous and laughable rather than
simply monstrous and in developing his argument through
running and sometimes almost surrealistic jokes as well as through

violent language and grotesquely ugly behaviour. Viewed as a whole Bell's cartoons, for all their satirical sharpness, have a playful quality lacking in the consistently angry work of Steven Berkoff.

Beginning on 13 April 1982, Bell constructs out of his daily cartoon strip *If...* a mock heroic narrative based on the epic voyage, great feats of arms and final triumph that runs roughly parallel to events occuring simultaneously in the real world. However, his invasion force, unlike the real one, is comprised of three distinct parts. The first is a comically diminished version of the actual task force that becomes engaged in a battle with albatross and penguins and, more important, in an internal conflict between Commander Jack Middletar's uncritically heroic and Able Seaman Reg Kipling's sceptical views of war. Discourse is even more obviously the real battlefield for the journalists and politicians who comprise the other two groups in the *If...* task force. Thus, both are launched by Bell on elaborately metaphorical invasions of the Falklands in which all distinctions are collapsed between the actual war and the linguistic battle being fought on the home front by Thatcher and a compliant media against the enemies of the Conservative Government.

The ability of the hero myth to distort understanding of war is central to the story that Bell weaves around the exploits of Middletar and Kipling. His tale, as the cartoon strip of 13 April 1982 establishes (Bell, 1982, p. 86), is structured according to the conventions of turn of the century adventure stories, a genre in which imperialist values are wedded to heroic narrative.[5] Thus, Bell offers as his title the rather portentous, 'Jack Middletar, Agent of Destiny'. Middletar himself is depicted as a square-jawed, keen-eyed, pipe-smoking figure out of the Richard Hannay, Bulldog Drummond mould and his first two pronouncements – 'We sail at dawn!' and 'Who knows what we're getting ourselves into this time, Mr Kipling!' – are redolent with promises of adventure and danger. The visual image of Kipling, Middletar's comrade in arms, is equally a product of imperialist adventure fiction. Short but stocky and with flat, plebian features, Kipling is the very model of the solid, working class type always ready to play the role of faithful squire to his aristocratic superior officer. The suggestion that Bell is taking the reader into a world where deeds of daring are performed for Queen and Country is reinforced by the use of heavy contrast black and white art work and, more specifically, by the introduction of a giant Union Jack into the title frame and by the presence in the last two frames of a huge rising sun whose beams fill the sky and illuminate the sea.

Middletar stays in character throughout the Falklands campaign and, when victory is won, 'broaches the grog' (Bell, 1983 p. 10; orig. pub. 24 June 1982) as a final gesture of comradeship with Kipling and their recent companion, the Penguin. That he remains unchanged is a testament to the power of heroic discourse to shape perceptions in the face of a contradictory reality, for the world in which Middletar lives is not at all the heroic one he imagines. Our first clue to this discrepancy between perception and reality is provided by Middletar's own name which, while implying that he is the reincarnation of the archetypal British sailor, Jack Tarr, also strongly suggests, as James Aulich has pointed out, that he cannot 'quite sustain the 'High Tar' of *Player's Navy Cut*' (p. 100) and therefore falls short of what the twentieth century at least expects of its heroes.

The final frame of the 13 April cartoon fully confirms Bell's debunking intentions. Having limited the reader's view to close ups of Middletar's and Kipling's strong, purposeful faces in the first three frames, Bell now offers a more distant perspective in which they are revealed to be setting sail not in a mighty aircraft carrier such as HMS *Invincible* but in a ludicrously small 'armoured punt' named, as we learn from a later strip, *Incredible*. The simple substitution of a tiny boat for the grand warship promised by the heroic style of the cartoon's earlier frames is enough to make Bell's satirical point about the ability of powerful traditional images to distort perceptions of reality. However, the point is enriched by the fact that the boat is a punt, an insignificant enough craft in itself but one that needs only to be shifted into the context of long sunlit afternoons on the Cam or the Cherwell to function as a central icon of that falsified ideal landscape known as 'deep England'.

As the Middletar-Kipling narrative unfolds the burden of Bell's critique of the obfuscating ability of heroic images and language is borne by a series of exchanges between his two major characters. Despite his name, Kipling is not locked into an imperialistic vision of the nation and its noble destiny. On the contrary, he rejects official rhetoric in favour of his own cynical, clear-sighted and politically left wing analysis of the war with Argentina. Faced with the unreceptive Middletar, Kipling employs theatrical performance and costume as well as direct and ironic

comment as vehicles for the communication of his message. Theatre
is, for instance, the medium chosen by Kipling for his first attempt
to challenge Middletar's complacent reading of their situation.
Thus, when Middletar warns that the price of failure will be the
fall of Margaret Thatcher, Kipling immediately asserts the existence of a gap between the national interest and the Prime Minister's
party-political interests by waving a white handkerchief in the
air while calling out, 'We surrender' (1982, p. 88; orig. pub. 15
April 1982). Kipling further undermines Middletar's heroic
conception of the war by manoeuvring his captain into admitting that political reality makes it impossible to sink an enemy
ship and that his ambition 'to deliver a clean punch where it'll
hurt Johnny Gaucho the most' can be realized only through the
ludicrous gesture of firing on albatross in order to destroy
Argentina's 'guano industry' (1982, p. 89; orig. pub. 16 April 1982).
Kipling adds a further dimension to his subversive interpretation of the Falklands War by pointing out how 'bloody silly' it
is for Thatcher to have supplied the very arms that Argentina is
using against the task force (1982, p. 89; orig. pub. 17 April 1982).
He then dramatizes his contention that the 'whole affair is nothing
but a staged media event' (1982, p. 95; orig. pub. 1 May 1982)
designed to improve the Conservatives' electoral chances by
dressing up as Thatcher, complete with Party rosette.

Kipling's critique of media manipulation is fleshed out by his
reaction to the attempts of the *Daily Mule*'s Barry Blockhead to
cast him in the plucky, resilient role customarily assigned to the
lower ranks in British military myth. First, in response to questions
about his morale, Kipling play-acts the matter of fact professional
killer always ready to take action in defence of his country.
However, by directing a demonstration of his skills in unarmed
combat at Blockhead, he makes the point that his real enemies
are not albatross, penguins or even Argentinians but the politicians and compliant press whose manipulation of public opinion
has made possible the 'whole stupid *** business' with which
he is so 'brassed off' (1982, p. 93; orig. pub. 27 April 1982). Then,
in order to avoid any misunderstanding of the tiny drama he
has just mounted, Kipling explains that he cannot assume the
part assigned to him in Blockhead's heroic interpretation of
war because 'this whole insane debacle' has disillusioned him
about 'the possibility of the moral exercise of military might'
and has brought him to an understanding of 'the futility of all

armed conflict' (1982, p. 94; orig. pub. 28 April 1982).

With these words, Kipling broadens his specific attack on Margaret Thatcher's performance as a war leader into a Johnsonian definition of all war as immoral, insane and irrational and positions himself as a pacifist in order to assert his own capacity to make moral decisions, to act sanely and to think rationally. Challenged by Middletar to sustain an antiwar stance in the face of his sister's hypothetical rape by an Argentinian, Kipling further points up the the moral vacuity and deep-seated madness of the militaristic response obviously expected of him by making a hyperbolic proposal to immediately 'reduce his entire country to a pile of radio-active dust' (1982, p. 94; orig. pub. 29 April 1982). Kipling's view that nationalistic values are to blame for the widespread failure to subject war to rational or moral analysis is expressed in a later cartoon when, using mime as his medium, he answers Middletar's claim that penguins have 'no moral sense' because 'they know neither God nor Country' by grasping a fish in his teeth and flapping his arms (1982, p. 108; orig. pub. 27 May 1982).

Despite the range of tactics, verbal and physical, employed by Kipling in constructing his critique of militarism, inherited ideas about the nobility and purposefulness of war prove to be so powerful that nothing he says or does succeeds in changing Middletar's view of reality. Like Blockhead, who follows Kipling's impassioned cry of outrage against armed combat with the question, 'Yes, but apart from that. How is your *morale* keeping up' (1982, p. 94; orig. pub. 28 April 1982), Middletar seems incapable of hearing anything that contradicts his preexisting ideas about the nature of war. As a result, he responds to each of his adversary's subversive statements and gestures, not by questioning his own values but by locating Kipling within some of the spaces assigned to the excluded Other in heroic discourse. On various occasions, Kipling is postulated as 'a degenerate' (1982, p. 89; orig. pub. 16 April 1982); accused of 'mutinous rumblings' (1982, p. 89; orig. pub. 17 April 1982) and 'barefaced treachery' (1982, p. 106; orig. pub. 25 May 1982); termed a 'damned odd fish' (1982, p. 94; orig. pub. 28 April 1982), 'a transvestite'(1982, p. 95; 1 May 1982) and 'a pacifist' (1982, p. 94; orig. pub. 29 April 1982); and told he has 'taken leave of [his] senses' (1982, p. 106; orig. pub. 24 May 1982). Middletar's only positive response occurs when, blissfully unaware of its satirical intent, he praises Kipling's promise to launch a nuclear attack on Argentina as a return to sanity.

The unbridgeable nature of the gap between the rational moralist Kipling and the unthinking patriot Middletar is underlined by a final series of cartoon strips. In the first of these post-victory strips Middletar displays his patriotic and xenophobic credentials by hoisting the Union Jack, boasting that 'Johnny Gaucho has thrown in his poncho at last' and spouting Thatcherite slogans according to which Britain's military success serves as 'a triumphant vindication of our principled stand' and a clear warning to 'every tinpot dictator' about the continuing vitality of 'the British lion'. As Middletar continues to rant, so Kipling stands in stony-faced silence before finally seizing the chance to subvert his captain's nationalistic ourpourings by inserting into them his own description of the British lion as 'a blood-thirsty moth-eaten psychopath'. In response, Middletar accuses Kipling of being 'a treacherous, cynical bounder' (1983, p. 9; orig. pub. 21 June 1982), thereby making it obvious that he is no nearer to comprehending his crewman's perspective as anything but perverse than he was when they set out on their journey together.

Middletar's continuing inability to see beyond the confines of a view of war shaped by heroic discourse is even more clearly revealed by the cartoon strip in which he insists that Kipling and the Penguin join him in marking victory with a traditional 'broach[ing] of the grog' (1983, p. 10; orig. pub. 24 June 1982). Middletar can sustain a belief in the appropriateness of such a ceremony only because he has an understanding of his crew that derives, not from the real world, but from the many patriotic Second World War films, *In Which We Serve* being a prime example, in which a racially and socially diverse group of men become united by a common commitment to their country's cause (see Calder, p. 237). Thus, regardless of all the evidence of his crew's lack of fellow feeling, he tells Kipling that, despite being a 'damned odd egg', he is 'a decent sort underneath' and invites the Penguin to take part in the celebration because, while 'he may be an outright bounder', 'we've come through a lot together!!' (1983, p. 10; orig. pub. 24 June 1982). Neither the Penguin, who rejects the grog on religious grounds, nor Kipling, who stares grimly into his mug, responds appropriately. Nevertheless, Middletar proves to be sufficiently in the grip of his preconceived conception of reality to get thoroughly drunk while talking enthusiastically about his pride in Britain's ability to fight a 'well regulated, up-to-date, moderate and discreet war in this decadent age' (1983, p. 11; orig. pub. 25 June 1982).

For the most part, Middletar is simply the butt of Bell's rather good-natured jokes and emerges as a pathetic figure, easily confused by and impotent to respond to Kipling's quick-witted comments and antics. There is, however, a sinister dimension to Bell's portrayal of a man who is essentially a moral idiot, committed by a blind acceptance of nationalistic ideology to participate in whatever violent atrocities his Government deems appropriate. Middletar's darker aspect is brought into particular prominence in the later parts of Bell's Falklands narrative when, with the appearance of the Penguin, the xenophobic, paranoid and violent underbelly of his enthusiastic and almost schoolboyish patriotism is exposed. Kipling introduces the Penguin as his 'friend'. Middletar, however, is too firmly in the grip of a nationalistic view of the world to respond with anything other than suspicion and hostility to a former enemy, who mocks Thatcher by calling out 'Rejoice!!' (1982, p. 106; orig. pub. 25 May 1982), and an alien, who is later to enter Britain as 'an illegal black and white immigrant' (1983, p. 18). Thus, admittedly egged on by the anarchistic Penguin's refusal to cooperate, Middletar hurls a variety of accusations at the bird, subjects him to inter-rogation, repeatedly threatens him with a cocked gun, and finally shoots at him.

A further exploration of the deleterious effects of substituting a faith in national institutions for a morally rooted and rational analysis of current reality is made possible by the arrival on the *Incredible* of a foul-mouthed padre. Just as Middletar privileges unquestioning acceptance of a militaristic national mythology and the policies of the Thatcher Government over rational thought and moral judgement, so the padre has renounced his own spiritual and ethical responsibilities in favour of the irrational assump-tion that God expresses his will through the Church of England, as represented by the Archbishop of Canterbury, and, even stranger, public opinion. Thus, since 'every shade of opinion is united' in support of the Falklands War and since the Archbishop, in direct contradiction of Biblical teaching, has 'confirmed that turning the other cheek is just not on in this situation', the padre feels it is his 'moral duty' (*Guardian*, 2 June 1982, p. 25), as the man responsible for the navy's 'spiritual front' (1 June 1982, p. 21), to take issue with Kipling's pacifism.[6]

The tactics employed by the padre in dealing with Kipling serve to strengthen the connection Bell has already established between conformity to right wing ideological formations and irrationality, intolerance and violent behaviour. The padre first tries to convince Kipling of the error of his ways by twisting his arm up his back while exclaiming, 'Pull your socks up, you conchy bleeder' (1 June 1982, p. 21). He then demands that Kipling share his own irrational faith in the pronouncements of the Archbishop of Canterbury and the results of public opinion polls. Faced with reasoned arguments against giving moral weight to 'majority opinion' (3 June 1982, p. 25), the padre reacts by drawing a gun and threatening to blow Kipling's head off. He meets Kipling's subsequent argument that the Church of England, as 'a time honoured instrument of class hegemony', 'has got about as much bearing on contemporary reality as a bingo caller' (4 June 1982, p. 29) by accusing him of atheism. With this response the padre further confirms his inability to distinguish between God and an institution that claims to represent Him in the temporal world. In a last cartoon strip dealing with this character, Bell makes the point that such an equation would be sustainable only if God were actually the cruel, inept murderer who, in responding to the padre's call for Him to prove his existence by shooting down an 'Argie bargie' (5 June 1982, p. 14), accidentally kills a seagull instead.

The sequence of cartoon strips that deals with the journalistic branch of the three-pronged task force responsible for the recapture of the Falklands in the *If . . .* version of the war with Argentina provides Bell with opportunities to explore the moral and linguistic inadequacies of newspapers such as the *Sun*, which he satirizes as the *Morning Mule*. An important part of Bell's critique of the popular press derives from a running joke in which he displaces the actual soldiers dispatched to the Falklands to fight a shooting war with reporters ordered to 'go in at dawn' and save Thatcher's 'reputation' (1982, p. 91; orig. pub. 21 April 1982) by winning the war of words. In a complete reversal of the Middletar–Kipling plot, which explores the inadequacies of the schoolboy adventure story as a way of understanding war, this second plot employs heroic ideals as a benchmark against which tabloid journalists are judged and found wanting. Thus, several cartoon strips depicting reporters aboard HMS *Redundant* as they drill in preparation for an invasion of the Falklands are constructed around a contrast between the young heroes, healthy in body and mind, normally associated with this activity and the chain-smoking, round-shouldered, scruffily-dressed 'troops' who line up in front of their even less appealing commander, the balding and unshaven Harry Hardcastle. The extent to which this army of newspaper reporters falls short of the heroic ideal, with its connotations of courage, nobility of purpose and spirituality, is clearly demonstrated by the specific exercises that Hardcastle demands of them. In one cartoon strip, the reporters make Harry 'proud' by smoking and drinking heavily, by sticking their stomachs out while bringing their shoulders down, and by chanting 'Gung ho!' (1982, p. 90; orig. pub. 20 April, 1982). In another, Harry criticizes one reporter for the lack of cocktail stains on his lapel and then gets his men ready for battle with an address made up of examples of the type of nationalistic clichés they are supposed to use in their reports: '"Yes its war". "We attack at dawn"'; '"England expects every journalist shall do his duty"'; '"Forward with the facts!!" "Ours not to reason why"' (1982, p. 91; orig. pub. 22 April 1982).

Bell continues his analysis of the limitations of tabloid journalism by means of a cartoon strip in which Harry Hardcastle and his men seek to establish a beachhead on the Falklands. The use of heavy contrast black and white art work similar to that employed in the first Middletar-Kipling cartoon allows Bell to create an heroic visual image. This image, however, contrasts heavily with the message communicated by the cartoon's captions. Thus, as their assault craft approaches the beach, instead of alerting his men to the existential tests of courage and commitment awaiting them on enemy territory, as the conventions of the traditional adventure story demand he should, Harry offers them instruction in interview techniques based on banal questions such as, 'Do you have any useful hobbies?' and 'Do you really live on corned beef?'. The battlecry 'Bingo-o-o!!!' (1982, p. 92; orig. pub. 24 April 1982), uttered by the journalists as they charge out of the assault craft, is an obvious allusion to the game at the centre of the circulation war in which the tabloids were involved immediately prior to and during the Falklands War and serves as a reminder of the profit motives underlying the jingoistic, clichéd style of reporting advocated by Hardcastle.[7]

The final group of cartoon strips dealing with the part played by the tabloid press in the Falklands War focuses not on the failure of journalists, as represented by Harry Hardcastle and Barry Blockhead, to live up to heroic ideals but, more explicitly than before, on their inability to meet standards of responsible reporting. Far from seeking out a vantage point close to the front line from which they will be able to exercise, as Harry puts it, 'their journalistic integrity and a degree of objectivity that the military can never provide', Hardcastle and Blockhead have allowed themselves to be confined to a dark bunker. As a result, they are now reliant on the military for 'food, drink, fags, information, the lot' (1982, p. 111; orig. pub. 10 June 1982). Most important of all, though, their reports are no longer anything but conduits for the euphemistic view of the war promulgated by military briefings: 'Big show – our chaps – major targets softened up – . . . hard fighting – stiff resistance – big push – . . . tricky terrain – light casualties – frightened conscripts – . . . threw down arms – . . . our lads – welcome cuppa – royal wedding mugs – Argentinians lick wounds' (1982, p. 112; orig. pub. 12 June 1982). Hardcastle in particular has become so totally complicit in his own oppression that he deprives Blockhead's brief encounter with the actual war of any real meaning by recasting it in terms guaranteed to win the approval of the military authorities. Thus, he tells Blockhead that what he encountered was not war but 'an armed conflict' and that what he witnessed was not 'some bloke literally blown to pieces in front of his face' but 'a surprisingly light casualty being sustained' (1982, p. 110; orig. pub. 8 June 1982).

Besides pointing up the failings of tabloid journalism, Bell's intention in this group of cartoon strips is to expose the limitations of a Prime Ministerial message pitched so low as to find its most appropriate expression at the bottom end of the newspaper market where the profit motive guarantees that sensationalism will always prevail over a concern for the truth. In making this point Bell takes as his initial target the absurdity of the semi-official recognition Margaret Thatcher gave to the tabloid newspapers and their self-proclaimed status as organs of patriotic opinion when she refused to extend her attacks on the supposedly traitorous BBC (Morgan, p. 231–2) to include what Michael Foot called the 'hysterical bloodlust' (Morgan, p. 233) of the *Sun*. Thus, in the second of a sequence of cartoon strips set in a pub in England, Bell creates a deliciously exaggerated scenario in which a customer is arrested for 'treasonable talk' (1982, p. 103; orig. pub. 18 May 1982) in the form of an anti-*Sun* joke.

The connection between Thatcher and the tabloid press is exploited to even greater effect, however, in Bell's suggestion that the Prime Minister's message is nowhere more accurately communicated than by the *Sun*, thinly disguised in *If. . .* as the *Morning Mule*, because the version of Thatcherite ideology that it trumpets has been stripped of all trace of high ideals to reveal the xenophobic and violent impulses that lie at its heart. One story is, for example, headlined 'Argies Eat Babies' (1982, p. 103; orig. pub. 17 May 1982) and another reports on a new missile that can pick out Argie spies in any group of people and obliterate them selectively (1982, p. 104; orig. pub. 20 May 1982). Later strips reveal the *Mule*'s submasthead to be 'The Paper That Kicks The Argies Up The Bum', an obvious parody of the *Sun*'s 'The Paper That Supports Our Boys', as well as the headline, 'Our Boys Swat Argies Like Flies' (1983, p. 12; orig. pub. 28 June 1982).

As he develops the first two of his narrative threads, Bell thus becomes ever more insistent that, far from communicating a noble commitment to justice, self-determination and liberty, officially sanctioned discourse about the Falklands War is at root characterized by values usually associated with the extreme right of British politics. Given the drift of his argument, it is not surprising, therefore, that, in a sequence of much less good-humoured cartoons, Bell characterizes the Conservative politicians who complete his version of the task force as violent neo-Nazis.

The troops that take over the invasion of the Falklands from Hardcastle's journalistic platoon are made up of two groups, the Special Iron Lady Service and the Special Bike Service, that stand for the most right wing tendencies in the Conservative Government. Both the name of the Iron Lady Service and its hard-faced troops, all of whom are outfitted in Thatcher drag, serve to conjure up an image of Margaret Thatcher, who revelled in the soubriquet Iron Lady throughout the Falklands War, at her most militant and uncompromising. A cartoon frame depicting a troop of Ronald Reagans parachuting to the rescue of the Iron Lady Service reminds the reader of Thatcher's close relationship with an American President who shared her aggressive attitudes, particularly towards Communism. The presence in the foreground of this cartoon of one of the Reagans waving a cowboy hat and hollering 'Yee Haaa!!' (1982, p. 98; orig. pub. 5 May 1982) as he is parachuted down in a bed – to each corner of which Bell has added nuclear warheads in the front cover illustration of *The 'If. . .' Chronicles* – further underlines Reagan's militaristic tendencies through an allusion to the last scene in Stanley Kubrick's black comedy *Dr Strangelove*

(1964). In this scene a bomber pilot, conceptualized by Kubrick, who originally cast Peter Sellers in both parts, as an alter ego for a war-mongering American President very much in the Reagan mould, rides cowboy style on the descending bomb that will start the final nuclear war.

Bell invents the Special Bike Force, which is made up of Norman Tebbit lookalikes, because he wants to introduce into the conflict a Cabinet Minister who was actually little involved in the Falklands War but who, in his capacity as Minister of Employment, played a key role in some of the Thatcher Government's most vigorous attacks on the Welfare State. Tebbit's function in *If . . .* as an exemplum of the far-right tendencies of the Conservative Party is made clear by the obvious allusion in the name Special Bike Force to the infamous 1981 Conservative Party Conference speech in which Tebbit advised the unemployed to stop sponging off the state and follow the example set by his father who got on his bike in search of work during the Depression.

The thuggishness implicit in this reference to the Minister of Employment's scornful rejection of the state's obligations towards its disadvantaged members is made explicit by a sequence of cartoon strips in which Tebbit, now operating on the home front, recruits and trains violent skinheads, all of whom look like him, for service in his Tebforce. The lessons he presents to his trainees as part of 'Tebbit Theory I', in which a vicious and intolerant code of conduct is linked to demands for a return to traditional values, are a crudely parodic version of the Thatcherite political message and are intended by Bell to collapse distinctions between Conservative and National Front ideology. Thus, having blamed 'flabby minded socialist eyewash' for undermining 'the values that are traditionally held in highest regard – loyalty to family, church and crown', Tebbit offers as a 'solution to this essentially moral problem', the slogan 'Kill Pinkos Now!!' (1982, p. 101; orig. pub. 13 May 1982).

Bell completes his deconstruction of Thatcherite discourse with two cartoons in which the Conservative Party is represented as militaristic children. In the first, three frames depicting an overweight, ugly schoolboy engaged in an almost manic imitation of the motion and sounds of combat are followed by a fourth devoted to the caption, 'That was a Party Political cartoon strip on behalf of the Conservative Party' (1982, p. 100; orig. pub. 10 May 1982). In the second, Thatcher, Nott and Tebbit are portrayed as schoolchildren pretending to be various types of missiles; Thatcher calls out, 'I'm a Trident and you're all nuked', while Tebbit and Nott claim to be 'a ground to air Tebbit' and 'a corned beef seeking missile' (1982, p. 102; orig. pub. 15 May 1982).

In a series of cartoons whose subject matter ranges from the absurdities of armed nuclear punts and talking penguins to direct caricature of current politicians, Steve Bell, like Don Shaw and Steven Berkoff, thus offers a strong challenge to the Thatcherite reading of the Falklands War. As presented in *The Falklands Factor*, *Sink the Belgrano!* and *If. . .*, Thatcher ceases to be the noble leader who, inspired by a traditional British concern for freedom, justice and self-determination, achieved military victory abroad and a moral and spiritual revitalization at home. Instead, she emerges as a manipulative and inhumane person prepared to sacrifice hundreds of lives in order to secure her own political future and, in the view of Berkoff and Bell at least, to satisfy her violent urges.

Thatcher's prestige was, of course, so great by the end of the Falklands War and she had been so successful in constructing a framework of meaning around the war designed to advance her hegemonic ambitions that she was unlikely to be discredited by any single challenge. Nevertheless, while all three of the works under examination in this chapter must undoubtedly have met with a great deal of opposition, taken together they constitute a significant act of resistance to the authoritative position occupied by Thatcher. Shaw's play, broadcast less than a year after the retaking of Port Stanley, is, for instance, sufficiently indirect and reflective in its approach to its subject that it is likely to have persuaded even some of those still caught up in Falklands euphoria to ponder the issues at stake in the recent war with Argentina as part of a larger consideration of governmental discourse and behaviour in all wars.

Steven Berkoff's *Sink the Belgrano!*, on the other hand, is so visceral in its attack on Margaret Thatcher that, even five years after the end of the war, it received a generally hostile reception, typified by the review in *Plays and Players* in which Tony Dunn describes the play as 'inept and unsubtle' (p. 32) and likely to appeal only to Argentinians. Nevertheless, for anyone sceptical enough about Thatcher's conduct of the Falklands War to seek out the point of his intentionally offensive approach, Berkoff

offers valuable insights into the extravagantly overstated nature
of the official Falklands myth.

The original publication of the cartoon strip *If . . .* in the liberal
newspaper, the *Guardian*, guaranteed Bell an audience receptive
to his skilful deconstruction of mainstream Falklands discourse.
This is not to say, though, that Bell has simply preached to the
converted. Subsequent publication in book form has made *If . . .*
accessible to a much wider audience, at least part of which is
likely to have been seduced by the playful and good-natured
tone of much of his Falklands narrative into giving serious
consideration to his ultimately rather savage treatment of the
jingoistic rhetoric used by Thatcher to stir up an atavistically
hysterical response in the British public.

Considered as a group, then, *The Falklands Factor*, *Sink the
Belgrano!* and *If . . .* are likely to have had some success in cutting
the Prime Ministerial colossus down to size. As a result they
have helped create a climate of opinion receptive to the more
wide-ranging critiques of the Falklands myth that will be examined
in the chapters that follow.

Notes

1. Shaw's indirect approach to the Falklands War of 1982 prevents him
   from commenting directly on the stylistic failings of Thatcherite
   discourse. However, it is likely that he intended his characterization
   of parliamentary debate in 1771 as meaningless noise to apply equally
   to what went on in the House of Commons in 1982. Jonathan Raban's
   account of the emergency debate of 3 April 1982, in the course of
   which he hears 'a low growl of warning', 'a gathering rumpus' (1986,
   p. 105), 'din' and the sound of 'grown men baying like a wolf pack'
   (p. 107), is certainly consistent with the eighteenth-century political
   discourse dramatized in *The Falklands Factor*.
2. Donald Greene, the editor of the edition of Johnson's *Thoughts* to
   which I am making reference in this chapter, points out the allusion
   to *Paradise Lost* (p. 371).
3. In a letter to the author, Christine Slattery of the BBC Broadcast
   Archives confirms that the version of *The Falklands Factor* transmitted on 26 April 1983 did not include the superimposed images from
   the Falklands War. An article in *City Limits* claims that this montage
   was deleted from the television play on the orders of producer Louis
   Marks' superior, Brian Wenham, who regarded the material as
   'politically naive, unsound and unnecessary' ('Falklands Flurries',
   p. 4). Wenham was supported in his decision by Ian Curteis. The

last minute nature of the decision to censor Shaw's play is indicated by the references in John Naughton's review of the *The Falklands Factor* to the excluded material. Naughton, who had presumably viewed an advance copy of the television play, refers to the closing sequence as 'courageous' (p. 29). The British Film Institute houses videotapes of both versions of *The Falklands Factor* in its collection.

4. For well-balanced analyses of the *Belgrano* incident and its aftermath see Dillon, pp. 154–220 and Freedman, pp. 275–88.

5. The genre has its origins in boys' magazines such as *Chums*. Adult versions of the genre were produced by writers such as John Buchan and 'Sapper'. See MacDonald, pp. 31–55, for a discussion of *Chums* magazine and Stafford, pp. 489–509, for a discussion of Buchan and Sapper and other writers of espionage adventure stories.

6. The sequence of cartoons dealing with the padre are not included in Bell, 1982 or Bell, 1983. I have therefore cited the page number as well as the date of publication in the *Guardian*.

7. See Tom Bairstow's article entitled 'The Fleet Street Warriors Who Turn from Bingo to Jingo in the Battle of the Sagging Sales' for a witty account of the context out of which Bell's presentation of the tabloid press springs. Bairstow is at his sardonic best in his account of the battle between the *Daily Express*'s 'Double Quick Bingo' and the *Star*'s 'world-shattering . . . bingo championship' (p. 8).

3

Opportunists and Hooligans: Thatcherism in *The Ploughman's Lunch* and *Arrivederci Millwall!*

In *The Ploughman's Lunch* (1985) and *Arrivederci Millwall* (1987, 1990), the two works under consideration in this chapter, the focus of attention shifts away from Margaret Thatcher herself and onto that curious blend of nostalgia and neoconservatism known as Thatcherism.[1] McEwan's film and Perry's play/television film,[2] also use very different techniques from those employed in *Sink the Belgrano!* and *If.....* Thus, rather than rely on the alternative exaggeration of cartoon, they seek to counter Thatcher's mythic vision of nation through a rigorous conformity to the conventions of social realism.

McEwan and Perry's commitment to realistic conventions is evident in differences between their central characters and those that appear in Thatcher's mythic narrative. Although a composite of Thatcher herself and outstanding members of the task force such as Colonel 'H' Jones, the protagonist of the Prime Minister's Falklands story is a simple, archetypal figure who meets a number of challenges before achieving full heroic stature by defeating the Argentinian villain in a final decisive battle. James Penfield in *The Ploughman's Lunch* and Billy Jarvis in *Arrivederci Millwall*, on the other hand, are three-dimensional characters with personalities far too complicated to yield up their full significance in a single climactic piece of plotting.

The fundamental difference between McEwan's and Perry's techniques and Thatcher's is further underlined by their contrasting approaches to physical space and contemporary reality. The action in Thatcher's heavily mythologized and hence dehistoricized version of the Falklands War takes place against a stylized and unspecific backdrop of threatening ocean and almost featureless terrain. McEwan and Perry, on the other hand, use identifiable locations and make reference to actual events in order to imbue their sometimes almost documentary works of fiction with a strong sense of social specificity. Thus, the upper middle class world into which James Penfield is seeking entry in *The Ploughman's Lunch* is evoked quite precisely by location shooting in places such as the Burlington Arcade and the Barbican Art Gallery. Frequent references to the Falklands War, and the use of the 1982 Conservative Party Conference at Brighton as the setting for one of its major scenes, grounds the film even more firmly in contemporary British reality. *Arrivederci Millwall* weaves both the Falklands War and the 1982 Football World Cup into its otherwise fictional plot and the film version makes use of authentic South East London working class locations such as New Cross Baths and the Walthamstow Greyhound Stadium.

The distinctiveness of *The Ploughman's Lunch* and *Arrivederci Millwall* emerges most clearly, however, from a consideration of the role played by the Falklands War in the plots of the two works. As we have already seen in Chapter 1, Margaret Thatcher subsumed the complex political and military realities of the war within a simple mythic quest that moves forward purposefully before terminating dramatically and conclusively with the Argentinian surrender. The same events, however, are never more than an intermittent presence in *The Ploughman's Lunch* or *Arrivederci Millwall*, both of which eschew the opportunities for decisive closure offered by the British victory in the Falklands in favour of continuing their loosely structured and episodic stories on towards much more open-ended conclusions.

McEwan and Perry make such extensive use of realistic, and even documentary, techniques in order to be able to claim the kind of authority for *The Ploughman's Lunch* and *Arrivederci Millwall* that can only be conferred by a rootedness in real physical space and a fidelity to lived experience. As a corollary, they are also suggesting that the primary function of the fantasy world of myth, Thatcher's preferred vehicle for communicating her vision of the nation, is to conceal deliberate falsehoods rather than to communicate higher truths.

What might seem an excessive concern on the part of McEwan and Perry with enhancing the credibility of their fictional works

becomes fully justified once we recognize that it is their goal in
The Ploughman's Lunch and *Arrivederci Millwall* to construct
understandings of Thatcherism that run counter to the widely
accepted one propagated by Thatcher herself. Clear pointers to
the broader political aims of *The Ploughman's Lunch* and *Arrivederci
Millwall* are provided by the many references to the Falklands
War introduced into both works and by the intermittent appearance of Margaret Thatcher, usually on television but in person
during the Conservative Party Conference scenes in *The Ploughman's Lunch*. However, neither McEwan nor Perry is a polemical
author and there is little overt political debate to be found in
either *The Ploughman's Lunch* or *Arrivederci Millwall*. Instead, they
rely mainly on convincingly presented characters to carry the
burden of their critiques of Thatcherite ideology. Thus, at the
centre of both *The Ploughman's Lunch* and *Arrivederci Millwall*, as
the analysis that follows will seek to demonstrate, is a committed Thatcherite of a very different kind from either the noble
and patriotic soldier or the forward looking 'captain of industry' familiar to anyone who has read Thatcher's Falklands speeches.

THE PLOUGHMAN'S LUNCH: THE THATCHERITE HERO AS CYNICAL OPPORTUNIST

When Ian McEwan began work on *The Ploughman's Lunch* in 1981
his intention was, as he explains in the introduction to the film's
published script, not only to ask some broad questions about
morality in politics but also to attack a specific target: the recently
elected Conservative Government and its commitment to what
he considered a cynical and morally bankrupt ideological agenda
(McEwan, p. v). McEwan's task was made more difficult when,
with the unexpected outbreak of the war with Argentina in April
1982, Prime Minister Thatcher's previously stuttering attempts
to turn the British public into contortionists, looking simultaneously
back towards a presocialist past and forward towards a neoconservative future, suddenly bore fruit. At the same time, though,
the Falklands War served McEwan's needs by providing him
with a new and sharper focus. Thus, in a second and final draft
of *The Ploughman's Lunch*, McEwan is able to develop a compre-
hensive and damaging reassessment of many of the major themes
of Thatcherite ideology. These include class relations, social

hegemony, entrepreneurship, professionalism, history, the myth of 'deep England', and Britain's international status.

The subject of class relations offers a useful starting point for an analysis of *The Ploughman's Lunch*, not only because it reveals the depth of McEwan's loathing for the Conservative Government's political programme but also because it is fundamental to an understanding of James Penfield, the opportunistic and ruthlessly self-seeking young television journalist who is the film's main character and the conduit for all of McEwan's political themes. Penfield is willing to adopt either left or right wing political positions according to the demands of the occasion. Nevertheless, his actual priorities have been shaped almost exclusively by a neoconservative agenda and he sees himself as belonging to an enterprise culture in which the pursuit of individual goals overrides traditional class affiliations and values. The subservient role assigned in Thatcher's Falklands myth to people whose origins, like his own, are working or lower middle class clearly has no appeal for the aspiring Penfield. Thus, even though he is still in touch with his father, who runs a small shop, and his terminally ill mother, James is almost completely alienated from his roots. His visits to his parents' 'nondescript pre-war semi' (p. 7) are rare and brief, he has little to say to his father and he lies in order to excuse his absences. In separate conversations with his putative girlfriend, Susan Barrington, and with her mother, Ann, Penfield denies all familial ties by claiming that both his parents are dead.

James Penfield never speaks about his reasons for cutting himself loose from his parents but it is obvious that he has discarded them as irrelevant to his personal ambitions. His preferred company consists of sophisticated friends such as the journalist, Jeremy Hancock, and the television researcher, Susan Barrington, who can help him in his present career and enhance his social status, or people such as the publisher, Gold, who wield power and influence in fields where he hopes to make progress in the future. McEwan, however, calls Penfield's choices into question by creating a marked contrast between his parents, dignified and loving people with strong conceptions of family, home and community and the shallowly cynical Jeremy, the self-regarding Susan and the crassly materialistic Gold. McEwan's point is that, whatever he gains materially by liberating himself from what he would presumably see as the shackles of outmoded class loyalties,

Penfield can never compensate for the loss involved in exchanging a richly human environment for one that is shallow and meretricious.

Even more significant in terms of McEwan's critique of Thatcherite ideology, it finally turns out that James Penfield's belief that class distinctions have become irrelevant in an entrepreneurial Britain is extremely naive. He may speak and dress like his chosen companions; he might feel at one with the 'truly ambitious' Susan Barrington when she talks about 'progress' and 'tak[ing] responsibility for [one's] own happiness' (p.9); and he may be rich enough to buy Jeremy Hancock outrageously expensive drinks in a fashionable cocktail bar (p.11). Nevertheless, in the final analysis, neither Jeremy nor Susan considers James their equal.

In the course of *The Ploughman's Lunch* McEwan drops a number of fairly broad hints intended to make the viewer, if not James Penfield, fully aware of the deep-rooted class consciousness shared by Jeremy Hancock and Susan Barrington. Susan's sense of the innate inferiority of working class people is evident, for example, in her patronisingly supercilious account of a meeting with a group of trade union officials, 'all incredibly fat and beery, huge trousers and braces. And *so* sweet' (p. 32). Jeremy, as is his way with most subjects, turns James's class into a joke. He describes Susan, for instance, as 'a glamorous young lady way above [James's] station' (p. 10). On another occasion, having persuaded Penfield to drive the three of them to the Conservative Party Conference, he then reduces him to the status of chauffeur with the mock command, 'Brighton, James' (p. 30). However, like many jokes, Jeremy's have an origin in real prejudice. This finally becomes clear even to James when, speaking for once without irony, Jeremy seeks to justify the romantic betrayal of his supposed friend by arguing that he has 'known Susan for more than fifteen years' and that they are 'old allies' (p. 34). The military metaphor employed here underlines the fact that for Jeremy Hancock differences of class provide the basis for distinctions so absolute as to exclude a person of lower class origins, such as James Penfield, from considerations of common decency let alone friendship.

The effect of McEwan's analysis of class relations is to suggest that there is a devious logic underlying the contradictory roles assigned to those at the lower end of the social scale in Thatcherite ideology. Whether working and lower middle class people remain subservient to a ruling class of questionable benevolence or participate fully in a theoretically classless enterprise culture, the end result is the same as far as McEwan is concerned; they will be deprived of the traditional affiliations and loyalties that constitute their only source of power and identity. The first role, much favoured by Thatcher during the Falklands War, is one that she tried to impose on the working class by undermining the strength of the trade unions; the second superficially more attractive one is, as James Penfield's experience shows, a chimera intended to persuade the lower classes to betray themselves.

In order to understand the full extent of James Penfield's victimization, it is necessary to go beyond plot and character and consider the visual logic of *The Ploughman's Lunch*. For most of the film, Penfield, a self-interested liar who is always seeking an advantage, seems more exploiter than victim. However, a consideration of the manner in which director Richard Eyre structures his shots makes it obvious that we are intended to view James as a victim even before his betrayal by Jeremy Hancock and Susan Barrington. Although he is on screen throughout *The Ploughman's Lunch*, Penfield is never allowed to dominate the frame. Instead he is consistently shot in ways that suggest anxiety, alienation and weakness.

All three elements are present in an early episode during which he travels to work. Anxiety is the dominant emotion in an opening tracking shot of Penfield pushing his way hastily through crowds while glancing at his watch. A cut to an oblique angle medium shot of Penfield, screen centre and in focus, apparently oblivous to the other out of focus Underground passengers who press in on him from both sides, perfectly captures his alienation. And, finally, weakness is emphasized by the relationship established between Penfield's tiny, scurrying figure in the foreground of a low angle extreme long shot and that bastion of the establishment, the headquarters of BBC Radio in the Langham building, which looms in the background. These and similar visual devices are repeated throughout *The Ploughman's Lunch*, climaxing in a final freeze frame of the still anxious and isolated James Penfield, glancing at his watch as he pointedly ignores his father and the clergyman who stand beside him at his mother's grave. The overall effect of the film's visual style is to make the viewer intensely aware of the extent to which the pursuit of Thatcherite goals has caused Penfield to sacrifice not just his ethical standards but also his ability to relate to other human beings.

As constructed by writer McEwan and director Eyre, the social world that James Penfield is ambitious to join excludes not just the lower classes but also black people and socialists. It thus possesses the racial and political homogeneity of 'England', the idealized nation that it is Thatcher's ambition to recreate. None of James's colleagues at the BBC is black and the crowds who feature in several London street scenes only once include a black person, in the shape of a universally ignored street sweeper. Even in the Brixton neighbourhood where he lives in obvious anticipation of being in the forefront of a wave of gentrification, Penfield only once encounters black people, a group of boys playing football in front of his lock-up garage. This brief moment of physical proximity is, however, rather more effective than McEwan and Eyre's metaphorically motivated and very contrived exclusion of non whites from London's multiracial landscape in communicating the exclusivity of the white and black communities encouraged by Thatcher during her years in office. As he drives out of the garage, insulated in his sleek Jaguar, Penfield pointedly refuses to acknowledge the presence of the boys; they, in turn, ignore him and continue to play their game the entire time his car is passing amongst them.

Besides being white, the people with whom James Penfield works at the BBC are never heard to express any opinions even vaguely to the left of centre. Neither do the social circles in which Penfield moves include a wider range of political opinions except for the one that he briefly enters during two visits to the left wing historian, Ann Barrington. However, his trips to Norfolk have almost nothing to do with an interest in becoming better acquainted with Ann's ideas or those of her Polish socialist friend, Jacek. Instead Penfield's goal is to advance his relationship with her Thatcherite daughter, Susan, and to obtain information for a book on Suez that he is preparing for the right-wing Goldbooks. Ann's subsequent attempts to create a personal bond with James are categorically rejected. Similarly, although the women at the Peace Camp treat him as a 'friend' (p. 20) and lend him tools to mend his flat tire, Penfield later dismisses them as 'vegetarians, hippies, disturbed housewives . . ., mad' (p. 23). Encountering the Peace Women again as they demonstrate outside the Brighton Conference Centre during the Conservative Party Conference, Penfield walks by without a second glance.

Because of their marginalization the poor, black and left wing people occasionally encountered by James Penfield serve simply to underline the social and racial homogeneity and political conservatism of the Britain depicted in *The Ploughman's Lunch*. This Britain, however, bears little resemblance to the paradisal place lost, according to Thatcher, as a consequence of mass black immigration and postwar socialist hegemony. Although free to pursue their own agenda without the supposedly corrupting influence of alien forces, the Thatcherite elite Penfield aspires to join nevertheless turns out to be uniformly selfish, manipulative, materialistic and, above all, deceitful. This is a damning assessment of right wing Britain and, in order to justify it, McEwan weaves into the action of *The Ploughman's Lunch* rigorous rebuttals of three of the main arguments used by Thatcher, particularly during the Falklands War, to give moral authority to her vision of the nation. These are the arguments concerning the social usefulness of entrepreneurial enterprise; the contribution of professionalism to the dignity of both individual and nation; and the function of the past as a repository for the nation's spiritual and moral essence.

McEwan's sharpest critique of entrepreurship is to be found in those parts of *The Ploughman's Lunch* that bring James Penfield into contact with the publisher, Gold. Unlike the military example used by Thatcher in her Cheltenham speech, the book trade is a genuine model of capitalist endeavour. Nevertheless, it is also one with much more obvious potential for playing a useful social role than other entrepreneurial activities, such as currency speculation or property dealing, that flourished during the Thatcher years. We might well assume, for instance, that education would be an important goal for a textbook company such as Goldbooks. However, the owner of the company, Gold, who according to Jeremy Hancock is 'about to become very rich' (p. 3), appears interested in books only for their commodity value. He is sufficiently amused, for example, by a young employee's assumption that Goldbooks might aspire to the standards of Faber and Faber to make it the subject of an anecdote he recounts during a party to launch his company's book on the Cold War. At the same party, he has no sooner been told that James Penfield is one the book's contributors than he directs his attention towards 'our sales team' (p. 2). This conception of books as commodities is reinforced by an unidentified voice, but almost certainly Gold's,

that later raises itself above the hubbub of the party to announce
that 'nobody reads books during a recession' and to complain
that 'none of them will get off their backsides and sell books'.[3]

McEwan's loathing for the crassly materialistic Gold is particularly evident during the scene in which the publisher lunches
with James Penfield at Langan's in Piccadilly. The restaurant,
which is plushly furnished and bathed in a rich golden glow, is
a kind of temple to the pleasures of expensive food and drink
and Gold seems determined to make the most of what it has to
offer. Thus, he is distracted from Penfield's enthusiastic monologue
about his proposed book on the Suez crisis first by the appearance of a trolley laden with desserts, then by the waiter's offer
of coffee, about which he speaks to James with his mouth full,
and finally by the ordering and flaming of sambuccas. After lunch,
the cigar-puffing Gold leads James into the Burlington Arcade,
another shrine to conspicuous consumption, where he abruptly
terminates their conversation by plunging into a shop in pursuit
of something that has caught his eye in the window display.

For Ian McEwan, it is greedy materialists such as Gold who
represent the true spirit of Thatcher's much vaunted enterprise
culture. He is thus implicitly objecting to the connection developed by Thatcher between the nurturing of an entrepreneurial
spirit and the rekindling of the nation's spiritual and moral core.
McEwan's objection emerges even more clearly from an examination of James Penfield's role in the Langhams/Burlington Arcade
scenes. As described by James, the book on the Suez crisis that
he pitches at Gold during lunch is a direct product of the mood
of national optimism inspired by 'this Falklands business'. His
intention in writing it, he goes on to say, is thus to break away
from 'all the moralising and talk of national humiliation that is
now the standard line on Suez' (p. 5). In order to achieve this
goal, Penfield plans to develop a revisionist reading in which
the war with Egypt becomes both an honourable attempt to defend
the 'ideal' of the British Empire and the last occasion when Britain
acted 'independently' and was therefore in touch with the authentic
self it has 'discovered . . . again' in the South Atlantic.

However, as soon as Gold points out that the book will be
aimed at American Colleges, which constitute a 'growth area'
for 'twentieth century history', James revises his thesis to elimi-
nate any implied criticism of the United States for its refusal to
support Britain's invasion of Egypt. Thus, he gives the United

States the role of 'a good ally ... who doesn't back you up in your mistakes', a change of emphasis that will force him to seriously modify his original position regarding the value of Britain's independent stance over Suez. Faced with a choice, then, between propounding an idealistic view of the nation and making a profit, Penfield puts profit first. By behaving in this way, James Penfield fully conforms to McEwan's definition of the true Thatcherite: a person for whom talk of the eternal nation and its essential spirit will never be more than a 'performance' (p. 6) designed to mask a real agenda constructed around the pursuit of power and wealth.

A similar scepticism informs Ian McEwan's treatment of professionalism, a key term in Thatcher's list of entrepreneurial virtues. In this instance McEwan approaches his subject in an extremely direct way by allowing two of his neoconservative characters, James Penfield and Susan Barrington, to define how they view themselves as professionals. For Susan, professionalism is simply synonymous with the pursuit of power. Her position is made clear by the explanation she gives for failing to side with the women in her office when they objected to male bias in current affairs reporting. To act as a woman and support the feminist position by resigning would have involved, in Susan's view, taking 'the not-power path' of 'sisterly feelings, masochism and frustration' whereas to behave as a 'professional' demanded that she take the path of 'power' and 'keep working' (p. 4).

Susan's definition of professionalism is an obvious product of naked self interest. Nevertheless, it possesses a certain crude vitality. James Penfield, on the other hand, has reduced professionalism to mere technique. As he defines it, the term refers to the skills involved in 'ending a broadcast on the dot, having everything run smoothly, selecting a running order that makes sense, knowing instinctively what you can and cannot do'. There is obviously very little emotional or spiritual sustenance to be derived from such mechanical achievements and James describes how the pleasure he once took in technical mastery soon turned into 'numbness' (p. 9).

All but the least experienced of Penfield's colleagues seem to suffer from the same affliction. The Editor-in-Chief, for example, fails to communicate any sense of mission and uses daily staff meetings to expound tediously on the proper usage of the word 'finally' (p. 4) or to insist on an even-handed policy of news reporting that guarantees blandness. His audience, as the panning camera reveals, is too bored to respond with anything stronger than expressions of tired resignation. By making a fetish of technique, this kind of professionalism not only diminishes individuals but also the institutions for which they work. Therefore, it is not surprising that McEwan's version of the BBC is a shadow of the great national institution that once employed people, including Ann Barrington's first husband, who were 'passionate' enough to resist attacks on the Corporation's 'independence' (p. 17) of the kind made during the Suez crisis.

As defined and practised by Susan Barrington, James Penfield and the BBC, professionalism clearly has none of the resonance, dignity or moral force that it acquired during the Falklands War through association with the efforts made by the armed forces in the defence of the realm. Instead, like other terms in Thatcher's language of national regeneration, it is exposed by McEwan's close scrutiny as nothing more than a typically ugly product of the selfish individualism and moral vacancy that, in his view, lies at the root of neoconservative ideology.

The role played by history in the right wing Britain of *The Ploughman's Lunch* provides McEwan with still more opportunities to point up the essential hypocrisy and cynicism of Thatcherism. Most of the characters in *The Ploughman's Lunch* are preoccupied with the past but none of them would propose, except in the self-serving spirit that informs James Penfield's reading of the Suez crisis, that it functions as a kind of fixed reference point, a source of essential truths about the nation. On the contrary, they view history as endlessly fluid and always capable of being reshaped or 'fabricat[ed]' (p. 30), as Matthew Fox puts it, to serve the ends of personal profit or new right ideology.

Both Gold, the publisher, who, as we have already seen, regards history as 'a growth market', and Fox, a director of television commercials who admits to earning 'so much money at what I do that I can't begin to defend it', are acutely aware of the money to be made from manipulating the past. Fox, for example, is quite frank about the ways in which the advertising industry exploits 'the national memory' (p. 25). On one occasion he describes the 'fantastic response' he got to a commercial for 'some new lager' that comprised 'a series of vignettes of Kings and Queens – Henry VIII, Mary. . . , Elizabeth I and so on' (p. 24). On another he allows James Penfield to watch him film a commercial that creates an idealized, nostalgic and hence falsified version of prewar, middle class family life in order to promote a bedtime drink.

The point being made here – that these images of 1930s family life are 'fabricated' rather than given – is reinforced by the simple but effective technique of placing the viewer in the middle of a cosy, intimate sitting room before pulling the camera back to expose it as merely a set surrounded by the paraphenalia of film making and located at the centre of a cold and impersonal hangar-like sound stage. McEwan's point is further reinforced when Matthew Fox, in an anecdote that provides the film with its title, tells James Penfield that, far from being 'traditional English fare' (p. 25), the Ploughman's Lunch is in fact 'an invention of an advertising campaign they ran in the early sixties to encourage people to eat in pubs' (pp. 29–30).

The susceptibility of the past to ideologically motivated manipulation is revealed several times during *The Ploughman's Lunch*. An announcement about an upcoming edition of *Woman's Hour*, for instance, suggests that, far from being even-handed, the BBC is colluding with the Thatcherite agenda by offering a version of history as a compendium of Britain's glorious achievements. Thus, the programme is to open with Commander Freddy Bracknell 'talking about his four years as a German POW in Stalag Three' (p. 1), followed by John Clayton 'reliving the thrills and perils of Everest'. Ironically, a third item is concerned with the ways in which 'the governments of Eastern Europe distort their recent past in history books to suit their present policies and allegiances' (p. 2). Later in the film, the child Tom Fox's recitation of a list of English monarchs, which omits the Cromwells because 'they don't count' (p. 17), suggests that the school system is also engaged in shaping history towards right wing ideological ends. This point is made more explicit when, in the course of a conversation inspired by Tom's list, the socialist, Jacek, criticizes the British establishment for suppressing an alternative 'subversive' history that records the achievement of what he, as a Pole, considers to be 'enviable freedoms' (p. 24).

Finally, in a climactic scene shot at the Conservative Party Conference held in Brighton shortly after the Falklands War, we hear Margaret Thatcher deliver a speech in which she seeks once again to dignify Britain's victory over Argentina by locating it within a version of national history that displaces temporal realities with the concept of eternal spirit: 'The spirit of the South Atlantic

was the spirit of Britain at her best. It has been said that we
surprised the world, that British patriotism was rediscovered in
those spring days. Mr. President, it was never really lost!'
(p. 33). Of all the falsifications of history identified in their film,
Thatcher's is obviously the one that McEwan and Eyre are most
concerned to discredit. Therefore, in his capacity as director,
Richard Eyre offers several visual cues designed to ensure
that the viewer sees the Prime Minister's speech as a fraudulent
performance.

The most effective of the devices used to cast a pall of deceit-
fulness over Thatcher's speech involves frequent cutting between
images of the the Prime Minister at the Conference podium and
shots of those model Thatcherites, James, Jeremy and Susan on
the Conference floor and in the Press balcony during the moments
when the truth finally emerges about the network of lies underpinning their triangular relationship. Eyre's other main device
for destroying Thatcher's credibility involves a reprise of the
technique used in the television commercial scene. Thus, tight
shots communicating the television audience's view of Thatcher
– standing impressively at the centre of a raised platform,
flanked by Conservative luminaries and in front of a brilliant
blue backdrop on which is inscribed the slogan, 'The Resolute
Approach' – are interspersed with longer shots intended to draw
attention to the technicians and to the clutter of cameras and
cables responsible for the creation of the televisual image. Later,
the camera lingers in the hall after the Conference has ended in
order to record the dismantling of the platform and the removal
of the backdrop, thereby identifying the scene of Thatcher's triumph as a set and her as a performer. The sum total of Eyre's
directorial decisions is to shrink Thatcher's inspirational address
to the same dimensions as all the other exercises in historical
manipulation scattered throughout the action of *The Ploughman's
Lunch*. The only difference, it is suggested, between Gold and
Fox on the one hand and Thatcher on the other is that, whereas
they are selling books and lager, she is selling a new right image
of nation.

McEwan completes his analysis of the gap between the social
realities of Britain under Conservative rule and Thatcher's authentic nation with several scenes set in Norfolk during which he
explores the myths of 'deep' England and of British independence. First, McEwan takes advantage of the shift of location

from city to country to call into question the validity of the network of associations implicit in the phrase 'deep England', particularly the belief that certain rural settings possess a special
quality that enables English people to get in touch with their
essential selves. The burden of McEwan's point is carried by James
Penfield, once again functioning as the film's representative
Thatcherite.

In leaving London for Norfolk, Penfield is obviously not motivated by any Wordsworthian longing to exchange 'the din of
cities and towns' for 'the beauteous forms' of nature. On the
contrary, as a dissolve from the brownish-yellow map of Egypt,
pinned up over the desk at which he is writing his book on
Suez, to the similarly coloured Norfolk landscape suggests, not
only is James taking his urban preoccupations with him but he
is approaching the country somewhat in the spirit of a soldier
making a sortie into enemy territory. This metaphor is reinforced
later when Jeremy Hancock mockingly awards 'General Sir James
Penfield' a medal for 'services during the Norfolk campaign'
(p. 31). Clearly, the aim of James's incursion into the country is,
as always, to gain an advantage for himself; by visiting Ann
Barrington he hopes to get material for his Suez book and to
make progress in his relationship with Susan. Thus, if he ever
notices the golden light that often falls across Eyre's richly photo-
graphed Norfolk landscape, he is more likely to be reminded of
the atmosphere of wealth created by a similar light in Langan's
in Piccadilly than he is to be moved to an aesthetic or spiritual
response.

Despite the camouflage provided by a tweedy cap, James
Penfield is, then, out of his element in the country. This alienation is most evident in two scenes set amongst fields and sand
dunes in which high angle extreme long shots reveal James as a
tiny, vertical figure dwarfed by the vast horizontal landscape.
Shots of enormous ploughed fields and a soundtrack of slow,
mournful music are particularly effective in making James Penfield
look helpless and lost at the point during the first of these scenes
when he is forced to abandon the security of his Jaguar and trudge
off into the unknown in search of help with a flat tire.

Penfield's destination turns out to be a Women's Peace Camp
and, as he approaches, ever louder rumbling and whining sounds
intrude into the peaceful woods through which he is walking.
Finally, with his emergence into a field where he is faced with

shimmering, grey images of huge transport planes inside a tall wire fence, the noise becomes deafening. Like earlier shots of low-flying fighter planes screaming across a glorious landscape of sea and sand dunes, this bizarre scenes serves to debunk Thatcherite mythology by providing evidence that, even if it once existed, there is no longer any corner of rural Britain that retains the pretechnological purity embodied in the concept of deep countryside. However, because what Penfield is seeing is an American airbase, the scene also exposes the lie implicit in Thatcher's postulation of Britain as a powerful nation capable of standing alone militarily and of pursuing an independent foreign policy. Indeed, far from being an autonomous sovereign state, Thatcher's Britain is exposed as nothing more than a client of the United States helpless to prevent the American neoimperialist behemoth from inserting its monstrous military machine into the very heart of the English countryside.

By the end of *The Ploughman's Lunch*, Thatcherism has been shown up as cynical, manipulative and dishonest. The film does not, however, offer much immediate hope that this pernicious ideology will lose credibility with the British public. On the contrary, McEwan goes to some pains throughout *The Ploughman's Lunch* to emphasize the ability of official voices to drown out oppositional and alternative discourses. Beginning with the film's opening shot, a close up of a teleprinter churning out a news story, which is soon followed by shots of a typist at work and of James Penfield using a photocopying machine, *The Ploughman's Lunch* consistently draws attention to the technology of public communication. The foregrounding of cameras in the television commercial and Conservative Conference scenes are obvious examples of this. Others include close ups of the typewriter on which James Penfield hammers out his Suez book, the use of broadcast booths and projection rooms as the location for several scenes, and the almost ubiquitous presence of television sets reporting the Falklands War. On one occasion, newspapers, books and a television set are all included in a single deep focus shot. Even the art show that James and Susan visit at the Barbican features works based on print and newspaper images. However, despite the multiple forms in which it exists, communications technology is used almost exclusively in *The Ploughman's Lunch* to promote the ideological and political positions of the Conservative Government.

Attempts by protest groups such as the Peace Women to gain access to the organs of mass communication are frustrated in part by their own lack of sophisticated media skills. It is extremely naive of Carmen, for instance, to believe that crumpled hand-outs of the kind that she gives to James Penfield can provide an adequate basis for the 'national coverage' (p. 21) her group craves. However, the unwillingness of what McEwan presents as a solidly right-wing media to provide a vehicle for the communication of any opinion that runs counter to their own view of the world makes a much more significant contribution to the silencing of the Peace Women. The consequent marginalization of dissent is captured most effectively in the contrast between the small group of protestors chanting their noisy but often unintelligible slogans outside the Conservative Party Conference hotel and inside, Margaret Thatcher, whose message is getting across loud and clear not just to the delegates seated before her but to an entire nation of television viewers, radio listeners and newspaper readers.

Other oppositional political voices are restricted either to the classroom, as is the case with the polytechnic lecturer who offers his students a critical assessment of Britain's role in the Suez crisis, or to private gatherings such as the dinner party during which Jacek and Ann Barrington discuss contemporary Britain from a socialist perspective. Much the same is true of overtly nonpolitical but nevertheless alternative discourses. The poet, Edward, for instance, publishes in the specialist *Times Literary Supplement* rather than in a mass market newspaper and gives readings in half empty community halls while the voice of religious belief is heard only once in the film and then by the small group of mostly elderly, working class mourners who attend Mrs Penfield's funeral.

The main hope offered by McEwan would seem to reside in the fact that *The Ploughman's Lunch*, the master discourse to which all of the discourses embodied within it are subordinated, is both oppositional and less marginalized than the voices of protest that are heard within the film. It is certainly true, as McEwan admits in the introduction to the published script, that *The Ploughman's Lunch* lacks the 'nursery tale aesthetic ("but where's the good guy")' required to win 'mainstream cinema investment' (p. vi) and distribution. Nevertheless, because of its conventional narrative mode, its use of realistic conventions and its contemporary subject matter, *The Ploughman's Lunch* has been able to locate itself somewhere on the fringes of popular culture and has managed to reach a fairly wide audience of television viewers, film goers and video renters. The film is therefore capable, especially in concert with other works that embody political themes in accessible fictional narratives, of at least chipping away at the distortions, fabrications and outright lies out of which, McEwan would argue, Thatcher's new right hegemony is constructed.

ARRIVEDERCI MILLWALL: THE THATCHERITE HERO AS FOOTBALL HOOLIGAN

One such work, which quite directly echoes *The Ploughman's Lunch* in its concern to expose the flaws in Thatcherite ideology, is *Arrivederci Millwall* by Nick Perry. Despite its fictional treatment of football hooliganism, a topic of widespread interest during the 1980s, *Arrivederci Millwall* is unlikely to have come to the attention of many people in its original manifestation as a stage play written by an unknown author and performed first on the metropolitan margin at the Albany Theatre in Deptford and then at the Edinburgh Festival by a group of Cambridge University students. However, the publication of the script by Faber and Faber and, even more significant, the reworking of the play into a film for BBC television, directed by Charles MacDougall, gave *Arrivederci Millwall* sufficient exposure for it to be considered a genuine threat to Thatcherism.

Like Ian McEwan, Nick Perry is concerned to find ways of prying open the apparent monolith of Thatcherite ideology in order to expose its inherent flaws. The fault line at which he chips away is created by the network of contradictions that characterize the relationship of the Thatcher Government to football hooliganism. The gangs of football hooligans who were such a prominent part of the British social scene during the 1970s and 80s closely resembled the new right in their excessive patriotism, xenophobia, racism, anti-intellectualism and willingness to resort to violence.[4] Less obviously, the hooligans also shared the new right's commitment to materialistic and even entrepreurial values. Most gang members were not unemployed, as was commonly assumed, but were relatively affluent young men who dressed fashionably and sought through petty crime, or 'going on the jib' as they called it, to return from their often expensive football excursions with a net profit (Buford, pp. 27–9). In that many of them had connections with the National Front, football hooligans were even amongst the group of potential voters whose support Thatcher had sought by adopting racist policies in the late 1970s.

Yet, despite their Thatcherite tendencies, football hooligans were probably the most thoroughly demonized of all the groups that constituted Thatcher's enemy within. In addition to repeated verbal attacks on these 'troublemakers', whom she even compared to the IRA after the Heysel disaster (J. Williams, p. 11), Thatcher introduced a number of draconian measures intended to control hooliganism, including heavy and extremely intrusive policing around and inside football grounds, mandatory club membership and the segregation of rival supporters. Amongst the possible explanations for a hostility and a degree of attention that far exceeded the real social dangers posed by football hooligans, one of the most plausible in the context of the understanding of Thatcherism provided by *The Ploughman's Lunch* is implicit in the suggestion that Thatcher was unwilling to include the working classes in her new model society. This is certainly what John Williams is arguing when he points out the delicious irony in the Conservative Government's tendency to blame the very affluence that it was so proud of fostering in other social spheres for allowing 'England's young Calibans [to buy] their way out of their caves' (p. 12).

While acknowledging the validity of this analysis, Nick Perry is more inclined to propose that Thatcher's overreaction to football hooliganism is rooted in a need to deny the very real similarities that, as we have just seen, exist between her own and the hooligans' values. Perry makes his point in part by modelling the rhetoric of the gang of hooligans who are the main characters in *Arrivederci Millwall* on speeches made by some of the more right wing members of the Government during the Falklands debates in the House of Commons. He also introduces a series of metaphors into his play in which a connection is established between the British task force and the self-styled 'Millwall Task Force' that sets out from Southampton to invade Spain during the 1982 World Cup.

Ironically, when viewed from the perspective afforded by Perry's football hooligans, Thatcherism emerges as much less cynical than it does in *The Ploughman's Lunch*. Billy Jarvis and his gang are as greedy and materialistic as McEwan's characters but their patriotism is too heartfelt to be exploited for financial gain. Thus, when Harry Kellaway, usually the most entrepreneurial of the group, is asked how he expects to profit from organizing the football gangs of England for battle with the Spanish fans, he replies, 'Nothing. Absolutely not a thing. I want to do one thing in my life for love instead of money' (Perry, p. 77). However, this does not mean that Perry is any more sympathetic to Thatcherism than McEwan. On the contrary, his goal in exploring the value system of a group of unsophisticated characters, who are either incapable of or uninterested in packaging up their beliefs to make them appear either internally consistent or congruent with traditional British values of tolerance, moderation and community, is to expose Thatcherism as a mean-spirited, selfish and brutal creed built upon the twin pillars of material self-aggrandizement and violent behaviour.

The Thatcherite credentials of Billy Jarvis and his fellow Millwall supporters, Cass, Mal, Kenno and Terry are quickly established by the opening scene of *Arrivederci Millwall!*'s original dramatic version. Thus, in the course of his first monologue Billy pledges himself to 'progress', expresses a keen interest in developments in weaponry from the 'broken bottle' of his father's youth to the 'the Stanley knife' employed by modern hooligans, and offers a patriotic salute to 'Millwall and Saint George' (p. 6). The themes of violence and patriotism introduced here are developed later and connected to the further Thatcherite concern with history. However, the major emphasis in the early action of *Arrivederci Millwall* is on 'progress', which the model capitalist Billy considers to be synonymous with the cultivation of materialistic values: 'Everything's a fashion. . . . That's progress for you' (p. 5).

Billy's fellow gang members are equally materialistic. At first, they play a consumer role, showing off their acquisition of the latest fashions in football fan wear through the format of a mock fashion show: 'Malcolm is wearing a Tacchini track suit – (clock the label . . . North London is still wearing Lacoste, which we dropped months ago). The track suit retails at one hundred pounds' (pp. 5–6). Later, they shift into a variety of entrepreneurial roles, all of which are characterized by a single-minded pursuit of profit. Billy and Cass are, for instance, painters and decorators who have no time for the traditional working class concepts of honest labour and pride in workmanship, preferring instead to run their business according to the mottoes, 'Give us a slum, we'll show you a profit', 'You're in business to do business' and 'You've got to do it to them before they do it to you'. Thus, faced with the problem of an out-of-stock paint, Billy simply substitutes cream for mushroom because 'at fifty quid a day what does he [their customer] expect?' (p. 7).

Other members of the gang or, as Billy calls it, 'firm' (p. 17), an East End slang term that straddles the boundary line between the business and criminal worlds, feel no compunction about breaking the law in order to make a profit. For example, Mal, a true Thatcherite who taunts unemployed Northern football fans with Norman Tebbitt's infamous slogan, 'on your bike' (p. 24), fly-pitches 'genuine stolen property' (p. 8) on Oxford Street. Even more flagrantly criminal is the way in which the gang acquires goods for later sale in their local pub through the open theft of shirts from a clothes shop during a trip north in support of their team. In part, the robbery is simply a act of bravado designed to show the gang members disregard for authority. However, Billy's parting gesture of handing the manager a business card, professionally printed with a Millwall lion logo and the message, 'You have just met Millwall' (quotations without accompanying page numbers are taken from the film version of *Arrivederci Millwall*), suggests that they also consider the robbery a legitimate expression of the entrepreneurial spirit.

Thatcher, with her law and order agenda, would obviously have disagreed. Neither would she have reacted with anything other than outrage when Billy and his friends cheat the dole system. However, for Perry, the distinctions Thatcher draws between proper and improper ways of making money are based almost entirely on class. He makes this point by including in the dole queue Harry Kellaway, a somewhat older working class hooligan and entrepreneur, who is beginning to explore the often shady but more acceptable route to material success offered by the financial markets and who offers the advice, 'You got to speculate to accumulate' (p. 9).

Perry dismisses the possibility that Thatcher's frequently expressed objections to the obviously criminal entrepreurship involved in cheating the welfare system might have a moral basis by pointing up the quintessentially Thatcherite nature of the gang members' values. Thus, their view of Britain as a 'culture . . .

[whose] independence and freedom' are bound up in 'securing an honest [sic] profit' (75) and in which successful 'fiddles[s]' (p. 47) are admired, while anyone acting on principle is considered 'a mug' (p. 16), is one that might have been expressed, albeit in somewhat more refined terms, by any of the establishment figures in *The Ploughman's Lunch*.

Perry's analysis of the entrepreneurial behaviour and codes of his football hooligan characters has two obvious main goals. First, like McEwan, Perry is intent on pointing up the class biases built into Thatcher's supposedly equal opportunity society. Second, and more important for an understanding of *Arrivederci Millwall*, he is seeking to establish that, despised as they may be by Thatcher herself, Billy Jarvis and his friends are nevertheless imbued in the spirit of new right ideology. Therefore, in going on to explore the gang members' violence, patriotism and sense of history, Perry has as a further goal the illumination not only of a working class subculture but also of the dominant ideology of Britain in the 1980s.

Violence, although most obviously to the fore during their highly organized battles with rival groups of football supporters, in fact permeates the gang members' entire lives. This is particularly true of Billy. Thus, in addition to those times when we might expect him to behave violently, as in the vicious punishment that he metes out to Harry for beating up his friend, Terry, Billy relies upon a hard slap in the face to teach Terry a lesson about the evils of drug addiction, makes threats and engages in boisterous wrestling when he wants to show affection for his brother, Bobby, and delivers a bite on the bottom in order to express sexual desire for his girlfriend, Julie.

This tendency to react violently in a wide range of situations has obvious roots in childhood. A particularly formative event in Bobby Jarvis's life, for instance, occurred at the age of ten when he was forced to watch helplessly as a group of West Ham supporters attacked his father for wearing Millwall colours. Nevertheless, Perry does not encourage his audience to understand the violent behaviour of his characters as a simple product of their brutalized working class childhoods. On the contrary, he presents violence primarily as a product of the amorality of contemporary British society and as a way of filling the spiritual and emotional void that inevitably exists at the centre of lives dedicated to material gain. In other words, Perry is proposing an intimate link between violent behaviour and Thatcherite values.

Billy, a practising Catholic, listens to a sermon on the text, 'love your enemies, bless them that curse you, do good to them that hate you, and pray for them which despitefully use you, and persecute you' (p. 22). Violence does not, however, pose any moral problems for him and his scorn for Christian teaching is revealed in the film version of *Arrivederci Millwall* when, as a response to Julie's objections to being bitten, he offers the mock advice that she 'turn the other cheek'. The only law that Billy will acknowledge is the law of 'survival'. He claims to have learnt this principle while working in a slaughterhouse where he 'put bolts through the heads of living cows' (p. 66). It is more likely, though, to be a product of his acceptance of the neo-Hobbesian creed of self interest promulgated by the new right.

Kenno has a similarly reductive view of experience that he derives from the Thatcherite buzz word 'self-discipline'. As employed in neoconservative ideology, this term has no particular ethical or moral signification. Therefore, there is nothing to prevent Kenno, who draws on his own experience of the Conservative Government's 'short, sharp shock' approach to young offenders, from transforming 'self-discipline' into a synonym for acts of mindless violence: 'I'll tell you what you boys need. Three months in a detention centre. Makes a man of you, that does. Teaches you self-discipline. That's what it taught me. How to fight and how to fight proper' (p. 62).

What Billy and Kenno's explanations of their approach to experience reveal, then, is that, for all its stress on law and order, Thatcherism actually creates an amoral and self-interested environment that is extremely hospitable to violence. In Thatcher's Britain, however, Perry further suggests, violent behaviour is not just acceptable, it is almost essential. As Billy indicates when he complains that 'nothing ever happens here' (p. 33), he and his friends get very little real satisfaction from their lives and suffer from an anomie that has its source in an incompatibility between the materialistic goals that they pursue so avidly and their needs as human beings. Apart from the sustenance provided by the gang members' 'friendship' (p. 16) with each other, which Cass at least values, only fighting can satisfy these needs. At the most basic level, successful combat serves a 'therapeutic' function by producing an intense feeling of well being. As Bobby puts it, 'I mean you straighten your arm and it's like years of silt come dredging up from the bottom of your gut' (p. 34). In addition, fighting provides these Thatcherite hollow men with an identity lacking in other aspects of their lives. Thus, for Billy, a firm sense of self is bound up in being 'best at something' and, as he boasts, 'when the name of the game was chinning people, we was second to none' (p. 24). Similarly, Terry's self esteem is greatly enhanced by the appearance of his photograph in a newspaper story about gang violence: 'I'm a star' (p. 28).

The violent incidents in which Billy and his friends become involved are not, then, as one might at first assume, a byproduct of their loyalty to Millwall. On the contrary, it is the violence itself that is important; football games simply provide a convenient excuse and occasion for acts of hooliganism. In the original dramatic version of *Arrivederci Millwall*, an older Billy offers a retrospective analysis of his youthful experiences as a football hooligan, in the course of which he admits that there is nothing inherent in Millwall F. C. that makes the team worth fighting for: 'What was all that fighting for? . . . A football team, a shitty poxy wanky tenth-rate third-division fucking USELESS . . . football team' (p. 7). Team loyalty is important only because, without it, the gang would lack both the internal cohesion produced by a shared cause and a clearly defined enemy. In effect, then, they are mimicking what happens on the field by choosing sides and engaging in a contest. Given this kind of thinking it is only logical that, once Millwall has completed its game of football with a Northern rival at Cold Blow Lane, Billy's gang should take on their supporters in a bloody knife fight at Whitechapel underground station.

Using this analysis of the connection between violent behaviour and team loyalty as his starting point, Nick Perry then goes on to a broader assessment of the connection between Britain's military aggression against Argentina and the patriotic fervour with which the public responded to the outbreak of the Falklands War. The essence of his argument is that, like Billy and his friends, the nation as a whole has become enthusiastic about violence in order to fill the moral and spiritual void created by the spread of Thatcher-inspired materialism and that the function of patriotism, like that of team loyalty, is simply to provide an excuse and an occasion for violent acts.

The connection Perry is forging between the activities of a despised subculture and those of a self-proclaimed imperial nation is reinforced early in *Arrivederci Millwall* when Billy compares the blue and white shirted Millwall with 'Saint George' (p. 6), the patron saint of England. Billy's later claim that the contrast between the 'aggressive' style of English football and 'fancy continental stuff' reflects an essential difference between the national characters of Britain and of other nations serves a similar function. By blending together an account of the 1982 European Cup Final, during which Aston Villa supporters sang 'Rule, Britannia!' in response to Spanish chants of 'Argentina, Argentina' (p. 38), and belligerent excerpts from the emergency debate of 3 April, Perry indicates that there is nothing idiosyncratic in the equation Billy draws between team and nation.

Perry makes several other direct allusions to the Falklands War in order to sharpen his analysis of the wider social implications of violent behaviour amongst football supporters. Thatcher's vainglorious predictions about the inevitability of Britain's triumph in the South Atlantic find a clear echo, for example, in Billy's assertion of his gang's intrinsic superiority over all rivals: 'But one thing you can rely on: London's always first. And first is first, second's nowhere. London talks, England walks. South London to be exact. . . . Argies start at Calais, civilization stops at Watford' (p. 5). Similarly, when Billy claims that his attack on Harry Kellaway was necessary in order to 'keep the peace' (p. 18), he sounds very like Margaret Thatcher putting a pacifist interpretation on her decision to go to war with Argentina. By adding, 'You have to give it 'em strong' (p. 18), Billy expresses a faith in the curative powers of violent action very similar to that of the Conservative member who argues – in one of the speeches from the emergency debate introduced into *Arrivederci Millwall* – that 'the government must now prove by deeds to ensure that foul and brutal aggression does not succeed in our world . . .' (p. 38).

Falklands parallels become particularly pronounced during the 'Second Half' of *Arrivederci Millwall* which deals with the gang's trip to Spain for the World Cup. Like the recently departed task force Billy and his friends embark from Southampton on what is, from their point of view, a mission of great national importance. Thus, they no longer see themselves as simply Millwall supporters but as an English 'Army' that is 'gonna take Bilbao [the site of England's first-phase games]' (p. 61). Their enemy, literally the Spanish, is transformed by Harry Kellaway into the Argentinians on the grounds that 'a spic is a spic' (p. 76).

Earlier in *Arrivederci Millwall* both Billy, in his evocation of

Millwall and Saint George, and Kenno, who claims after a successful fight with rival supporters that 'we have done our duty' (p. 26),
demonstrate an awareness of how effective an appeal to patriotic
values can be in giving a sense of purpose to pointless hooliganism.
It is therefore inevitable that, with victory in the recent Falklands
War to inspire them and deeply conscious that they are now
supporting England rather than Millwall, the members of the
gang will turn to *amor patriae* in order to justify violent acts
committed during their trip to Spain. Thus Kenno says of the
gang's riotous behaviour in a restaurant, 'You can't blame us
for being patriotic. There's a fucking war on, you know' (p. 71).
Examples of the gang's extensive use of the language and symbols of patriotism include the whistling of 'Colonel Bogey' as
they march down a Spanish street, the humming of 'Rule,
Britannia!' in defiance of brutal Spanish police, and the sporting
of Union Jack flags and T-shirts. Mal has even told his fiancée
that, in cancelling their wedding to go to Spain, he is 'putting
[his] country first' (p. 63).

In one of several expressionistic scenes during which Perry
deviates from the otherwise realistic style of the stage version of
Arrivederci Millwall, this patriotic discourse rises to a crescendo
when Billy and his friends, now joined by the supporters of other
clubs and calling themselves 'England' (p. 87), engage a group
of Spanish fans in an orgy of pointless violence. Terry sings 'Rule,
Britannia!' as he is overwhelmed by superior numbers in a prelim-
inary skirmish and, as the main battle begins, the ghost of Bobby
Jarvis cries out, 'SONS OF ENGLAND, ARISE!'. Then the Chorale
delivers a speech, replete with echoes of some of Thatcher's
more charged utterances during the Falklands War, in which
the ugliness of violent behaviour is concealed under a cloak of
national destiny:

> Always in the lives of great nations comes the moment of deci-
> sion, comes the moment of destiny. And this nation again and
> again in the great hours of its fate has swept aside conven-
> tion, has swept aside the little men of talk and delay and has
> decided to follow men of movement, who say go forward to
> action. (p. 82)

So persuasive is this patriotic rhetoric that Billy undergoes a transformation, made literal by the inscription of the Union Jack on

his face, in which he ceases to be a hooligan seeking the thrill provided by acts of violence and becomes first his country's champion and then the country itself: 'These colours on my face I wore with pride, and not for camouflage. Like the Polish cavalry we're charging at tanks with a clatter of swords and a flag and a drum . . . Like this war paint: you ent got a face. Just a Union Jack' (pp. 80–1).

In addition to exposing Britain under Conservative rule as an inherently violent society in which the ugly impulses responsible for its military entanglements are concealed beneath a layer of patriotic rhetoric, Nick Perry's exploration of the connections between the football hooligan subculture and mainstream British society serves as the vehicle for an analysis of the jingoistic and racist aspects of Thatcher's idea of nation. In order to understand Perry's argument, it is necessary to start with his analysis of the role played by bonding and excluding in shaping violent cultures.

When Billy and his friends function as Millwall supporters, questions of identity seem fairly straightforward. Other fans of Millwall, easily recognized by their blue and white colours, fashion choices and South London accents are considered allies and those who follow rival teams are immediately revealed as enemies by their different colours, clothes and regional accents. However, even within the relatively uncomplicated world of football hooliganism, the rules are not always consistent. Cass's inclusion in Billy's gang reveals, for example, that race is not a crucial factor when it comes to deciding who is acceptable as a Millwall supporter. The Northern fans with whom Billy's gang fight at Whitechapel, on the other hand, seek to set themselves apart from Millwall supporters not just by regional differences, as is implicit in addressing Billy as 'you cockney shite', but also on racial grounds: 'Eh lads: leave the nigger to me. I'll give him a dig' (p. 25).

Even team loyalty is ultimately arbitrary despite its frequent origins in family and neighbourhood. For Mal, the fact that his girlfriend, whom he describes as a 'dozy bitch', 'likes Chelsea one week , Tottenham the next' (p. 63) is attributable to the inability of women to understand the essentially masculine codes of the football supporter. However, Harry Kellaway, once a West Ham supporter (p. 36) but now torn between Tottenham Hotspur and Millwall (p. 37), is equally vacillating in his affiliations. Some slipperiness of definition is, of course, inevitable in any socially-constructed group. However, and this is Perry's main point, precision becomes virtually irrelevant when identification with a club is simply a means of facilitating violent behaviour.

Most of us would probably assume that the issues involved in choosing sides for fights between gangs of football supporters have very little relevance to the much weightier business of organizing the opposing forces during national conflicts such as the Falklands War, which Perry brings into prominence towards the end of the 'First Half' of *Arrivederci Millwall* with Bobby Jarvis's embarkation as part of the task force. Such is certainly the view of a television commentator heard announcing, 'This is no longer a game', over film of HMS *Hermes* setting sail for the South Atlantic. However, Perry demonstrates in the 'Second Half' of *Arrivederci Millwall* that there are indeed some striking similarities between the two spheres.

Billy and his friends do not begin to think of themselves in national rather than club terms until they set out for Spain for the World Cup. However, there is a richly comic moment much earlier in the play/film that clearly suggests that the gang's new and apparently more substantial identity is in fact no more stable than their old one. This occurs when that most basic of national institutions, the 'Great English Breakfast', is instantly defamiliarized by the Italian cafe owner's translation of Billy's order into 'DUE SALCICCIE UOVO PANCETTA PATTATINE FRITTE E LA PANE FRITTO!' (p. 15).

Once the action of *Arrivederci Millwall* has moved on to Spain, Perry has ample opportunities to flesh out the serious implications of this comic suggestion by demonstrating how arbitrary even a national identity can become when it is arrived at by a process of inclusion and exclusion whose sole purpose is to facilitate opportunities for violent confrontation. Clearly he has in mind Thatcher's simultaneous expansion and contraction of the term British to include the Falkland Islanders and to exclude various enemies within. His point emerges with particular clarity when Billy expresses a willingness to embrace under the rubric of England all those previously despised supporters of rival teams: 'We wasn't Millwall no more. We wasn't Liverpool or Man Ewe, West Ham or Chelsea. We was an army that day, a fucking army. We was England' (p. 87).

The bonding together of groups formerly characterized by

difference is made possible by a polarization process fundamental to all nationalistic thinking and particularly pronounced in the militant variety embraced with equal enthusiasm by Billy Jarvis and Margaret Thatcher. Thus, gangs of young thugs, who until recently had been bitter enemies, need only to construct a Spanish Other in order to become united under a common identity. According to Billy and his friends who, of course, have almost no real knowledge of the country or its people, Spain and the Spanish are the antithesis of all the qualities that make the British great; the country is 'a right hole' (p. 61) and the people have poor 'hygiene' (p. 59), speak an inferior language (p. 62), eat disgusting food (p. 64), and lack any concept of 'respect' (p. 69) or 'discipline' (p. 73). Harry Kellaway, having added laziness, cowardice, viciousness, cruelty to animals and women, and deceit to the list of national vices, completes this process of demonization by proposing that, as 'dagos' and 'spics' (p. 76), the Spanish are synonymous with the hated Argentinians.

Because of its xenophobia, militant nationalism emerges as even more sinister than football hooliganism, at least as practised on the domestic front. Furthermore, as Cass points out in response to Harry's outrageous claim that 'a spic is a spic. Anyone of them will do [to kill]', xenophobia is only a short step away from racism, a form of dehumanization that, as we have already seen, is not integral to identities created around team loyalty:

Cass: How about me then?
Billy: You ent a spic.
Cass: What am I then? An 'Englishman'? You reckon Harry looks at me, he sees an 'Englishman'? Look at me, Billy. What am I? How far away must I stand before you can see me what I am? A hundred yards, am I still your friend? . . . Can't you see? Kick a dago, kick a nigger – what's the fucking odds? (p. 76)

Harry's response of 'I couldn't have put it better myself' (p. 77) and the speed with which Billy attaches the label 'nigger' (p. 79) to his former best friend both demonstrate the accuracy of Cass's analysis.

Nick Perry completes his reassessment of Thatcherism with a scene, excluded from the more consistently realistic film version of *Arrivederci Millwall*, in which an hallucinating Billy observes

and then participates in an 'historical tableau or pageant' (p. 82).
This tableau is comprised of figures that bear a close resemblance
to those summoned up by Thatcher in the course of her attempts
to define the Falklands War as a moment of destiny when the
essentially peace-loving people of England once again demonstrated their country's greatness by taking up arms in defence
of Christian values, the rule of law and the right of self determination. However, while the King, who is loosely based on
Shakespeare's Henry V, the Knight, the Para, the Peasant and
Gloriana, a name often given to Queen Elizabeth I, all echo the
Thatcherite version of our Island's glorious story, they also offer
an alternative reading of the past as a sequence of acts of mindless violence.

Thus, interspersed amongst references to the 'English', a 'mighty-
hearted', 'noble' and 'peace-loving people' (p. 83) who take 'God
[as their] right and strength' (p. 84) and who are willing to sacrifice their lives 'in the name of Queen and Country, in certain
hope of victory' (pp. 85–6), are a number of statements of blood-
thirsty intent and expressions of scorn for the Christian values
expressed in Gloriana's address to her 'loyal subjects': 'Lord, make
me an instrument of thy peace. Where there is hatred, let me
sow love; where there is injury, pardon; where there is darkness,
light; and where there is sadness, joy' (p. 86). In speaking of the
upcoming battle, for instance, the Knight expounds with relish
on the violence he intends to inflict on his Spanish enemies: 'The
time has come, the time for action – cook a broth with bone and
water, / thicken it with Spanish blood; / roast their greasy hides
for crackling' (p. 83). When speaking in this voice the English
cease to be mighty-hearted and noble and become instead 'a nation
of butchers' (p. 84) whose battle cry is 'I AM A WARRY BAS-
TARD, I AM!' (p. 85). As butchers and warry bastards, the English
scorn 'conscience [as] a word that cowards use' (p. 82), mete out
rough justice to the Peasant for questioning their violent intent,
and callously reject his desperate plea, 'as your fellow man, your
mother's son, your brother: have mercy' (p. 85).

The clash between conflicting national visions that develops
as these widely differing sentiments are expressed is given dramatic voice through the melange of competing discourses Perry
creates by making the figures in his tableau shift back and forth
between the grand language of Shakespeare, the foul-mouthed
Cockney of the Millwall football hooligan and the occasional plain

speech of the soldier. Both the King, who tells his troops that 'half your force is adequate / to blight the full-blown flower of Spain: / the other half may lie a-bed', and the Knight who says, 'Account yourself a lucky man who dwells within the Wooden Walls of England, environed with a Great Ditch from all the world besides' (p. 83), tend to speak in Shakespearean cadences. Occasionally, however, they each resort to hooligans' Cockney; it is the King, for instance, who utters the aggressively skinhead cry of 'I AM A WARRY BASTARD, I AM!' while the Knight greets the arrival of the enemy with, 'It's off! It's off! The dagos are coming, mob-handed!' (p. 86). The plain voice of the soldier, which falls between these rhetorical extremes, is heard when the Para describes his death in the Falklands – 'I died up on Wireless Ridge / bending to dimp my cigarette' (p. 82) – and when the Peasant recounts his fate at Valparaiso in 1592: '[The Spaniards] cut off our hands, feet, noses and ears, / and tied us to trees to be tortured by flies / and other beasts' (p. 84).

Of the three competing discourses, the soldier's matter-of-fact manner of speaking the plain facts of violence, about which he has first-hand and painful knowledge, is clearly the most authoritative. Yet, this voice is rarely listened to in the Thatcherite England of *Arrivederci Millwall*, as has already been demonstrated by Billy's inability to learn either from his sailor brother, Bobby, who tells him 'no one has to fight' (p. 31) and that there are 'no hard men' (p. 35), or from the veteran of Northern Ireland who reveals how unappealing violence is to those who have experienced the horrors of real warfare: 'It's a great life, lad. It's good crack scraping your oppo off pavement. It's a reet laugh getting shot at by twelve-year-old micks' (p. 72). The Shakespearean and Cockney voices, on the other hand, experience no difficulty in being heard because they transmit similar messages that strike a resonant chord in a modern Britain where the influence of Thatcherite ideology runs deep.

The congruency that exists in *Arrivederci Millwall* between high and low discourses derives from the fact that, once plucked from their original context in *Henry V* where they function as part of a complex meditation on nationalism and war, Shakespeare's words become nothing more than a grandiloquent vehicle for the transmission of a creed of violence communicated much more directly by the outbursts of Billy Jarvis and his friends. Perry communicates his point extremely graphically at the climax of the historical pageant when Billy takes over the role of Henry V and recasts his Agincourt speech in the much more appropriate argot of the football hooligan:

> Dear friends – there's mugs at home
> in front of the box
> or down the pub
> or shagging their tarts
> who'll kick themselves
> and bite their lip
> in years to come
> because they was not here today
> to fight with us – this crew, this fighting crew,
> this band of ruckers, this England! (p. 88)

A similar transformation is achieved a little earlier in the tableau when Gloriana or Elizabeth I, already recognizable as the Para in drag, tears off her costume to reveal herself as a football hooligan dressed in a Bulldog Bobby T-shirt. The purpose of this piece of mime is to once again displace Thatcher's fiction of contemporary Britain as the glorious product of a noble history with a portrayal of an ugly and violent nation. By choosing Gloriana rather than Henry V as the regal figure who turns into Bulldog Bobby, Perry is directly implicating Thatcher, who was of course often compared with Elizabeth I during the Falklands War, in the thuggishness that became so rampant during her time in office.[5] Perry reinforces the connection between monarch and Prime Minister by introducing a reference to 'Saint Francis of Assisi' (p. 86), the subject of one of Thatcher's most infamous speeches, into the 'address' to 'her loyal subjects' that immediately precedes Gloriana's transformation into Bulldog Bobby.

With this depiction of Thatcher as football hooligan, Perry completes his deconstruction of neoconservative ideology. However, thorough as he is in anatomizing Thatcherism and British society under Conservative rule, he is no more ready than McEwan to offer an immediate alternative. The original dramatic version of *Arrivederci Millwall* finally sidesteps the political issues with which Perry has been dealing by offering a purely personal and not very plausible resolution in which Billy, chastened by the extreme violence of the climactic battle between English and Spanish football fans and mellowed by marriage and fatherhood, simply outgrows his affection for Millwall and his love of fighting. In sharp contrast to the evasive ending of the play, the film version of *Arrivederci Millwall* concludes with a dark statement about the consequences of living by the values of a violent society. This statement is implicit in director Charles MacDougall's decision to open the film with a shot that is repeated at the end, where it belongs chronologically. In the shot a policeman is typing up a report of Cass's murder, thereby suggesting that once Billy has embarked on the violent course that the film is about to chart, there is a dreadful inevitability about the final and self-defeating act that leaves his best friend dead and himself at the mercy of the hated Spanish police.

However, this uncompromising second ending does not bring Perry any closer to answering in any but the most tentative way the question of how the violent culture created by a Thatcherite hegemony might be challenged. In both play and film casualties and veterans of war provide a valid but ignored perspective on the ugly realities that lie beneath the glamorous surface of violence and there are occasional glimpses of real bonds of friendship amongst the gang members that point to the possibility, albeit unrealized, of an alternative to their community of hatred. In the end, though, the main hope offered by *Arrivederci Millwall*, as is the case with *The Ploughman's Lunch*, resides in its author's ability to contribute yet another voice to the growing chorus that seeks to make itself heard above the clamour of the dominant Thatcherite discourse.

Notes

1. *Arrivederci Millwall* was originally written as a stage play and later adapted for television by its author. In this chapter the two versions will be treated as a single hybrid text except for those few occasions when there are significant differences between them. In translating *Arrivederci Millwall* from stage to screen, Perry made only two major changes. He completely rewrote the ending and eliminated the occasional shifts from realism to surrealism.
2. In naming McEwan and Perry as the authors of *The Ploughman's Lunch* and *Arrivederci Millwall* I am doing less than justice to the roles played by Richard Eyre, the director of *The Ploughman's Lunch*, and Charles MacDougall, who directed the televised version of *Arrivederci Millwall*. However, whenever I speak specifically about visual rather than textual

aspects of the two films I will attribute authorship to the two directors.

3. Neither of these statements appears in the published script of *The Ploughman's Lunch*.

4. For discussions of the relationship between football hooligans and the new right see Aulich, pp. 91–2; Chambers, p. 29; Samuel, I, xxxiv; Williams, J., p. 17.

5. Antonia Fraser has suggested that Thatcher wwwwas not only frequently compared to Elizabeth I during her time in office but also liked to take on the role of the task force's 'Armed Figurehead' (pp. 314, 317–18). Fraser would therefore presumably see references to Margaret Thatcher not only in the fact that Gloriana is a name for Elizabeth I but in her also being the Para in drag.

4

Writing the Imaginary Britain: *Kingdom by the Sea* and *Coasting*

Paul Theroux's *The Kingdom by the Sea* (1983) and Jonathan Raban's *Coasting* (1986) are both records of journeys around Britain. Theroux set out to travel by foot, train and bus around the entire British coastline, starting in a westerly direction, while Raban planned to circumnavigate the country in his boat, *Gosfield Maid*, after sailing eastwards from Fowey in Cornwall. By coincidence they began their journeys within a few days of each other, just as Britain was going to war with Argentina over the Falklands, and the bulk of their respective narratives focuses on the period April–May–June, 1982. Theroux and Raban's common goal is to achieve an understanding of the British people and their way of life – thus encompassing the country metaphorically while circling it literally – and ultimately to create and communicate a national mythology.

In time span and purpose, then, *The Kingdom by the Sea* and *Coasting* have a good deal in common with the Falklands speeches of Margaret Thatcher and her political supporters and the reporting and editorials of the pro-Government media. Also like the Thatcherite forces, which unfolding events inevitably make their major reference point, Theroux and Raban recognize that the appropriate vehicle for the communication of a national mythology is the quest narrative. From this point on, though, Theroux and Raban deviate from the Thatcherite model since, as post-modernists, they are unwilling to grant absolute authority to any interpretive framework, including the archetypal. Thus, beginning with a demonstration of the arbitrary nature of their own and, by implication, Thatcher's mythic structures, Theroux and Raban become engaged in thoroughgoing deconstructions

117

of the mainstream Falklands myth that finally clear the way for the development of alternative national stories. Viewed from the postmodern perspective adopted by Theroux and Raban these stories are, of course, no less provisional than Thatcher's. Nevertheless, and somewhat paradoxically, they acquire a degree of credibility and hence authority from their authors' willingness to lay bare the rhetorical underpinnings of any truth claims that they might make. As a result, both *The Kingdom by the Sea* and *Coasting* are able to mount serious challenges to the official Falklands myth.

POSTMODERN PERSPECTIVES

Theroux first reveals an intention to milk the mythic potential of his journey when he compares himself to 'the prince in the old story, who ... disguises himself in old clothes and ... hikes the muddy roads, talking to everyone and looking closely at things, to find out what his kingdom is really like' (Theroux, p. 8).[1] Theroux's insistence that a journey begun on May Day will develop according to the logic of a fairy world still kept alive in many English villages by the choice of a May Queen (p. 9) further prepares the way for mythic understandings of the people and creatures he meets, the adventures in which he becomes involved and the places he visits.

Armed with a fortune teller's prediction that he will 'survive' (p. 23) whatever trials might be awaiting him, Theroux encounters a variety of mythic figures in the course of his travels, including 'sea monsters' (54), the 'ghosts of Henry James, Paul Verlaine, Tess Darbeyfield, Mary Shelley' (p. 95), 'goblins' (p. 124), and a 'wicked witch' (243). Dracula lurks on the cliffs at Whitby (p. 385) and Theroux suspects the 'robust, rosy-cheeked' Mrs Chandler, who looks like 'she [feeds] off [her husband] at night' (pp. 156-7), of vampirism. Even the Devil's son puts in an appearance during a television lounge viewing of *The Omen* (pp. 165-6). Several of Theroux's adventures involve landladies who are mysteriously seductive and attempt to divert this latter-day Sir Gawain from his quest: '"Why don't you stay tonight." She meant it and seemed eager, and then I was not sure what she was offering' (p. 158).

Equally charged with mythic associations are Theroux's repeated experiences, albeit vicarious, of death by water. These include Virginia Woolf's drowning in the Cuckmere River (p. 62) and the accidental death of an unnamed woman swept off the breakwater into Whitby harbour (p. 383). Amongst the places Theroux visits are Harlech Castle, 'the very image of the gray mass of round towers high on a sea cliff that children dream about after a bedtime story of kings and princesses and dragons' (p. 204); 'Welsh landscapes' full of 'blurred castles and giants and dragons that were actually cliffs' (p. 185); the Scottish Cuillins with their 'fairy-tale strangeness' (p. 337); and the northwest coast of Scotland, 'a setting that was straight out of *Dracula*' (p. 329).

Raban also allots himself an archetypal role, in his case that of the son of 'a storybook dragon' (Raban, 1986, p. 18), and as he travels he comes across the 'Cylops' in the shape of the 'slowly turning head [of a tourist] culminating in the lidless mauve eye of a Yashica or a Nikon' (p. 206). Many of the places through which Raban's journey takes him undergo a similar process of mythic transformation. The British Isles are, for instance, likened to the Cyclades (p. 52) and Portland Race is said to belong 'with the legendary horrors of mythology', being much bigger and more powerful than 'the piddling whirlpool of Charybdis' (p. 155). Night time London is in its turn changed into a 'labyrinth' full of people trying to shout their way out and Aberdeen becomes at once 'the Byzantium of eastern Scotland' and 'its Sodom and its Gomorrah' (p. 287).

An even more striking feature of *Coasting*, however, resides in the qualities it shares with *Gulliver's Travels* and *Alice in Wonderland*. On the Isle of Man, for instance, with its 'little houses, little gardens, little farms . . ., everything looked squashed and Lilliputian' (p. 60) and throughout his journey Raban experiences disturbing changes in size and shifts in perspective. *Gosfield Maid* seems 'to grow to the size of a cargo ship the moment she enter[s] the river [Yealm]' (p. 103) and 'England [has been shrunk] to a country half the size of the one in which [Raban] grew up' (p. 168) by motorway building in the 1960s and 70s. By way of contrast the distance between 'The South and The North' takes on 'legendary' dimensions when experienced at a sail boat speed of four to six knots, so that Hull is 'approximately 2,400 miles from Tower Bridge' (p. 246). A major shift in perspective occurs when a vantage point on board his boat allows Raban to

experience 'houses and trees [as] wander[ing] about the landscape' (p. 119).

Theroux and Raban finally part company with Margaret Thatcher
and those who mimic her version of the Falklands War, however, by refusing to blur the lines between real events and archetypal narrative. Theroux, for instance, emphasizes the arbitrariness
of the mythic role assigned to May Day in his tale by laying
bare the mechanics of the narrative strategy by means of which
he has suppressed the date's socialist associations and its
'politically neutralized' role as 'Spring Bank Holiday' (p. 9) in
order to foreground its fairytale connotations. The constructed
nature of not only Theroux's but also Raban's narrative is even
more firmly established by the frank and even playful manner
in which each acknowledges that he recognized in advance of
his journey the possibilities inherent within its circular route for
the creation of an archetypal structure.

Thus, early in *The Kingdom by the Sea*, Theroux states quite
baldly, 'As soon as I decided on this coastal route for my itinerary, I had my justification for the trip – the journey had the
right shape; it had a logic; it had a beginning and an end' (p. 6).
Similarly, Raban, who actually sailed in British coastal waters
for four years, muses on the incompatibility between the incon-
clusiveness of real travelling which, 'once you have gone past
your original point of departure . . ., has no destination and no
ending', and the reader's 'insist[ence] on travelling in a more
orderly sequence and demand [for] a strict and conventional
economy of literary means' (p. 50). He then promises, with tongue
firmly in cheek, to satisfy his audience by organizing the messy
reality of his journey into 'the usual epical–pastoral–tragical–
comical–historical–amorous and lonely story – of innocence lost,
ritual tests and trials, the holy terrors, funny interludes, romances
caught on the wing' (p. 49) and concludes with a one-paragraph
summary of this story that terminates in a conclusively italicized,
'*The End*'. The playfulness of these comments about literary
convention is underlined when Raban interrupts himself to describe
how a storm is tossing a three-volume set of *Tristram Shandy*
around the saloon of his boat in a kind of mimicry of the 'panic-
stricken' (p. 50) state that has long afflicted unwary readers of
Sterne's famously frustrating novel and is likely to be the fate of
anyone who takes his own statement of narrative intent at face
value.

The potential authority of Theroux's and Raban's archetypal narratives is further undermined by the failure of either *The Kingdom by the Sea* or *Coasting* to reach the 'end' so confidently promised by their authors. Despite a reference to the possibility of being 'duffilled' (p. 396), a verb he invented after an incident recounted in *The Great Railway Bazaar* in which a fellow traveller, Mr Duffill, was left stranded in Domodossalo as the Orient Express pulled out of the station, Theroux does literally manage to complete the circle by returning to Southend. However, he denies readers the satisfaction of a decisive closure by terminating his narrative with a hesitant beginning: 'I started down the long pier toward shore, trying to figure out a way of getting home [to London]' (p. 433). Raban's ending, as we might expect from his reference to Sterne, is equally subversive in that *Coasting* closes with him poised between a beginning – *Gosfield Maid* will take to sea again once the weather improves – and efforts to bring the writing of his book to a conclusion:

'How is it going?'
'Slowly.' I typed *Slowly. . . .*
'Where have you got to?'
'*Not far. Only here where we are now, before we go* –' (p. 301)

By laying bare the machinery underlying their texts, Theroux and Raban clearly announce themselves as postmodernists for whom, 'in the absence of a centre or origin, everything [becomes] discourse' (Derrida, p. 151). Viewed from this postmodern perspective, myth ceases to occupy the privileged position accorded it in Jungian psychology as a deep structure capable of communicating absolute truth and becomes instead simply a narrative strategy, one of the plethora of discursive systems through which reality is always mediated and meaning produced. By taking a postmodern stance, Theroux and Raban put themselves in a position to undermine the authority not only of their own works but also of other myth-based narratives, including the one that communicates the Thatcherite understanding of the Falklands War and its implications for Britain as a whole. Thatcher may express herself in terms of absolutes, may achieve decisive narrative closure, may organize her world view around rigid binary oppositions of good and evil, and may claim to be in touch with a transcendental national reality but, so Theroux and Raban's

postmodernist argument would have it, these are no more than
rhetorical strategies designed, paradoxically, to conceal the
rhetorical basis of the truth claims they convey.

Theroux's and Raban's challenges to 'logocentricism', Derrida's
term for the concept of a 'presence' outside the system of language,
and therefore to Thatcherite attempts at conferring the status of
truth on what are merely flawed ideological constructs are not
limited to a foregrounding of the mechanics of the mythic method.
On the contrary, they continue throughout *Kingdom by the Sea*
and *Coasting* to counter Thatcher's strategy of passing off her
own linguistic practices as transparent carriers of absolute truth
by repeatedly drawing attention to the inability of their own,
and by implication, all texts to escape the confines of language.
An important part of Theroux's and Raban's projects is to insist-
ently postulate Britain as a 'variously interpreted' (Theroux,
p. 93) text. By so doing they are able to fragment the monolithic
eternal nation constructed by Thatcher as a fundamental ground
for her ideological system. Perhaps even more significant, though,
is Theroux and Raban's refusal, in yet another distinctively
postmodern move, to offer themselves as anything other than
the deeply subjective and limited chroniclers of patently unheroic
journeys since, by so doing, they call into question Thatcher's
presentation of herself as simultaneously the oracular teller and
infallible hero of her own tale.

Theroux employs several different methods in order to foreground the written status or 'textuality', as Barthes would term
it, of *The Kingdom by the Sea*.[2] For example, he overtly fictionalizes
many of the people he meets during his travels. Thus, on the
train to Margate, having boasted that 'it [is] one of my small
talents to be able to tell a person's name by looking at them',
Theroux confidently asserts that a man who strikes up a conversation with him is named 'Norman Mould' and that 'those old
people up front – they were the Touchmores. The little girl drinking Tizer – Judith Memery. The man behind the *Express* – Roger
Cockpole' (p. 11). The effect of this use of a technique fundamental to the novelist but usually anathema to non-fiction writers
is to draw attention to the issue of generic convention and thus
to foreground the fact that Theroux is producing a text rather
than simply recording what he experiences in some kind of transparent language.

Textual production assumes a similar prominence on those

occasions when Theroux acknowledges that what he writes is not a unique transcription of internal and external reality but is, on the contrary, deeply indebted to other pieces of writing. During his travels in Northern Ireland, for instance, Theroux admits to giving the name 'Mooney's' to his hotel in Belfast 'because it greatly resembled Mrs. Mooney's flophouse in James Joyce's story "The Boarding House"' (p. 304). Shortly afterwards, in an unacknowledged but easily recognized piece of intertexuality, his description of the weather turns out to be a slightly modified version of the final lines of 'The Dead', another story from *Dubliners*: 'Rain was general all over Ireland, falling on every part of the dark central plain, softening the Bog of Allen and blackening Belfast still more' (p. 305).

The centrality of writing to Theroux's project is most obviously asserted, however, when the owner of a bookshop asks him 'to write me a nonfiction book about travelling around the British coast'. Her request makes Theroux so self-conscious about the process in which he is, of course, already involved that he begins to think of his journey in terms of the text into which it will eventually be tranformed: 'I . . . started towards Anstruther, thinking: That was a page, and here's another page, and there's probably a page in Anstruther' (p. 361).

During the incident in *Gosfield Maid*'s saloon described earlier when 'hellfire sermons [were] colliding in mid-air with three panic stricken volumes of *Tristram Shandy*, and *A Sentimental Journey* [was] making a break for it through the galley' (p. 50), Raban similarly collapses all distinctions between text and action. However, it is usually the gap between what happens and how it is transmitted in language that is emphasized in *Coasting*. This gap yawns particularly wide on the occasion when a complete stranger is able to transform Raban's understanding of his own experiences by filtering them through the conventions of adventure fiction. At first Raban is struck by the differences between the 'glum and lacklustre' (p. 244) voyage in which he believes he is involved and the 'rhapsody in blue, punctuated by wonderful characters' (p. 243), the 'glorious summer excursion through wonderland, with a dash of heroic danger added, like Tabasco, to sharpen the cocktail' created by the American tourist, Harvey Swanson. However, he soon finds that literary convention has the power to make him reformulate what he thought he already knew at first hand: 'There were some crazy characters to be

encountered in my voyage too. If you were looking for a
memorable player in the Masque of Britain, could you do better
than find a Minneapolitan of Swedish extraction [i.e. Swenson],
wearing Dress Gordon, and pretending to be a house guest at a
shooting party in a Scottish baronial lodge' (p. 244).

The textualizing process is equally to the fore in Raban's
announcement that he is seeking out Aberdeen, not as a new
experience, but as an already scripted 'success' story that will
play an 'essential part' in his 'own plot' (p. 287). The power of
the impulse to textualize continues to be felt when, having ended
up in one of Aberdeen's sewage outfalls surrounded by shriek-
ing birds rather than in the already written glamorous city, Raban
quickly modifies his narrative goal: 'I thought, at least this feels
more like real life than my imaginary boom town, and if a
boom town is essential to this story, won't the birds do just as
well?' (p. 290).

In postmodern gestures that more directly challenge Thatcherite
essentialism, both Theroux and Raban postulate Britain, as an
'imaginary' place susceptible to repeated textual reshapings
(Theroux, p. 253; Raban, 1986, pp. 15, 246). Thus, Theroux, who
begins *The Kingdom by the Sea* with the remark that 'Britain [is]
the most written-about country in the- world' (p. 1), later claims
that it is a place that has 'seldom been seen plainly, without
literary footnotes' (p. 421) and that 'literature has the capacity
to turn the plainest corner of England into a shrine' (p. 127).
Examples of the way in which Britain exists only as it is written
abound in *The Kingdom by the Sea*. Carrickfergus, for example, is
known to Theroux even before his train reaches the station because
he is familiar with the poetry of Louis MacNeice who grew up
there and wrote about it (p. 267). Similarly, Theroux's experience of Ilfracombe is shaped by what Henry James wrote as he
'tiptoed around the town in 1872' (p. 150).

Britain functions most strikingly as a text, however, in those
extreme cases when a place becomes known almost entirely
through a single piece of literature or when its identity is disseminated amongst a range of discursive systems. Theroux comes
across examples of the one extreme in Devon, which is *Lorna
Doone* country (p. 156) even for people who have not read the
book, and Wigan, where he is always conscious that whatever
he sees is 'what Orwell had seen' (p. 242) or, more accurately,
written. At the other extreme are the Highlands of the clear-

ances which Theroux understands variously as 'an early chapter
in the history of Scotland, . . . a melodramatic painting by Landseer'
and, in the version constructed by his guide's impassioned commentary, 'a lingering injustice' (p. 341). The ability of competing
discourses to wrench Britain into very different shapes is also
evident in the comic contrast between Wordsworth's description
of the Rheidol Valley as 'woods climbing above woods, / In
pomp that fades not' and the dismissive comments of a group
of 'pale tattoed thirteen-year-olds smoking cigarettes', for whom
it is simply, 'fulla fucken trees' (p. 198).

The Britain of *Coasting* is no less a product of writing than
that of *The Kingdom by the Sea*, although Raban's sources are
generally much quirkier than Theroux's. Thus, Raban devotes
his first chapter to a review of the diverse but always unsatisfactory Britains created by the highly eccentric outcasts who have
preceded him on his voyage. These range from the 'evangelical
philanthropist' (p. 22) John MacGregor's urban slum in desperate need of '"strong Tory government" and a great Christian
crusade' (p. 24) to the Catholic neofascist Hilaire Belloc's disgusting democracy crying out for a domestic 'Mussolini' (p. 32).
However, an even more striking example of the ability of writing to give meaning to place is provided by Raban's analysis of
T. E. Brown's poetry, which has had such an impact on the way
in which Manx people understand their island that many of them
can 'recite whole pages at a time' (p. 67). That Brown's Isle of
Man is a construct rather than a reflection of an actual place
with an identity already shaped ahead of its literary representation is underlined by the gap that Raban explores between the
persona of 'the "roughish" sort of chap' (p. 66) adopted by Brown
for his 'immense dialect poems' (p. 65) and the real man, 'who
took a degree at Oxford, then spent a lifetime teaching at an
English public school, Clifton College' (p. 66).

Britain as a whole is subjected to equally thorough textualization
by the workings of the heritage industry since, as Raban puts it,
'the essence of being a good tourist' resides in 'ignoring everything you actually [see] and listening instead to what the guide
[tells] you that you should see' (p. 232). An example of what he
is getting at is provided by the tour guide whose words are able
to transform London from the decaying, ugly, 'bad dream country' with which Raban has long been familiar into a 'wonder-
fully simplified' (p. 233), 'picturebook city' (p. 232). The guide's

'skill' is particularly in evidence when, as a result of his quickly improvised spiel, 'Camelot Tower' ceases to be a 'ripe example of 1960s English council housing' and becomes instead something 'kind of . . . *sweet*' (p. 236).

At a more personal level, Raban reveals how his teenage immersion in the films of James Dean and the works of the Beats enabled him to experience 'Harold Macmillan's England' (p. 160) as 'an imaginary America of bums and hobos, crash-pads and one-night stands' (p. 161) and 'the A33 from Bournemouth to Southampton [as] Highway 1 . . ., going South to LA and San Diego' (p. 162). A similar textualization along American lines displaces the 'grey . . ., gloomy . . ., and genteel' Aberdeen that Raban visited when he was sixteen with 'a boom town' full of 'all-day, all-night saloons, their granite walls drumming with the amplified sound of Dolly Parton and Johnny Cash' (p. 286).

Theroux and Raban complete their dismantlings of the conception of myth as vatic narrative, and thus of Thatcher's attempts to claim absolute authority for her national myth, by the manner in which they construct their dual roles as hero and narrator of the adventures recounted in *The Kingdom by the Sea* and *Coasting*. The version of self that Theroux wishes to present to his readers is first revealed by his choice of 'vague alien' (pp. 5, 126, 197) from amongst the several subject positions, including the much more dignified 'passionate pilgrim', offered by the epigraph to *The Kingdom by the Sea*. Equally incompatible with an heroic conception of self are Theroux's confession that he is 'as bad and lazy as everyone else' (p. 3) and his wry observation that, 'as a man of forty with a knapsack', he must look like 'a serious crank' (p. 68).

Neither, Theroux points out while describing his plan to travel around Britain by a combination of footpaths, branch lines and green buses, does he look upon his journey as an opportunity to seek out heroic challenges: 'I did not intend a stunt or a test of strength or a public display' (p. 8). Any tests that do occur are met with a caution verging on timidity quite alien to traditional ideas of the hero. Thus, Theroux 'hold[s] his breath' (p. 14) and remains a passive observer while a gang of Skinheads rampages through his railway carriage and he moves on in search of alternative lodgings (p. 158) rather than expose his chastity to the test posed by a seductive landlady.

Raban's sea voyage obviously has far more heroic potential

than Theroux's tame wanderings by land. Portland Race is, for example, 'much bigger, much more powerful and has claimed more lives than the piddling whirlpool of Charybdis' (p. 155). Raban, however, constructs a flawed self that is closer to Theroux than to the 'heroic prophetic outcasts' (p. 34) in whose wake he is following. As a 'coaster' (p. 21), Raban is as much slacker as sailor and he readily acknowledges a fear 'of going anywhere near' Portland Race. Thus, he waits 'for perfect weather and a neap tide before daring to creep round its outskirts' (p. 155). To make matters worse, he is so 'giddy with exhilaration at having got past the Race' (p. 157) that he loses concentration and almost collides with the Cherbourg-Weymouth ferry. The scene ends with Raban 'tumbl[ing] harmlessly in the ferry's wake', 'an obvious figure of fun' (p. 158) to a party of French schoolgirls.

Only once, when taking his parents on board in order to provide them with 'a slice of heroic adventure', does Raban postulate a more glorious role for himself. This attempt to create a persona that 'combine[s] all the essential properties of Joshua Slocum, Captain MacWhirr and a Guernsey slaver' serves in the end, however, to simply reinforce Raban's lack of heroic stature. Although originally conceived of as 'a voyage of discovery', the actual excursion, during which Raban finds himself stuck 'in the middle of a floating vicarage garden fete' (p. 179) made up of Sunday afternoon recreational sailors, turns out to be nothing more challenging than what his mother calls 'going boating' (p. 181).

An even worse fate awaits Raban's Oedipal plan to belatedly displace the father whose monstrous image has towered over him in childhood and beyond by 'pilot[ing] my parents across the lonely face of the sea in a neat reversal of roles [in which] the son would turn father, with all the father's air of calm and baffling expertise in the world'. In the event, far from demonstrating his maturity, Raban reveals that he 'doesn't know the ropes' and is finally forced to relinquish the wheel to his father who, with 'beard glint[ing] in the sun' and 'comfortably in command of the occasion' (p. 180), then begins to issue 'captain's orders' (p. 181).

Theroux and Raban also develop a number of strategies intended to strip their roles as narrators of the authority usually claimed by the teller of mythical tales. The space that this particular postmodern gesture opens up for a reassessment of the rhetorical

strategies employed in the mainstream Falklands myth emerges
with particular clarity from a consideration of Theroux's narratorial
persona. In his assertive, confident tone and his fondness for
sweeping generalizations and categorical judgements, Theroux
strongly resembles Thatcher. His narrative, however, is frequently
contextualized in such a way as to call into question the equation
between an authoritative manner and genuine omniscience
that gives so many of Thatcher's pronouncements their air of
infallibility.

One example is provided by Theroux's encounter with a colony
of artists in Hastings. Although he has no prior acquaintance
with these people, Theroux soon offers a number of the decisive
snap judgements to which he is prone. On this occasion, however, the inadequacy of his characterizations of his new friends
is almost immediately exposed by juxtaposition with an insider's
more informed viewpoint. Thus, 'Sara Milverton', whom Theroux
takes to be 'a secure fulfilled person' has had 'a terrible time',
her fellow artist Rooney informs him, married to a man who
has been 'manic for eight years'. Similarly, Orlock, whose joking
manner epitomizes for Theroux the 'optimistic romance and spir-
ited intimacy' (p. 55) of the artistic colony, is quickly transformed
by a few knowledgeable words from Rooney into a desperately
alienated man with seventeen stiches in his arm from a recent
suicide attempt. Even more chastening is Theroux's discovery,
made during a visit to the home town of a man treated as a
comic figure in *The Great Railway Bazaar*, that 'he had not known
[the now deceased Mr Duffill] at all'. Far from being 'a little
crazy', as he had seemed during their brief encounter on the
Orient Express, Duffill turns out to have been 'brave, kind, secret-
ive, resourceful, solitary, brilliant' (p. 401) and much admired in
his native Barrow for his 'adventurous life' (p. 397).

The reliability of Theroux's frequent grand generalizations is
also called into question by the existence of unacknowledged
inconsistencies amongst several equally assertive interpretations
he offers of the significance of the British tendency to look out
to sea. Early in his journey, Theroux declares the practice to be
'an experience of nothingness' (p. 42) and, in similar vein, 'a
way out of England – and . . . the way to the grave' (p. 98). By
the time he gets to Holyhead, however, he seems equally convinced that people look out to sea in search of an alternative to
a British interior that has been 'eroded by ten thousand years of

admiring scrutiny' (p. 222). Finally, on his return to Southend, Theroux claims, still with an air of complete confidence, that the British demonstrate their 'quiet . . . hopeful[ness]' by 'forever standing on a crumbling coast and scanning the horizon' (p. 431).

In addition to those occasions when context undermines his authority as a narrator, Theroux occasionally offers direct comments on the subjectivity of the individual perspective. A meeting with Jonathan Raban in Brighton, for instance, causes him to observe that 'all trips are different, and even two people travelling together have vastly different versions of their journey' (pp. 65–6). The appropriateness of this statement can be confirmed by a reading of the quite dissimilar accounts of Theroux and Raban's meeting that appear in *The Kingdom by the Sea* and *Coasting* (Theroux, pp. 65–8; Raban, 1986, 195–9).

The question of narrative authority is much more overtly thematized in *Coasting* than it is in *The Kingdom by the Sea* because Raban presents himself as a victim of the illusion concerning centred structure that, from a postmodern perspective at least, has long plagued Western thought. Jacques Derrida defines the error in the following way: 'The concept of a centred structure is in fact the concept of a play based on a fundamental ground, a play constituted on the basis of a fundamental immobility and a reassuring certitude, which is itself beyond the reach of play' (pp. 150–1). Raban anticipates that his boat, *Gosfield Maid*, will provide this fundamental ground and expects to remain 'at a slight oblique angle to the rest of society on shore' (p. 114) throughout his coastal voyage, thereby gaining a privileged vantage point close to but nevertheless outside and beyond the influence of Britain, the structure he is trying to define. So long as he remains at sea, Raban argues, he has 'absolute freedom' (p. 5) and is located in 'a wilderness [that] serves as an elemental point of continuity from which it's possible to measure the pace of the civilization on its outer rim' (p. 39).

However, no sooner has Raban postulated himself as 'a private person – in the Greek word, an *idiot*' (p. 48), content to run his ship while 'Mrs Thatcher [runs] hers as she please[s]' (p. 140), than the word 'idiot' begins to take on its more commonplace English meaning. Following a childhood dominated by a father who 'was England . . ., the Conservative Party in person, the Army in person, the Church in person, the Public School system in person, the Dunkirk spirit in person, Manliness, Discipline, Duty,

Self Sacrifice and all the rest' (p. 18), Raban would like nothing
more than to assume the detached stance of the outsider. This
choice, though, is simply not open to him any more than it is to
the rest of us and, in the course of his voyage, he is caught up
repeatedly in the play of the very structures that he is intent
upon immobilizing.

Thus, as he looks at television pictures of 'the first ships sail[ing]
from Portsmouth [en route for the Falklands] (p. 114), Raban
discovers that his 'scepticism about this political adventure [is
not] waterproof' and he is left 'blubbering with silly pride in
Queen and Country' (p. 115). Similarly, although he begins his
visit to the Britannia Royal Navy College in Dartmouth in the
stance of a disinterested researcher seeking insight into the anachronistic impulses stirred up by the Falklands War, Raban ends
up 'stranded' in his insecure boyhood past: 'Talking to the Captain, I felt that I was being interviewed for a place in the college
and was being found wanting on every account' (p. 125). Neither
can Raban maintain his equilibrium once he sets foot for the
first time since his teenage years in Lymington, despite an initial scan through his binoculars to assure himself that there is
'no sign, anywhere, of 1959. Not a single scowling youth on the
foreshore' (p. 160): 'it was hard to recover my landlegs as the
streets rose and sank in a sickmaking swell. On home ground
one moment, in bottomless water next, I floundered up Quay
Hill and out into the High Street' (p. 164).

Any lingering illusions Raban might have about his special
powers as an author are shattered when actual experience inter-
venes to disabuse him of the essentialist idea underlying the
privileged position that he had previously claimed for life aboard
Gosfield Maid. During his visit to Lyme Bay, the site of a major
lobster fishery, Raban encounters a number of unemployed men
who have responded to the free enterprise spirit of the 1980s by
'turn[ing] to the sea as the last place where a man without capi-
tal might make an independent living', only to discover that 'they
were coming too late, to a sea which was rivalling the land in
making men who worked on it redundant' (p. 147). The economic forces at work in Thatcher's Britain are revealed, then, to
extend out into the ocean. As a result, and contrary to Raban's
Wordsworthian notion of Britain's coastal waters as a 'wilderness' (p. 39) beyond the influence of cultural forces, the sea turns
out to be not very different from a coal mine or a steel mill.

CHALLENGING THE FALKLANDS MYTH

Implicit within Theroux's and Raban's postmodern contextualizing of their own archetypal narratives is, as we have already seen, an extremely effective challenge to the official Falklands myth. This challenge also lays the groundwork for a more direct assault on the no longer monolithic framework of meaning erected around the Falklands War by Conservative politicians and the tabloid press. Having lost the privileged status conferred on it by the transformation of messy reality into myth, and therefore no longer able to terminate the play of signification, the Thatcherite version of the Falklands War now becomes nothing more than a typically subjective, unreliable and provisional set of discursive practices not only susceptible to critical analysis but also vulnerable to repositioning within rival discourses.

In moving from a postmodern assessment of Thatcher's rhetorical practices to a more direct attack on the mainstream Falklands myth, Theroux and Raban offer scathing analyses of tabloid and parliamentary manifestations of the voice of Thatcherite orthodoxy and draw attention to the mixture of scepticism, indifference, nostalgia and bellicosity with which the British public 'reads' the supposedly inspiring official version of events. The end result of their efforts is to raise serious questions about the validity of Thatcher's claims to be unifying a previously fragmented body politic around widespread consent for her essentialist tale of an ancient nation rising once again to take on the challenge provided by a moment of national crisis.

Apart from one reference to 'Maggie's ... nonsense' (p. 336), Theroux's reassessment of the Falklands myth is based almost exclusively on his reading of what a politically aware bus driver identifies as 'Tory' (p. 114) tabloid newspaper headlines. Squeezed into the tight space occupied by the headline in conventional journalistic practice, the Falklands myth ceases to be at all noble or full of high purpose. Instead, it takes on intolerant, xenophobic, quarrelsome and, above all, violent characteristics. The *Sun*, for example, responds to the sinking of the *'General Belgrano* and the twelve hundred dead men' with 'SUNK!', 'the first', Theroux comments, 'of many gloating headlines' (p. 31). A later 'gutter press' headline, 'ARGIES LOSE TWO!' (p. 94), causes Theroux to comment that 'all the headlines exulted when Argentina suffered casualties, but British losses were somewhat understated, and most of the time it was reported in the language of British sports reporting' (pp. 94–5).

For Theroux the tabloid version of the Falklands myth is not only ugly but often based on blatant lies. Mrs Wheeker, a woman he meets in a cafe at Mawgan Porth, is totally convinced by the tabloid claim that, 'We're in this all alone'. Nevertheless, as Theroux points out, the statement is untrue and denies the simple fact that 'the United States had given material support to the British' (p. 145). Later, faced with 'more gloating' stories in pro-Government newspapers claiming that the new 'Falklands spirit' has inspired 'the travelling public' to 'cop[e] magnificently with the [railway] strike', Theroux draws on his own direct experience as a would-be passenger to state, in a laconic mimickry of the tabloid headline, 'More lies' (pp. 404–5).

Theroux also explores the gap between official claims that the Falklands War is uniting the British public around a noble common cause and the actual response of those he encounters during his travels. For Theroux, the mythic interpretation that Thatcher and her supporters have imposed upon the war rarely achieves its goal of stirring up the people of Britain into a patriotic frenzy. The Lucketts, a couple he meets on their way to Southampton to 'see the *Queen Elizabeth II* set sail for the Falklands', are, for example, obviously motivated in part by pride. Nevertheless, the embarrassed way in which they euphemistically refer to 'this Falklands business' (p. 79) when speaking of the great national crusade suggests to Theroux that, 'if it had been raining, they would not have gone' (p. 80). A Deal landlady, Mrs Sneath, also fails to respond with much enthusiasm to the news of the sinking of the *General Belgrano*, displaying instead a sense of guilt that she seeks to alleviate with the feeble argument that the Argentinians had been planning to eat the Falkland Islanders' 'British sheep' (p. 30).

Later, Theroux is struck by how, although there is 'a kind of disrespect these days in not turning on [the television]', few people actually pay much attention to 'the Falklands news': 'Donald was watching the moving arrows on the Falklands map and listening to Florence talking about ligaments, and he said, "I spent me 'ole life in 'ornchurch"' (p. 138). Those who do make the effort to understand what is happening in the Falklands seem to Theroux to be not at all 'jingoistic' and 'swagger[ing]' but, rather, 'ashamed and confused' at the defeat of 'pathetic, ramshackle, and unlucky [Argentina] with [its] conscript army of very young boys' (p. 152).

What enthusiasm there is for the Falklands War amongst a British population so fragmented that a Welshman is stirred only by the death of a man named Jones (p. 187) is the product, according to Theroux, of its ability to provide an outlet for the two regressive urges that, as we will see later, are central to his own myth of Britain. The first is the nostalgic reaction displayed by petit bourgeois people who express their dissatisfaction with life in contemporary Britain through an intense response to the physical remoteness and anachronistic military style of the Falklands War. Amongst their numbers are the 'army veterans on the park benches of Shanklin' whose hearts are 'gladdened' by news of 'bombing missions and aerial dogfights' (p. 84) and 'Mrs. Mullion and Miss Custis at the Britannia in Combe Martin, who, after some decent platitudes, wandered from talk of the Falklands to extensive reminiscing about the Second World War' (pp. 152–3).

The second urge is the violent one that typifies the reaction to the war of far-right Conservatives who begin to behave, in an ironic juxtaposition we have already observed in Nick Perry's *Arrivederci Millwall*, like the Skinheads and other of Britain's alienated youth encountered by Theroux at various points in his journey. Theroux's first experience of the ability of the Falklands War to provide a release for pent-up violent impulses occurs as he walks along the promenade in Blackpool and observes how people become 'snorting and vengeful-looking' while reading 'news of the bloody war' (p. 247). The class affiliations of such people become clear during a later encounter with a group of 'bluster[ing]' anglers, 'all Tories', who call 'the Prime Minister "Maggie"' and want 'to shoot the man being interviewed' on the television as well as 'half the Labour Party' (p. 336).

Raban also uncovers a revealing subtext to the official Falklands myth in television and tabloid press coverage of the war. His analysis is rather more complex than Theroux's, however, in that it insists on the existence of an intimate relationship between the violent and nostalgic aspects of this subtext and makes explicit connections between media and parliamentary discourse. Raban completes his subversive reading of the Falklands myth by identifying amongst the melange of high purpose, xenophobia, jingoism, intolerance, bloodlust, escapism and sentimentality that characterizes the discursive practices of both journalists and politicians a deep strain of cynicism and hypocrisy.

For Raban, as much as for Theroux, intimidatory headlines such as 'STICK THIS UP YOUR JUNTA!', 'INTO BATTLE!', 'FULL AHEAD FOR WAR!', 'DEADLINE TONIGHT!', and 'HIGH NOON!' (pp. 200–1), that 'squeal with infantile excitement at the prospect of the atrocities to come' (p. 200), are a distillation of the way in which right-wing tabloid journalists interpret the Falklands War. For 'the *Sun*, the *Mail* and the *Express*' (p. 150), the war is not ultimately a noble cause or a moral crusade to be entered into in a serious and sombre spirit but 'a national holiday' that offers an outlet for the 'bloodthirstiness and bigotry' (p. 158) of a British public transformed into 'whoop[ing] and [yell]ing ' 'schoolboys' (p. 100): 'The message of the headline writers was that nothing would give the British more satisfaction than to wipe that smile off Galtieri's face and crack the joints of both those thumbs' (p. 100). The moral vacancy of the tabloid press is fully confirmed with Raban's realization that much of the 'hatred' and 'bigotry' that fill its pages is not even genuinely felt. On the contrary, these ugly but potentially powerful emotions are 'mass produced' to serve the interests of the Government and to milk the full potential from 'a bestselling war' (p. 150).

Television cameras also function, in Raban's view, as 'offensive weapons' (p. 114). He notes, for example, how television creates a visual image of the Argentinian leader 'infinitely, luxuriously, more hateable than that of Hitler' (pp. 113–14) in order to encourage the British public to go beyond the 'unbridled distaste' (p. 113) it already feels for Galtieri's 'loathsome face' (p. 114). Similarly, 'bloodcurdling' television coverage of the task force during its voyage south becomes 'a form of warfare in its own right', an 'assault by photomontage, with flags superimposed over phalluses and songs over aeroplanes, gun-muzzles and bayonets', targeted at 'the Argentinian forces and their effete supremo [about] to be raped by the greater potency of the British' (p. 136).

However, the 'reporter's voice' that accompanies these violent images of the task force is 'an earnest pastiche of the Britain-can-take-it style of Movietone News in the 1940s' (p. 136), thus revealing that, even at its most bloodthirsty, the televisual presentation of the Falklands War is also deeply nostalgic. Nostalgia is even more to the forefront at other times. As Raban watches the fleet sail from Portsmouth, for instance, the image on his appropriately 'old-fashioned black and white' television set 'shatter[s] every few seconds'. This hardly matters, though, because what he is viewing, with its 'pipe bands, bunting, flags, kisses, tears, waved handkerchiefs', is 'such a famous picture' (p. 114) that it scarcely requires a specific representation in order for its meaning to be grasped and an appropriately sentimental response to be evoked.

This version of the Falklands War with its crass and sometimes patently hypocritical appeal to some of the British public's ugliest and most sentimental emotions seems on the surface to be seriously at odds with the Government's presentation of the struggle with Argentina as a moral crusade in defence of the weak against the strong. In Raban's view, however, this is not at all the case as he sets out to demonstrate through a searching analysis of the emergency debate of 3 April. Because the debate is transmitted on the radio, Raban is spared the distracting visual images of television. He is therefore able to pay close attention to tone as well as content while listening to speeches delivered by the Prime Minister and her colleagues. Consequently, he is able to identify a striking contrast between the surprising lack of conviction with which Thatcher sketches out for the first time the broad outlines of the official Falklands myth and the primitive fervour that 'claret-and-havana Tory voice[s]' put into blowing up their jingoistic, xenophobic and deeply nostalgic 'rhetorical balloon' (p. 105).

Thatcher sounds, to Raban's ears, like a 'cross nanny' about to send 'the children . . . to bed without any tea' (p. 104). She also keeps on 'putting her emphases in the wrong places', thereby exposing her declaration of supposedly heartfelt commitment to the Falkland Islands and its inhabitants as 'ghost-written' (p. 104). Her parliamentary colleagues, on the other hand, speaking in a language that communicates by sound rather than sense, give vent to a whole range of sincere but violent emotions. Thus, as he listens to a succession of Conservative speakers, Raban hears 'a long indigestion of approval' in response to a description of the Argentinian leaders as 'this jumped-up junta of barbarous men'; a 'low growl of warning' followed by 'roar[s] and jeer[s]' (p. 105) aimed at the speaker who dares to suggest that Britain should restrict its retaliation against the invasion to seeking Argentinian exclusion from the upcoming World Cup of Football; and a 'gruff' of assent and 'cheers' (p. 106) following an attack on the Foreign Office. Interspersed with this 'verbal bloodletting', which he also refers to as the 'sound of men baying like a wolf pack', Raban hears a strain of deep nostalgia. This nostalgia is first given voice when the Conservative benches respond to a description of the Falkland Islanders' 'British blood and bone' with 'the right kind of rousing tune'. It is also heard in the cries of 'Hear, hear!' (p. 107) that are inspired by a reference to 'the Duke of Wellington' at 'Torres Vedras' (p. 105).

The different ways in which the emergency debate fails to achieve the status of rational discourse leads Raban to two important conclusions about the structure of meaning erected by the Conservative Party around the Falklands War. First, when expressed in a speech so poorly understood by the deliverer that a momentary loss of concentration on Raban's part makes it seem 'as if [Thatcher is] drifting out of English and into Danish' (p. 104), the official Falklands myth emerges as a cynical and self-serving fabrication. Second, as Raban suggests through the mixture of animal and musical images that he uses to communicate the tone of the emergency debate, any genuine convictions Conservative members of Parliament might hold about the significance of the Falklands War spring from deeply atavistic sources rather than reasoned reflection.

A Governmental discourse whose main features are a parroted and transparently hypocritical evocation of noble goals and a passionately nonsensical expression of violent and nostalgic sentiments is scarcely less absurd in Raban's view than the hysterical outpourings of the tabloid press and the mixture of bloodthirstiness and nostalgia that passes for television news reporting. In order to underline the absurdity of what has just been broadcast from the House of Commons, Raban constructs a richly parodic version of the interchange between the Prime Minister and her parliamentary colleagues out of a comic dialogue he overhears in a bar. The Thatcher part is taken by Pepe the parrot with his repeated cries of 'Bye bye, shut up, hullo!' and that of her fellow parliamentarians by a 'florid man with fierce grey handlebar moustaches' (p. 108) who rants about 'football hooligans, the short sharp shock, welfare scroungers and how Mussolini made the trains run on time' (p. 109).

As they do for Theroux, so observations of public reaction to the Falklands War also play an important part in shaping Raban's sceptical view of official discourse. Thatcher's claims to have united the nation around a common cause lose much of their credibility, for instance, in the face of the uneven and frequently unenthusiastic response to the war that Raban encounters on his travels. The task force might receive the 'vociferous support' of the 'tweedy and choleric classes' (p. 200) but neither the 'fishermen' who visit Raban's boat in Lyme Regis nor the people he encounters in 'the seaside towns where *Gosfield Maid* [takes] up lodgings' (p. 201) seem to be 'in the least impressed by the sabre rattling' (p. 143) or show many signs of 'going wild with patriotic fervour' (p. 201). For most people, a friend tells Raban, the war is 'just something else that's on the TV' (p. 228), a view that receives support from the failure of ecstatic tabloid newspaper headlines to stir up any postvictory euphoria in Hull: 'I looked for signs of rejoicing on the wharves and in the streets around the Fish Dock, but if people were dancing in Hull, they must have been doing it very quietly, and indoors' (p. 269).

The war's only widespread appeal derives, in Raban's view, from the opportunities this 'phantasmal imperial exercise' (p. 117) provides for people to escape, if only temporarily, from the grim realities of life in contemporary Britain. Thus, for Raban, it is neither Thatcher's speech nor violent backbench ranting that captures the public's imagination but rather the most blatantly nostalgic parts of the parliamentary debate, during which Britain can be overheard 'talking in a dream' (p. 107) about 'the naval fleet . . . sailing backwards, into last year's autumn, or maybe some other autumn belonging to the Duke of Wellington or another monarch' (p. 106).

The mood of a nation living 'a daydream' (p. 187) in which it is out on a public school 'field day' (p. 135) circa 1959 is most completely expressed in two texts quoted by Raban in *Coasting*. The first is a letter 'written in a dream' by a Welsh Guardsman shortly after embarking on the *QE2* in which he tells his 'Dear Mummy' about 'the green fields of England' and his determination 'to do [his] duty to [his] country and [his] men' (p. 116). The second is a song, 'I Love This Land' – performed by Vera Lynn, 'the "Forces Sweetheart", from a thousand ENSA concerts and wartime radio broadcasts' (p. 186) – that 'enshrine[s] a wonderful, vainglorious untruth' about the immortality and immutability of Britain, thereby 'stat[ing] – more nakedly than anyone had dared to do so far – the terms of the daydream in which Britain was living in 1982' (p. 187).

Although the exercise in 'History on the cheap' in which the
British people become engulfed during 'the spring of '82' (p. 153)
seems generally free of the violent emotions expressed in the
media and by many of the speakers in the House of Commons
debate, Raban does suggest, on at least one occasion, that for
the public at large, as for journalists and politicians, there are
close links between nostalgia and violence:

> Standing alone in the world was what the British liked to believe
> that they did best. It brought out the Dunkirk spirit, which
> was now busily being rebottled as the Falklands Spirit . . . It
> brought out, in the British Isles at large, all the crabbiness, the
> xenophobia, the determination to take the rest of the world
> down a peg, the hunch-shouldered go-it-alone-ism, of the Manx
> – and of the Falklanders themselves. (p. 219)

By his insistence here and elsewhere in *Coasting* on the connection between violence and nostalgia, Raban is almost certainly
proposing that these very different emotions serve a similar function. For Raban, violence, which has the ability to consume the
individual's entire attention, can be just as effective as nostalgia
in providing a distraction from the unwelcome demands of the
present. His position is thus similar to that of Don DeLillo's
character, Murray Jay Siskind, who argues in *White Noise* that
'war is the form nostalgia takes when men are hard pressed to
say something good about their country' (p. 258).

ALTERNATIVE NATIONAL MYTHOLOGIES

The final and boldest strategy employed by Theroux and Raban
to extricate the Falklands War from the privileged position it
occupies in the Thatcherite myth of Britain is to incorporate it
into their own deeply subversive national myths. As post-
modernists, Theroux and Raban are not, of course, seeking to
displace Thatcher's truth claims with any absolutist assertions
of their own. From a postmodern perspective, the Falkland Islands
and, by implication, the war that was fought there are, after all,
simply a 'blankness' capable of '*signifying*' 'nothing or everything'
(Raban, 1986, p. 113). However, because of their willingness to
point up the provisionality of what they write and to foreground

their discursive practices, it is likely that many readers will be persuaded that Theroux's and Raban's interpretations of the contemporary British situation have more credibility than Thatcher's.

Both Theroux and Raban share Thatcher's vision of Britain as a nation in decline. However, their depictions of the superior past, their explanations for this decline and their prognostications for the future are all radically at odds with hers. Theroux, for instance, creates a much less romantic picture of the past than Thatcher does. This is not to say, however, that his past is necessarily closer to historical fact than hers for, like Thatcher's, Theroux's past is largely a projection of his own fantasies. The past that Theroux conjures up in his imagination is an essentially petit bourgeois one, characterized by qualities such as comfort, convenience, compromise, practicality and operating primarily by a pragmatic standard of usefulness.

On one occasion, Theroux expresses his idea of the perfect Britain through a description of the quintessential High Street – with 'shops selling sensible, practical merchandise', plentiful 'tea shops; a busy bus route' and 'a park bench every twenty yards' – which he offers up to the reader as 'a resumé of middle-class English civilization' (p. 57). Even closer to the heart of Theroux's idealized conception of the British past, however, is the branch line railway which he regards as 'the highest stage of civilization' (p. 136) because it manages to be 'useful' (p. 148) and 'serviceable' (p. 84) without 'disturb[ing] . . ., spoil[ing] . . . [or] alter[ing] the landscape' (p. 136). The image of 'the train on a rocky shore, rolling through the storm' (p. 115) at Teignmouth or 'moving majestically through the dale' 'where the River Esk widened just above Whitby' (p. 381) is, for Theroux, not only 'one of the most beautiful sights in the world' (p. 115) but the epitome of a perfect compromise between industrialization and nature: 'It was the machine in the garden, but it was a gentle machine' (p. 136).

Images of urban landscapes created to serve commercial or industrial ends but nevertheless aesthetically pleasing and/or compatible with nature also illustrate the central role played in Theroux's vision of a superior past by a spirit of compromise between contending interests, particularly the human, the natural and the materialistic or economic. Thus, Theroux admires the 'elegance' of 'late-Georgian terraces' (p. 104) in Weymouth and the 'ample contours' (p. 391) of Scarborough. Even more striking to him is the way in which the use of 'fine polished versions' of the local granite as a building material makes Scottish coastal towns such as Oban look as if they have been 'thrown out of the ground' (p. 316). Another example of an appropriate balance between the constructed and the natural is Sandwich, 'a lovely place surrounded by flat green fields' (p. 25).

There are, of course, many places in Britain, such as Wigan – where Orwell, writing as far back as the 1930s, found 'labyrinths of little black houses blackened by smoke, festering in planless chaos round miry alleys and little cindered yards' (p. 241) – that are not so easily accommodated within the imaginary townscape of Theroux's idealized past. Even here, though, Theroux identifies in the useful and productive labour that used to go on in Wigan, 'a kind of grubby vitality' and a sense of 'possibility' completely absent from its 'lifeless' (p. 242) postindustrial present.

As the survival of Weymouth, Scarborough and Sandwich clearly demonstrates, fragments of this idealized past are to be found in Theroux's version of contemporary Britain. He is particularly struck, for example, by the way in which a 'still sturdy' Tenby has 'been maintained' and has 'mellowed' (p. 180) and, of course, he is delighted whenever he comes across a still functioning branch line. However, Theroux is convinced that such survivals are incompatible with the current political ethos and are therefore the result of accidents or of special circumstances. This ethos is identified by Theroux as a Thatcherite one in which profit is always given priority over human or environmental considerations. Under such a profit-driven regime, towns that have lost their economic base are simply left to rot regardless of the needs of their inhabitants. These include Holyhead which has 'blacken[ed] like an extremity with gangrene' (p. 222), Belfast which is in its 'death agony' (p. 268) and Jarrow which looks like it has 'just lost a war' (p. 375). Worst of all is the 'great silence' that has replaced the 'racket of [Wigan's] machines' (p. 243).

Neither is survival guaranteed even for those services and buildings that continue to have an obvious function. Many of the branch lines still in operation, for example, continue to meet a real need for public transportation. However, Theroux is acutely aware that any, like the line from Ashford to Hastings, that are 'useful but unprofitable' (p. 50), are in imminent danger of closure. Inevitably, they will be replaced by 'dangerous speedway[s] of dinky cars and whining motor bikes' (p. 388). Similarly, any 'grand [and still serviceable] Victorian structure', such as the ferry station at

Rock Ferry, is likely to be demolished to make way for buildings 'made of corrugated plastic sheets bolted to iron pipes' that 'do not need repainting' (p. 231) and are therefore cheaper to maintain.

Wherever innovation rather than neglect or closure has followed from a concern with profitability the result is usually even more dispiriting. Industrial development can lead, for instance, to a 'ten mile' strip of buildings, all of them 'frail and temporary' (p. 174), as it does on the outskirts of Bristol. Even worse is the 'four-legged oil rig look[ing] like a mechanical sea monster defecating in shallow water' (p. 350) that is the source of Aberdeen's new prosperity. The particular scorn that Theroux reserves for the privileging of profits over a respect for nature is underlined in this instance by his use of excremental imagery. Theroux is no less scathing when he describes the 'three or four gigantic gray slabs' of the 'Trawsfynydd Nuclear Power Station', as a 'monstrosity', amongst 'lovely mountains' (p. 215).

According to the analysis of contemporary Britain developed in *The Kingdom by the Sea*, the emergence of a vast new service economy, which Thatcher regarded as the likeliest source of future national prosperity, has caused further damage to both urban and rural landscapes. Theroux notes, for example, the contrast between the 'sublime charm of the [original] twisty streets and stone cottages' (p. 125) of St Ives and the 'ridiculous' paraphenalia associated with its tourist industry: 'the postcards with kittens in the foreground of harbour scenes . . ., the bumper stickers, the sweatshirts with slogans printed on them . . ., and the shops full of bogus handicrafts' (pp. 125–6). Equally destructive products of increased tourism are the 'caravan settlements [which are] always hideous and always in the loveliest coves' (p. 203) and the 'sleazy paradise[s]' (p. 164) of Butlins Holiday Camps.

As far as Theroux is concerned, then, change motivated entirely by the profit motive is almost always a form of vandalism with serious negative consequences for the human spirit. The spiritual dimensions of such acts of economically inspired despoliation are brought into sharp focus by successive descriptions of the 'torrent of traffic' that has displaced 'Dickens' birthplace'; of the 'gas station' standing on the site of the house where 'Shelley wrote "Grant, O Darkling Woods, My Sweet Repose"' (p. 81); and of the typical 'defunct church' 'made into a bingo hall, or else torn down and a gas station built in its place' (p. 82).

Given the dehumanizing tendencies inherent in the process of

change that he observes throughout his journey, Theroux can
envisage Britain's future only as the bleakest and most violent
of dystopias. The ever-increasing value accorded to money in
what is, despite pockets of prosperity, a country in economic
decline thus promises a future of 'hard-edged horror' (p. 357) in
which the poor will 'be dangerous and pitiful' and 'probably
hunt[ed] . . . for sport' by 'the rich' (p. 52) and in which every
city will have its 'Control Zone' and be 'sealed' (p. 287) like Belfast
or Derry. The only relief likely to be available to the underclass
in this repressive future will be found in the 'coastal town of
the future', the 'tinselly New Jerusalem' (p. 161) of Butlin's, a
'prison'-like place 'in which people [will be] treated more or less
like animals in a zoo' (p. 164).

For Theroux, death is written everywhere on 'the face of the
future' (p. 252), metaphorically in his comparison of Butlins with
'Jonestown' (p. 160), literally in the concentration camps predicted
by a poem he sees inscribed in a bus shelter (p. 224), and most
definitively in several intimations of nuclear apocalypse. These
include a Scotsman's prediction that 'there'll be naebody left'
after the 'Third World War' (p. 315), Theroux's description of
the Windscale (now Sellafield) nuclear power plant as possessing
'the simplicity and proportions of an enormous tomb' (p. 252),
and the strong sensation that Theroux experiences amidst the
empty landscape of Cape Wrath of being transported into 'the
world after a catastrophic bomb' (p. 340).

In direct contradiction, then, of the Thatcherite vision of a capitalist nirvana, Theroux foresees that the relentless pursuit of selfish
and materialistic goals will end with the transformation of Britain into 'a pulverized civilization' (p. 170). Put in another way
more in keeping with the mythic methods employed by Thatcher
and Theroux, Britain will be become a wasteland. This particular image of nation is foregrounded as Theroux passes close to
Cliftonville where, 'in 1921', T. S. Eliot was 'having a mild nervous
breakdown' (p. 21). Thus, as he walks on Margate Sands, Theroux
comments that, 'I could connect nothing with nothing' (p. 16), a
direct echo of the words of the Thames maiden who lost her
virginity there in *The Wasteland*. Eliot's poem is also obviously
very much in Theroux's mind when he describes a clairvoyant
in Broadstairs as 'the wisest woman in Europe' (p. 22).

Theroux finally incorporates his interpretation of the Falklands
myth into this subversive national story, thereby completing his

assault on the authority of Thatcherite ideology. This process begins with Theroux's suggestion that, as they move ever closer to a wasteland situation, the only responses available to all but the few British people with positions of power will be to either retreat even further than they do now into nostalgia or to commit acts of increasingly savage violence. Each person's response, however, will be the product, as is already the case, not of individual choice but of social class, the petit bourgeoisie behaving in an escapist manner while the alienated young conduct themselves in angry and aggressive ways. Theroux demonstrates his thesis by recounting an incident in which a railway carriage comes to stand for the present and future nation.

Thus, as he travels on a Bank Holiday train to Southend, Theroux is able to observe how 'neatly dressed' (p. 10) families and elderly people perform elaborate tea-drinking and sandwich-eating rituals, conduct highly stylized conversations about the weather and each other's health, and conform to strict standards of formal behaviour as a way of withdrawing into a world where they can pretend that 'the Sunday peace of . . . jogging train[s]' (p. 14) is still a reality even as a group of 'insectile and dangerous' looking Skinheads rampage through the carriage, screaming obscenities and fighting amongst themselves. For Theroux, who notes the Skinheads' 'Union Jack' (p. 13) tattoos, both types of behaviour are characteristically British and yet so incompatible with each other that he has difficulty 'remember[ing] Dickens or Merrie England or "this sceptred isle" or the darling buds of May [while] so near the seven roaring Skinheads' (p. 15).

By emphasizing how deeply entrenched are the coping mechanisms employed by the two groups of British people who play a part in the railway carriage scene, Theroux makes it clear that, as far as he is concerned, there is little hope of any widespread spirit of fresh hope emerging from the Falklands War. On the contrary, he would argue, the war is important only to the extent that it provides the British public with new outlets for expressing nostalgic and violent tendencies already well established as their main ways of dealing with an ever-increasing sense of helplessness and despair. Theroux further emphasizes that the Falklands War is not unique in stimulating a petit bourgeois tendency towards nostalgia by focusing attention at various points in his journey on the 'romanticized' (p. 87) view of smuggling adopted by Isle of Wight tourists; on Mr Pitchford's memories of 'two-tier buses, very big ones, drawn by horses' (p. 90); on a card in a shop window headed 'Catholics – Remember These Words?' and announcing a mass in Latin (p. 91); and, above all, on the behaviour of railway buffs who spend their free time travelling by steam train on short stretches of private railway line.

Theroux, who values the past only in so far as it can provide a practical model for the present, is generally unsympathetic towards these different expressions of the nostalgic impulse. As far as he is concerned, 'reminiscing', the characteristic discourse of nostalgia, is usually synonymous with 'gloating or boasting, or even lying' (p. 90). In order to illustrate his point, Theroux calls attention to the way in which people who are desperate to escape an unsatisfactory present fabricate a glamorous past by transforming the 'grubby and mendacious' (p. 88) activities of smugglers into heroic and courageous deeds.

Nostalgia is cast in an even more unfavourable light by Theroux's acerbic comments about the railway buffs he frequently encounters on his travels around the British Isles. Much to his disgust, railway buffs, who spend their time on private lines such as the 'twenty-five miles operating between Minehead and Taunton' (pp. 166–7), are 'not really interested in going anywhere'. Instead, they '[pretend] to be passengers', their itinerary being always 'there and back' (p. 167), and occupy themselves during their simulated journeys with spurious 'memories of the old days': 'Crikey, Rafe, don't it take you back?' (p. 168). The eminently useful branch line trains are therefore of no interest to these people unless the service is 'soon to be swept away', in which case they will indulge in 'joy-riding', something Theroux regards as 'worse than indecent' and 'a mild form of necrophilia' (p. 147). Railway buffery is seen at its most absurd in the behaviour of a man who, having gone as far as he can on a reopened narrow gauge line, prefers to travel the 'twenty-seven stop-and-go miles back to Bangor' in his 'little Ford Cortina' rather than make use of a convenient diesel train, which he scornfully dismisses as 'a tin box' (p. 26).

This assessment of the role played by nostalgia in contemporary British life serves to flesh out Theroux's own revisionist national myth; equally important, it adds an extra dimension to his critique of the official Falklands myth by diminishing what Thatcher presented as a meaningful retrieval of the national heritage to self-indulgent wallowing in a romantically falsified past on a par with the pointless activities of railway buffs. Perhaps even more effective, though, in deglamorizing the Falklands War are the steps taken by Theroux to connect what is happening in the South Atlantic to the ugly strain of violence that he has uncovered in contemporary British culture. This connection is firmly established by the juxtaposition of details of daily life in Britain and snippets of war reports. Thus, on one occasion, while watching the television in anticipation of Falklands news, Theroux hears instead of 'two women . . . murdered ("savagely") in some woods near Aldershot' (p. 91). Similarly, as he walks through Combe Martin, Theroux first eavesdrops on a news reporter announcing that 'seven more Argentinian aircraft have been shot down' and that 'so far four hundred and fifty men had been killed in the Falklands' fighting' (p. 150–1) and then comes upon a motorcycle gang of 'the wildest and scruffiest youths' who model 'themselves on Hell's Angels' (p. 151). Finally, in probably the most telling juxtaposition, Theroux strays into the Aberporth rocket range, where 'the incautious walker risked being blown up' (p. 195), shortly after learning about the deaths of 'two hundred and fifty men' in the equally rural setting of 'a small sheep station at Goose Green' (p. 194).

Theroux is also clearly alluding to the Falklands War when he employs military metaphors to further evoke the violent spirit abroad in Britain. Thus, Butlins at Bognor, with its 'sounds of bugles' and 'barracklike' (p. 73) buildings, resembles an army camp, people lying on the beach look like the 'war wounded' (p. 169), and the economically depressed town of Jarrow appears to have 'just lost a war' (p. 375). As he walks through this militarized landscape, Theroux compares himself to a 'commando' (p. 160) and, while in Yorkshire, prepares for a possible encounter with Barry Prudhon, an actual former commando turned psychopathic killer (p. 379).

Raban's equally subjective view of the past is somewhat less affirmative than Theroux's because, as the renegade last in line of a Tory, Church of England, military family, he has often experienced Britain as insular, snobbish and xenophobic. Nevertheless, he identifies loss rather than gain in the historical processes of his own lifetime. During the 1950s, when he saw himself as an 'angelheaded hipster' teenager, for example, Raban hated the 'bourgeois burg' of Lymington. Returning there in 1982, however, and observing the displacement of the 'retired gentry' (p. 164) and 'rear-admirals' (p. 165) by 'barbarians of the new'

(p. 166), with their 'gold-card' (p. 168) funded conspicuous consumption, their 'marinas' 'quarried out' of 'the saltings', and their fibreglass yachts, 'big plastic toys [that spend] most of their time lying idle' (p. 166), Raban finds himself 'indignantly on the side of the buffers' (p. 167). Raban's dislike is intensified by the fact that each marina represents 'just a small tithe of the profits still to be made in Mrs Thatcher's England' and 'behind each mean-eyed boat' he sees 'the rich pickings of the property business, the money markets, the motor trade, North Sea Oil, silicon chippery or the legerdemain of tax accountancy' (p. 168).

These children of Thatcherism assume almost demonic proportions in Raban's suggestion that, just as they have 'violated the landscape and the wild things that lived there' (p. 167) in pursuit of their selfish pleasures, so they have more generally attenuated the natural world through their business activities. Thus, as a consequence of property development, the 'exquisite' River Yealm, with its 'country silence, its steep terraces of dripping evergreens and its glassy water' (p. 103), has been diminished to 'an estate agents' desirable view' (p. 108).

The situation worsens for Raban with the discovery made in the course of his journey around the British coastline that, at the same time as a network of profit centres has been developing and speculative opportunities have been increasing, 'three million [have been left] unemployed' (p. 202) by a widespread decline amongst the older industries that once produced the basic essentials needed to sustain the very life of the nation. Fisheries all around the coastline have been ruined by falling fish stocks and, as a result of Iceland's victory in the Cod War, the Fish Dock in Hull, where ten years ago 'you could walk from side to side and end to end across the decks of the boats' (p. 255), is now almost empty.

The coal industry is in no better shape and, in Blyth, which he considers 'a small, proud, embattled bit of serious life' (p. 285), Raban encounters 'the dusty silence, the spaces between people, [that are] the outward and visible signs of the fact that . . . one man in three [is] out of a job' (p. 273). Returning briefly to his home in London, Raban once again comes across emptiness and silence where there was once purposeful and productive activity. Thus, as he sails through the 'wasteland' of the ruined docklands, Raban is struck by the fact that, even though it is 'a weekday afternoon, still inside working hours, . . . there [isn't] a human being in sight' (p. 225).

However, the industrial decline responsible for transforming Hull into 'a stricken city' (p. 264) like Beirut and for condemning the long-term unemployed of Southampton to eke out their lives 'stacked in concrete towers' (p. 176) is not what Raban finds most distressing about contemporary Britain. He is more troubled by the fact that, in a situation where the Conservative Government is intent 'in making a rapid shift from "high tech" through "low tech"' to a '"no tech"' (p. 210) service economy, the only hope for once flourishing towns such as Rye resides in seeking to make 'a profit . . . out of [their] own dereliction' (p. 209). Raban calls this route to salvation 'the merrying of England' (p. 188), a term he uses to describe a process involving the exploitation of the nostalgic impulses experienced not only by British people but also by visitors from abroad.

An example of what Raban means by 'merrying' or, as he also calls it, 'History on the cheap' (p. 153), is provided by the widespread creation in recent years of Morris dancing sides, all of which offer themselves as the 'inheritors of an unbroken British tradition' 'stretch[ing] back through the mists of time' (p. 195). The much less consoling truth of the matter, Raban points out, is that Morris dancing was a lost art until revived by Cecil Sharp in the 1890s and inspired little real interest until the 1950s.

In its more large scale, fully commercialized manifestation, the merrying of England involves turning the whole country into a massive theme park and its population into actors, the 'dramatis personae' of 'a jovial masque' for tourists entitled *'Britain'* (p. 212). The process is particularly far advanced in Rye with its 'Ye Old Tucke Shoppe and Simon the Pieman' restaurants and shops with 'no remotely useful things for sale' (p. 207). Rye, to Raban's keenly postmodern eye, has become a simulacrum, a copy without an original. Thus, he notes that the 'Rye Town Model, a perfect scale replica of the place', is 'redundant, for Rye itself [is] a model town', making the Town Model a 'model of a model, a picture within a picture, the second step of an infinite regression' (p. 209). This regression will never achieve a point of rest because the model/picture lacks an origin in the actual town that once smelt of the blood of 'whole sides of meat' (p. 214) rather than of 'a floral-scented underarm deodorant . . . that give[s merryed Rye] the dehumanized loveliness of a glossy colour photograph' (p. 206).

In Raban's myth of Britain, the future comes in several different versions. One, in which Raban briefly seems to share Theroux's

violent vision of the future, takes the form of the apocalypse
promised by a sunken munitions ship that 'could blow up at
any moment going off with a bang that would take most of the
people of Sheerness and Wallend with it' (p. 222). Another, which
also has violent overtones, is prefigured in the disappointing end
to a dream of economic revival that occurs when Raban, searching in the fog for the boom town of Aberdeen, ends up bobbing
in 'the city's main sewage outfall' amidst a 'crazed and deafening orgy' of thousands of birds 'jabbering, like a rioting crowd
in a Middle Eastern city' (p. 289). The most likely future, though,
is that which is embodied in Raban's claim that 'there is no logical end to the possible merrying of England on the Rye Town
model'. In this future, envisioned by Raban as a time when there
will be 'a foreign tourist for every single dwelling in the land',
'streams of buses [will] shunt [tourists] from Anne Hathaway's
Cottage to ruined car factories in Dagenham and Oxford, to
defunct coal mines, closed-down universities, deserted tower
blocks', all of which will have been transformed into 'living
museums' (p. 211).

Like Theroux, Raban completes his deconstruction of Thatcherite
mytholwogy by finding a place for his revised reading of the
Falklands War and its significance in his own deeply subversive
myth of Britain. In Raban's hands, the Falklands War ceases to
be a moment of destiny in which the nation returns briefly to
the past before springing forward into a more hopeful and pros-
perous future. Instead, with each parliamentary or journalistic
attempt to make events in the South Atlantic 'signify . . . Honour,
Tradition, Loyalty, Community, Principle . . .', the whole web and
texture of being British' (p. 113), the war becomes more thoroughly implicated in the merrying process and less able to claim
any function more dignified than that of encouraging the people
of Britain to give credence to a falsified version of the past as
national heritage. If the function of the Falklands War is indeed
to facilitate the transformation of Britain into a theme park and
its 'spoil[t]' inhabitants into mere actors with no 'secure sense of
their own identity' (p. 212), then it can no longer be regarded as
an emblem of rebirth. Instead, it simply marks one more stage
in the nation's decline.

Theroux and Raban are prepared to follow Thatcher, then, in
viewing the Falkland Islands as 'us in looking-glass reverse'

(p. 102), as Raban whimsically puts it on discovering that the two countries occupy the same latitude in their respective hemispheres, so that Port Stanley is 'the Hemel Hempstead of the Southern world' (p. 101). What they are not prepared to do, though, is to accept Thatcher's interpretation of the significance of the islands and the war that was fought there as definitive. Neither, though, do they make absolutist truth claims for the alternative stories that they weave around the Falklands War. Whether the reader is more convinced by Theroux's argument that the future will be violently repressive or Raban's that it will be characterized by an ever more stultifying exploitation of the British people's nostalgic impulses is not finally of much importance. What really matters is that they have reopened the play of signification surrounding the Falklands War formerly closed off by Thatcher's use of powerful archetypes. By so doing they are making an important contribution to the process of reintroducing the Falklands War and, by extension, Thatcherite hegemony into the arena of political contestation.

Notes

1. The archetype of disguised nobility is also in evidence when Theroux, in an obvious echo of the story of the Frog Prince, compares his situation in a narrow room with a high ceiling to 'sitting in the bottom of a well' (p. 216).
2. See Johnson, B., p. 40 for a discussion of the distinction that Barthes draws between 'work' and 'text'. Johnson defines 'textuality' as 'the manifestation of an open-ended, heterogeneous, disruptive force of signification and erasure that transgresses all closure'.

5

Em-Bodying the Disembodied: *Tumbledown, Resurrected* and the Language of Chivalry

Understandings of war in the twentieth century have been largely shaped according to the conventions of two competing discursive systems. As a result of the disillusioning experiences of the Great War, official discourse has been denied any but the most occasional access to the language of chivalry with its ennobling images of wounding and death. Therefore, it has generally relied upon a euphemistic vocabulary to camouflage the injured bodies that are, as Elaine Scarry points out, the fundamental object and inevitable consequence of combat (pp. 63–4). During the Vietnam War, for instance, the American military establishment almost always used comforting circumlocutions such as 'discreet burst', 'friendly casualties', 'meeting engagement', and 'light losses' (Herr, pp. 222–3) when describing battles in which hundreds of soldiers and civilians were torn apart by high velocity bullets and mortar fire or burned by napalm. The real identity of the casualties resulting from the allied bombardment of Iraq during the Gulf War was similarly obscured by a techno-bureaucratic language in which the civilian dead and wounded became merely 'collateral damage' and by the extensive use of terminology and images drawn from video games and action movies. An excellent example of the influence of popular cinema on Gulf War discourse is provided by the British newspaper report in which a missile attack on Baghdad becomes 'Luke Skywalker zapping Darth Vader'.[1]

The most important alternative to official discourse developed during this century has its origins in the plainly written accounts and stark pictorial representations of individual wounded and dead soldiers to be found in many of the poems, journals, novels and paintings of the First World War. The immediate target of writers such as Owen, Sassoon, Rosenburg, Graves and Blunden and artists such as Nevinson and Orpen was, of course, 'the old Lie' of chivalric myth in which the body is deprived of its vulnerable materiality by absorption into a system of disembodied beliefs about glory and heroism and by the promise of eternal life for the battlefield dead.[2] Wilfred Owen's 'Dulce Et Decorum Est', for instance, reaches its climax with a graphic description of a soldier's hideous death by gassing aimed at thoroughly exposing the inadequacy of the ideal of heroic sacrifice embodied in the poem's title.

Although originally designed to assert the mere materiality of dead and wounded bodies previously refined into the type of the wounded Christ, this set of discursive and visual practices has proven equally effective, particularly during the Vietnam War, in making visible what official euphemism seeks to hide from view. Thus, in spite of consistent attempts by the Government and its military spokesmen to sanitize what was happening in Vietnam, the American people's understanding of the war was ultimately shaped by the stream of images of individual death and wounding that flowed on a daily basis across television screens and the pages of newspapers and magazines. So completely did this reading of the Vietnam War displace the official version that for most Americans the war's definitive image is a black and white photograph of a naked and napalmed Vietnamese child which has been reprinted with sufficient frequency to achieve an almost iconic status. Similarly, if there is one book generally considered to tell the 'truth' about Vietnam, it is probably *Dispatches*, in which Michael Herr remorselessly and graphically catalogues example after example of death and mutilation. Typical of Herr's strategy is his description of a soldier hit by mortar fire who makes 'himself look at the incredible thing that had just happened to his leg, screwed about once at some point below the knee like a goofy scarecrow leg' (p. 32).

The ultimate failure of the rhetorical strategies employed by governmental and military sources to maintain public support for the Vietnam War may partially explain the decision made by Thatcher and her supporters to eschew euphemism when talking about the task force and its exploits in the South Atlantic in favour of a chivalric discourse virtually defunct since the early

days of the First World War. Of more immediate significance to
the shaping of official discourse during the Falklands War, however,
was Thatcher's recognition that the deeply anachronistic language
of chivalry could provide a particularly appropriate vehicle for
her attempts to postulate the struggle for the Falklands as an
essentially nineteenth-century exercise and thus as the first tangible
fruit of her promise to reclaim the national heritage. Consummate
political opportunist that she was, Thatcher must also have been
aware that, by using a vocabulary likely to strike a resonant chord
with the deeply nostalgic people of postimperialist Britain, she
could do a great deal to improve support for her deeply unpopular Government.

In the event, as we saw in Chapter 1, the language of chivalry
served the Thatcherite forces extremely well and opposition
attempts to redefine governmental discourse as jingoistic failed
to catch the attention of a public thrilled by the idea that their
country had once again become the nation that 'built an Empire
and ruled a quarter of the world' (Barnett, p. 150). However,
with the fading of the euphoria aroused by military success in
the Falklands, a process surely accelerated as film of some bloody
engagements on land and sea finally became available,[3] chivalric
rhetoric has proven no less susceptible in a contemporary context
to subversion by artists intent upon discrediting a language of
sacrifice and transcendence than it was during the Great War.

This avenue of attack has been exploited to particularly telling effect in two films, *Tumbledown* (1988), written by Charles
Wood and directed by Richard Eyre, and *Resurrected* (1989), written
by Martin Allen and directed by Paul Greengrass, both of which
are concerned with the wartime experiences of individual combatants. *Tumbledown* is the story of Robert Lawrence, a lieutenant
in the Scots Guards grievously wounded during the assault on
Mount Tumbledown, while *Resurrected* deals with another Scots
Guardsman, Private Kevin Deakin, who escapes bodily injury
but is heavily traumatized, first by his experiences as a stretcher
bearer and then by the seven weeks during which he wanders
lost and afraid in rugged Falklands terrain after fleeing the battlefield.[4] However, both films go beyond the tradition in which I
have located them. Whereas a poem such as 'Dulce et Decorum'
focuses entirely on the horrendous moment of injury, *Tumbledown*
and *Resurrected* also offer ironic analyses of the later problems
encountered by their protagonists in extricating the fact of their

bodily and/or psychic wounding and ultimately their sense of self from the chivalric myths in which they have become entangled.

TUMBLEDOWN: WARTIME MYTHOLOGY AND THE WOUNDED BODY

The events with which *Tumbledown* is concerned are narrated retrospectively by the film's main character, Robert Lawrence, in the course of a lunch party which he attends in 1985. As a storyteller Robert shows a scant regard for chronology, thus creating the impression that he is motivated more by a need to purge himself of a still-troubling experience than by a desire to provide his audience with a well-rounded narrative. However, more is gained than lost by the complex structure of *Tumbledown* because it not only reveals a great deal about the narrator's state of mind but also allows Wood to bring together episodes whose connection is thematic rather than chronological.

The first part of *Tumbledown* is constructed around a number of brief scenes that jump rapidly between three distinct time frames: the present, a day in 1985 when Robert Lawrence and his friend Hugh MacKessac drive to the Cotswolds to visit Hugh's friends, the Stubbs; the brief period between Robert's wounding on Mount Tumbledown on 14 June 1982 and his transfer to the hospital ship, the *Uganda*; and the weeks between the sailing of the *Canberra* for the Falklands on 5 April 1982 and the embarkation of the Scots Guards on 12 May, a time during which Robert and his regiment perform ceremonial duties in London. What is particularly striking about these scenes is the number of levels at which a congruence is established between the first and third time frames.

Most obviously, the action throughout both time frames is extremely colourful and charged with energy. The film begins in 1985 with a montage of shots in which rapid tracking and panning and a range of different angles and distances are employed to communicate the speed with which Robert's bright green Panther sports car passes through a landscape of vivid greens, yellows and blues. The action takes its rhythm from a soundtrack of jaunty military band music of the type favoured by 1950s war films such as *The Dambusters* and *Reach for the Sky*. This scene has parallels in several episodes from the pre-embarkation period in 1982, the most notable being the one in which a hand-held camera,

which creates jerky and frequently blurred images, follows Robert
and one of his men, Prothero, as they run, bouncing and leaping
like puppies, towards the morning inspection parade. On this
occasion, the characters' energetic movements take their rhythm
from the rock music which the viewer hears blasting from Robert's
Walkman. The colourfulness of *Tumbledown*'s opening sequence
of shots is matched by the bright reds that predominate during
scenes set in London. The Guardsmen parade in red dress uniforms
and train in red T-shirts; the officers' mess is carpeted in red
and green squares; and the bar where Robert and Hugh spend
their last night in England is bathed in red light.

Scenes from these two time periods are also congruent in that
they both project idealized visions of Britain. The Cotswolds
location shots and shots of the exterior and interior of the Stubbs's
Georgian farmhouse work together to suggest that Britain is a
rural idyll freed, as it is in the landscape paintings of George
Stubbs' famous namesake, from the ravages of time and social
change. The slow, dignified cadences of the later parts of the
music that accompanies the film's opening car drive hint at a
connection between this timeless perfection and a highly ritualized and militaristic culture. Ritualized militarism is also, not
surprisingly, the most prominent feature of episodes from the
April–May period of 1982, the first of which begins with Robert's
participation in the Ceremony of the Keys at the Tower of London.
By following this ancient ritual with a scene set in an officers'
mess whose walls are lined with prints of stately homes and
portraits of eighteenth-century soldiers, Wood is able to evoke a
Britain similar in its timelessness to the one created by the
Cotswolds scenes.

Sufficient correspondences are thus established to suggest a
considerable degree of continuity between Robert Lawrence's life
as it was before and as it is after the Falklands War. And yet
these scenes stand in stark contrast to the incident that separ-
ates them in time. As the action cuts away from the Cotswolds
to the Falklands, so a fertile landscape is replaced by rugged
and muddy moorland, brilliant sunshine by lowering clouds, and
sparkling colours by dull shades of khaki, green and brown. Most
important of all, though, the vitally energetic Robert Lawrence
has given way to an inert figure who lies moaning in the mud
as the chaos of a firefight swirls around him. The crucial fact
which this incident communicates by means of repeated close

ups is that half of Robert Lawrence's brain has been blown away.

The graphic presentation of Robert Lawrence's wounding immediately raises two questions. First, is it possible for Robert to have recovered sufficiently to be the same dashing young man in 1985 that he was before his injury? Second, how can a man who has suffered such grievous wounds still maintain the youthfully idealistic relationship to his homeland and its military institutions suggested by the visual and aural style of the film's first few moments? It takes the whole of *Tumbledown* to answer the second question, as I will be trying to demonstrate in the course of this chapter; the first is soon answered, however, because, physically, Robert is not the same at all and we soon learn that we have been deceived by the film's opening sequence. Robert seems fully functional while driving his sports car but once out of it he walks with a heavy limp, knocks over a glass of wine with his spastic left hand and admits to having limited control of his bladder. Even now, though, we have to rely on the response Hugh makes to Helen Stubbs' comment on her belated awareness of Robert's paralysis for an understanding of the full extent of his injury: 'Oh yes, he is – the whole of his left side basically. I swore he was dead when I saw him' (Wood, p. 11).[5]

However, this explanation simply raises a further question, the answer to which serves also to answer the question about Robert's continued idealism. The viewer's mistaken impression, as Helen Stubbs' confusion confirms, does not result from the filmmaker's desire to conceal the truth but from Robert Lawrence's. Why, then, is Robert striving so hard to deny what has happened to him? It would be wrong to assume that he simply wants to forget the terrible experience of his wounding. On the contrary, he is obsessed with it and, as soon as he enters the Stubbs' house, begins to describe what he went through in the moments after he was shot. However, there is an immediate discrepancy between the way in which the circumstances of his injury are portrayed by the film and the manner in which he talks about it that suggests that Robert is seeking to make the episode a good deal less ugly than it really was. For example, the matter-of-fact style in which he states, 'I was conscious all the time. I never lost consciousness' (p.8), completely excludes the tremendous pain that we see him suffering. Similarly, whenever jealousy compels Hugh to undermine the seriousness of his experience, Robert simply acquiesces. Thus, in response to Hugh's comment, 'It wasn't all covering ourselves in glory, you know. . . . Some of us had to spend the rest of the day and night on that sodding mountain', Robert replies, 'There you are. Glad I didn't' (p. 32).

Robert Lawrence's verbal style is clearly modelled on that of the laconic, self-deprecating protagonists of British war fiction and films and is intended to transform his experience of injury into an episode from the kind of chivalric fantasy for school-boys in which wounding rarely results in disability. The serious-ness of Robert's attempts to subordinate actual experience to fictional convention is made particularly obvious by his angry reaction when the jealous Hugh tries to steal his thunder by offer-ing up Drill Sergeant Terry Knapp, the first Scots Guardsman to be killed during the assault on Mount Tumbledown, as the even more glorious type of the warrior immortalized by death in combat:

Hugh:　　Got him straight between the eyes. Drill Sergeant, do you see? So well balanced on his feet he didn't fall. Braced they tell me. Nobody knew he'd been hit.
Robert:　That's crap. (p. 11)

Further evidence of Robert's determination to preserve the integrity of the fiction he has created around his wounding is provided when he makes Hugh confirm that his first words after being wounded were not a complaint about being cold but the much more gallant, 'Tell Sophie I love her' (p. 15).

The exploration conducted in *Tumbledown* into the reasons why Robert Lawrence feels compelled to construct a narrative so alien to the reality of his injured body begins early in the film during scenes that explore what it means to be a soldier. By foregrounding the element of performance in military behaviour, these scenes make the point that a soldier is expected to conform absolutely to the identity created for him by regimental culture. Thus, we first see the Scots Guards engaged in the Ceremony of the Keys, which takes the form of a heavily ritualized drama acted out before an audience of civilians. That those taking part are play-ing roles scripted entirely by somebody else is given particular emphasis when the Cockney, Prothero, adopts a Scottish accent for his challenge to the escort of the keys.

A sequence of shots focusing on the individual components of the Scots Guardsmen's uniforms and equipment helps to flesh out this point. A bayonet dominates in a low angle shot taken at

the beginning of the Ceremony of the Keys scene and this is
followed by a close-up pan across the faces of a line of Guardsmen that gives prominence to their chin straps and gun barrels.
In part, these and similar shots simply underline the ability of
military culture to impose an identity on its members by insist-
ing that they not only behave in a prescribed manner but also
adopt specific trappings and, consequently, the values these trappings represent. More important, though, by isolating the separate elements out of which the soldier is constructed, director,
Richard Eyre's montage further suggests that an identity derived
exclusively from such a limited discourse will be fragmented and
will leave its possessor without a coherent sense of self or the
capacity for individual thought and action.

Perhaps because he comes from a service family, Robert
Lawrence is an almost perfect product of military indoctrination. Hugh gives him the name 'action man' (p. 12) and Robert
describes himself as 'a real military shit' (p. 32). It is not surprising, therefore, that he conceptualizes the part he will play in the
Falklands War entirely in terms of military stereotypes. To fight
in the war is his *raison d'être* and weeks before he is posted overseas
Robert has fantasies in which he sees himself crouching, fully
armed, in the prow of a ship ready to leap into combat. Because
of the glory accorded death in battle by military mythology, Robert
finds it easy to contemplate the idea that he might die in the
Falklands. However, nothing in his indoctrination into the military mindset has prepared him to deal with the rather more likely
possibility that he will be maimed. This inability to comprehend
wounding as something with which he might be expected to come
to terms is made particularly obvious on the night before his
regiment's impending departure for the Falklands, when a drunken
Robert forces Hugh to promise that, 'When I'm maimed, mutilated,
my dick shot off, whatever, you [will] . . . finish me off' (p. 17).

Because of the juxtaposition of such incidents from his life before
the Falklands War with scenes set in 1985, it becomes clear very
early in *Tumbledown* that the actual experience of injury has scarcely
changed Robert Lawrence's views on maiming. He is able to
continue living not because he has come to terms with his physical
condition but because, at some level, he is able to deny the reality
of what has happened to his body. This denial is implicit in the
substitution of a sportscar for the wheelchair we might expect
him to occupy and is made explicit when he tells George Stubbs,

'You see, I hate cripples. Always have done. And I will not be one. That's what they don't seem to understand – I will not be a cripple' (p. 15).

As we have already seen, Robert has been predisposed to think in this way by his acceptance of the military view of death and wounding and, not surprisingly, his interactions with military culture during the middle sections of *Tumbledown*, which are fairly faithful to the chronology of Robert's long process of recovery, do little to encourage any reassessment of his attitudes towards the seriously wounded body. Less expected, though, is the failure of the narratives by means of which civilians give shape to their lives to be any more hospitable to the badly injured than those of the military. Thus, as we follow Wood's protagonist in his simultaneous attempts to reconcile his conditioned response to injury with the stark fact of his own terrible wounding and to come to terms with an ever-increasing awareness that there is no acceptable role for the physically disabled in any sector of society, so our initially unsympathetic attitude towards the apparently hubristic Robert Lawrence become a good deal more complicated.

The military reaction to Robert Lawrence can be divided into two categories. At an institutional level, the army is simply embarrassed by a shattered body that challenges its most cherished myths about wounding and death in battle. The attitude of the military establishment manifests itself with particular clarity in decisions made about Robert's role in the Falkland Islands Service at Saint Paul's Cathedral which takes place while he is still confined to a wheelchair. Although he is allowed to attend the service, Robert is denied permission to wear his uniform, is seated inconspicuously at the rear of the congregation out of the range of television cameras and, at the end, is kept waiting until everybody else has left. From an official viewpoint, it would seem that Robert has almost ceased to exist. This impression is reinforced when he arrives at an RAF rehabilitation hospital only to find that no one knows anything about him.

Individual servicemen respond much more positively to Robert but they are no more capable than the military authorities of acknowledging the implications of his highly visible bodily injury. Instead they insist on finding him a place within acceptable narratives of wounding. The most striking example of the inability of the military mind to deal with debilitating injury is provided by Robert's father, a retired wing commander who still sports an RAF moustache. It becomes obvious as soon as they are reunited at Brize Norton that, in order to make sense of Robert's injury, John Lawrence must locate it within heroic discourse. The real despair expressed when Robert greets him with the words, 'Daddy, it wasn't worth it!' (Wood, p. 35. These are Robert Lawrence's actual words. See Lawrence and Lawrence, p. 57), is clearly too much for John Lawrence and he displaces his son's interpretation of what happened on Mount Tumbledown with the more appealing version offered by Private Fraser. As if conscious of his role in the oral transmission of legend, John Lawrence is careful to repeat Fraser's exact words and to mimic his Scottish accent when passing on the story to his wife, Jean: 'You should have seen him, sorr. He was there with two rifles, blazing away, like that film, sorr, *True Grit*' (p. 37).

A need to mythologize is equally evident in John Lawrence's reaction to the news that Robert has survived major surgery. First he practices his delivery on Jean; then he seeks out his son, Nick, and regales him with a much more ebullient version of the same tale: 'I'm talking about Robert, Spud. Just heard. Thought I'd tell you. He came round from the operation and demanded double egg and chips at once or else, then another helping. How's that?' (p. 42). Clearly, the subject of this narrative is not the real Robert Lawrence but the fictional war hero who suffers no injury so serious that it cannot be cured by a combination of pluck and good plain British food.

Recognition of severe injury is, of course, anathema to the military because to do so would involve calling into question the heroic myths that make wars acceptable to those whose job it is to fight them. As a soldier Robert Lawrence should therefore have anticipated the inability of members of the armed forces to read what would seem to be the extremely legible text provided by his shattered body. What Robert has less reason to expect is that his body will be equally unintelligible to civilians. This lack of comprehension can be understood partly as a consequence of the renewed marginalization inevitably experienced by the maimed soldier as a result of Thatcher's success in persuading the British people to view the Falklands War through the lens of chivalry. However, *Tumbledown* also identifies elements within civilian discourses that make them intrinsically unreceptive to the injured body.

The speechless condition to which Robert's former girlfriend,

Sophie, is reduced during her first visit to the military hospital at RAF Rawton is,[6] for example, obviously in part a product of the blatant contradiction she experiences between the reality of his maimed body and the inspiring image of a glorious death in battle that motivated her to become involved in a pre-embarkation sexual reunion. However, it can also be explained in terms of the failure of her solipsistic Sloane Ranger discourse, in which the male is articulated mainly as sexual or dancing partner, to accommodate Robert's severe paralysis.

The same injured body that proves to be unintelligible to both the soldier and the Sloane Ranger is, of course, intrinsic to the medical subculture's definition of reality. It is therefore particularly ironic that Robert Lawrence continues to encounter incomprehension and rejection throughout his long period of hospitalization. The problem in this instance seems to be that, whereas in other areas of his life people cannot cope with the fact of his injured body, Robert is nothing but a body so far as the medical world is concerned. On one occasion, for example, a group of doctors remains oblivious to Robert's presence even as he supplies them with answers to their queries about the make and specifications of the high velocity rifle that wounded him. For them he is no longer a soldier whose job it is to know such things but a patient of whom nothing is expected except that he remain placid, pliable and, above all, silent.

Robert Lawrence's situation can be summed up as follows. Since the moment of his wounding he has ceased to be a soldier. This is communicated visually during the scene in the field hospital when his Northern Ireland boots and his SAS smock, both important parts of his military identity, are cut away from his body. Instead, Robert is, to use his own terminology, 'a cripple'. Acceptance of this fact is difficult enough for a man who has already expressed a strong preference for death over maiming. However, it is made almost impossible by the failure of those around him to acknowledge either what he is or what he has experienced.

There are occasions on which Robert nevertheless seeks to create a space for himself by speaking the ugly truth that in war bodies are 'blown apart'. However, whenever he does so people tend to respond with distaste or simple incomprehension. This is certainly the case with the nurse whose sentimental response to the 'poor horses' (p. 40) killed in the Hyde Park bombing inspires

Robert to describe exactly what happened to the men who also died. Only once, when he is befriended by an unassuming young doctor willing to share a beer and to talk, is Robert offered any help in coming to terms with the reality of his situation. Encouraged by this doctor, he even goes so far as to describe in quite graphic terms the destructive capabilities of a high velocity bullet such as the one that tore off the side of his head. In order to communicate how close Robert is at this moment to acknowledging the vulnerable materiality of his body, director Richard Eyre substitutes an extremely dramatic slow motion, close-up shot of a bullet splattering a tomato for the words that appear in the published script of *Tumbledown*. However, the short term presence of a sympathetic listener is not enough to sustain Robert in his efforts to accept such an alien view of his body. Thus, after daring to take the next step by asking about his future prospects, he is too upset by the doctor's frank answer that he will never again walk properly to continue the conversation.

Because his society does not offer and he is unable to create a narrative in which the wounded man is given an acceptable role, Robert Lawrence has little choice but to try to reassert the military identity around which his pre-Falklands life was constructed. This process begins at Brize Norton when the willingness of a Colour Sergeant to stand to attention before his prone figure and address him as 'Mr Lawrence, sorr' (p. 36) proves sufficient to shake Robert out of a state of despair.

From this point on Robert is, in his imagination, the figure identified in Wood's script as Bergen man, a 'lumbering silhouette' of a Scots Guardsman weighed down by a 'high-piled bergen [or backpack]' (p. 42). Identification with this fantasy figure allows Robert to envision his recovery as a military exercise, calling for the same qualities of self discipline and endurance demanded of Bergen man as he undertakes his trek across hard terrain. Clearly then, since he cannot find a story which will accommodate his injured body, Robert has decided to reshape his body in order to make it fit into an heroic narrative of wounding and recovery. He becomes obsessed with physiotherapy, which he retitles 'physioterroris[m]' (p. 54), thereby allowing him to approach it in the antagonistic spirit of Bergen man, and offers a definition of recovery fully in keeping with his renewed military persona: 'I'm going to march in a parade, in uniform, with medals, and show them this . . . My head. I'm proud of it' (p. 58).

One could argue that Robert Lawrence finds salvation by reinserting himself into military mythology. Certainly it is difficult to imagine how else he might have found the determination needed to learn to walk again. At the same time, though, he is clearly embarking on a path that leads to a dead end. Remarkable as his eventual degree of recovery is, he will never be fit enough to return to active service or even to march in a parade. Yet by pursuing this impossible goal, he has closed off all possibility of coming to terms with his actual bodily condition. The third and last section of *Tumbledown* teases out the ironies implicit in Robert's situation by once again juxtaposing scenes from different time frames.

The key to *Tumbledown*'s concluding episodes is provided when Robert Lawrence interrupts his narrative to show George Stubbs some gruesome photographs of his wounded head taken at the field hospital. The fact that he continues to carry and display these pictures long after he has decided to become Bergen man demonstrates that, at some level, Robert is still aware that his injured body has a tale to tell. The nature of this tale and the ways in which it accommodates experiences that go beyond the scope of Robert's own wounding can be best understood by considering two episodes from the film's earlier time frames that are introduced immediately before and shortly after he displays his photographs.

In the last of the dramatized recollections about his life in hospital Robert describes a meeting with an RAMC officer who asks him what it felt like to kill. It is, as Robert says, 'the sort of question you don't ask' (p. 69), but, having been invited at last to stray beyond the bounds of permitted discourse about war, he fully acknowledges for the first time the fact that he has injured others as well as experiencing injury himself. The particular act of injuring upon which Robert focuses is his clumsy and prolonged bayonetting of an already fallen Argentinian soldier. His recollection of this previously repressed incident is so detailed that we come to realize what a profound effect it must have had on him. However, having begun to open up, Robert, as he did in his conversation with the sympathetic young doctor, then shies away from further contact with painful reality by denying that he had any kind of emotional reaction to killing another human being.

When, in yet another time shift, the film finally dramatizes the assault on Mount Tumbledown, it becomes clear that this denial is intimately linked to Robert's denial of his own injury. During the depiction of the bayonetting episode the camera several times focuses closely on the Argentinian soldier's increasingly bloody face and mouth. The viewer is thus invited to see the bayonetting as a hideous experience, equally degrading for the victim, who begs for mercy, and for Robert Lawrence, who ignores his pleas. However, far from feeling shame, as the viewer might expect, or nothing, as he later claims, Robert is clearly elated by his murderous act. So much so in fact that he seizes the dead man's rifle and rushes to the summit of Mount Tumbledown where he raises his twin rifles aloft in a moment of triumph and calls out, 'Isn't this fun?' (p. 80), before being shot down by a sniper. By establishing a cause and effect relationship between these successive episodes from Robert Lawrence's experience of combat, Wood makes it very clear that the impulse that inspires the soldier to perform what military culture defines as heroic deeds and to suffer glorious wounding or death cannot be separated from the capacity developed in him by his training to perform acts of savage butchery. The terms 'hero' and 'killer' (p. 74), which Helen Stubbs views as incompatible, are thus revealed to be synonyms.

The two woundings in which he was involved on Mount Tumbledown obviously have the potential to tell Robert Lawrence some very important things about himself and about militarism. However, because he is so much a product of military indoctrination and because his injured body has blocked him off from those who might have been expected to provide help, Robert is unable to find a way to comprehend the significance of his own unusually intimate experiences of the materiality of the human body. The deeply ironic and unresolved situation in which this failure of perception leaves him is communicated, appropriately enough, by the two vivid bodily images with which *Tumbledown* ends.

First, the camera cuts from a silhouetted longshot of the triumphant Robert Lawrence abreast of Mount Tumbledown to a close up of his feet as he begins to crumple and then to several low angle pan shots of his falling body and the swirling sky above. A last shot of the sky is held for a few moments before dissolving to a mid shot of Robert, smartly dressed in blazer and panama hat, standing to attention on the Chelsea Barracks parade ground where he has gone to meet his regiment on its return from the Falklands. The narrative of wounding and recovery by means of which Robert is trying to connect these two images of his body is encapsulated in the regimental motto, 'Nemo Me Impune Lacessit' (nobody attacks me with impunity), visible on a plaque mounted on the wall behind his left shoulder.

For the viewer, though, the motto is a pathetic denial of the realities of injury; Robert has tumbled down for good and will never be able to get up and re-enter military life. This point is reinforced by further shots, now in close up, of the isolated and still figure of Robert, panama hat lifted in salute as the blurred shapes of energetically marching red-uniformed Scots Guardsmen pass between him and the camera. Even more indicative of his fallen status, however, is the fact that, because of his failure to break free from a military construction of reality, Robert will never be able to comprehend the text so vividly inscribed on his body and will, therefore, never be in a position to achieve the understanding of his situation needed before he can begin to develop a functional definition of self. Thus, the film ends with a still closer shot of Robert Lawrence staring hopelessly towards the camera. On the soundtrack the Corries sing 'Hush a Babe While the Red Bee Hums', a traditional song full of images of dying day and encroaching night that make it more lament for things lost than comforting lullaby for a man apparently fated to remain trapped within a boy's-adventure-story version of adult experience.

RESURRECTED: WARTIME MYTHOLOGY AND THE ABSENT BODY

Resurrected opens with a scene very like that in which Robert Lawrence must have frequently imagined himself playing the central part as he waited for an opportunity to sacrifice his life on the battlefield. The camera tracks across an idyllic English springtime landscape complete with picturesque village and distant hills. As it moves in closer and continues tracking across the churchyard we can hear birdsong mingled with voices singing hymns. Finally, a dissolve takes the viewer inside the church and into the midst of a memorial service for a dead Falklands soldier. The specific identity of the dead man, Kevin Deakin, is acknowledged by the presence of his photograph and by the use of his name in the sermon. The main purpose of the service, however, is not to memorialize Kevin Deakin but to locate him within the structure of the heroic myth that surrounds death in battle.

Thus, the church is filled with military iconography. Kevin's regimental hat and belt are placed next to his photograph; a bugler, in full dress uniform and at rigid attention, faces the congregation; a Guards' officer reads the lesson; bemedalled veterans are scattered throughout the congregation; and, at the end of the service, the bugler plays the Last Post. As a result Kevin comes to belong, not with his family and his neighbours, but with the dead of other wars, such as those whose names are engraved on the Second World War memorial picked out by the camera in a close up shot. Like these other dead he has become the type of the war hero, the man who willingly lays down his life in battle for the good of his country. The chivalric origins of this transformation from son and neighbour to sacrificial hero are made explicit by the clergyman's reference to Kevin's role in battle as being that of the good shepherd. The identification of Kevin with Christ is further emphasized by the officer's choice for his reading of a text dealing with resurrection.

Kevin Deakin's memorial service is, of course, very much in keeping with the official myth of the Falklands War. However, like Charles Wood and Richard Eyre in *Tumbledown*, what Martin Allen and Paul Greengrass set out to do in *Resurrected* is to call this myth into question. In both films, writer and director achieve their goal partly by deconstructing heroic myth and partly by demonstrating its power to destroy those caught up in it. Allen and Greengrass begin to reveal their sceptical attitude towards the Falklands myth with a cut away from a second close up of Kevin's photograph, in which his smartly uniformed figure is forever frozen at attention, to a shot of a weary soldier in grimy battledress struggling across a bleak Falklands landscape.

This cut serves to establish the same kind of distinction between actual events and a mythic reading of that Falklands War that we have already seen in *Tumbledown*. However, the full irony of the contrast created by cutting does not become evident until the viewer realizes that the man in the photograph and the struggling soldier are the same person. Kevin Deakin is not dead after all; he became separated from his regiment during battle and, after being lost for seven weeks, has now found a line of telegraph poles that will lead him back to the world of the living. By creating this rather bizarre situation the makers of *Resurrected* lay the groundwork for a thoroughgoing deconstruction of the phrase 'dead war hero'. Logically, these words should mean that a soldier has become a hero because there was something heroic in the manner of his death. What they actually mean, however, is that he is a hero simply because he died during a war. The oddness of the equation maintained with great consistency in chivalric discourse between death on the battlefield and heroism is thoroughly exposed by Kevin's reappearance because, as a living person, he is so clearly lacking in the qualities expected of the hero.

Kevin does not look at all heroic while he is stumbling towards rescue and he is addressed by the farmer's wife who opens her door to him not as shepherd but as 'poor lamb'. As a poor lamb Kevin immediately assumes the inglorious role of victim, the linkage between lambs and victims having been already suggested by the hanging sheep's carcasses that he passes on his way to the farmhouse. The accuracy of the farmer's wife's insight into Kevin's relationship to heroic myth is repeatedly confirmed as the film develops. Even after he has recovered from his gruelling experiences on the Falklands, for example, Kevin still lacks the physical attributes of the hero. Unlike Robert Lawrence, a well built and craggily handsome man with aggressive manners, Kevin Deakin is tall, gangly and rather gormless looking.[7] Neither does he possess the class credentials and early acquaintance with military culture required of the stereotypical war hero. Kevin's parents are working class and he joined the army not because he had ideas about seeking glory in battle, as Robert Lawrence did, but because, as he puts it himself, others 'made' him. Faced with the prospect of actual combat, Kevin volunteered for the pacifist role of stretcher bearer and, for him, the battle turned out to be neither a great adventure nor 'fun' but, rather, an horrific experience that left him haunted by the image of his dreadfully wounded friend, Johnny Flodden.

Once separated from the modifier 'dead', then, the soubriquet 'hero' clearly does not fit Kevin Deakin. This is immediately apparent to the military authorities and, in a move that recalls the treatment of Robert Lawrence during the Falklands Service, they make sure that Kevin and his family are kept well away from the celebrating crowds that greet the Scots Guards on their return to England. However, military mythology is particularly powerful at the moment of victory, especially when it is reinforced by newspaper headlines such as 'Falklands Battle Hero is Back'. As a result, Kevin's neighbours, the people who should know this unremarkable young man best, do not hesitate to fête him when he returns to the village. They are no more familiar with military culture than Kevin, however, and the celebrations they organize, although held in the appropriately named pub, The Volunteer, fail completely as a ritual confirmation of his heroic status.

The villagers greet the man who has supposedly become part warrior, part Christ with a group rendition of 'Hello Kevin', sung to the tune of 'Hello Dolly', and the evening that follows in the red, white and blue decorated pub is structured according to their past experiences of portentous national occasions such as the Coronation of Queen Elizabeth II and England's victory in the 1966 World Cup of Football. Although he puts himself forward to give the valedictory speech, Kevin's father has little sense of the appropriate discourse for the occasion and, when speaking of his son's reputed heroism, can offer nothing more stirring than a vague reference to being proud of 'what he did'. Only Kevin's teenage friends have any notion of how to treat a hero and they press him for tales of derring-do. Instead of seizing the chance to aggrandize his role, however, an obviously embarrassed Kevin responds with references to the inadequacy of the enemy that call into question any heroic interpretations of what happened in the Falklands.

Farcical as it may be, this scene is clearly not intended to mock Kevin or the villagers. On the contrary, it is the expectations imposed on them by an alien military culture that emerge as ridiculous. The function of the coming home celebration is thus to complete the debunking of heroic myth that has been the main focus of the first part of *Resurrected*. From this point on the film becomes less broadly satirical as it begins to examine how the role imposed on Kevin is not simply ludicrous and inappropriate but ultimately has the power to entrap and destroy him.

Unlike Robert Lawrence, Kevin Deakin has not internalized heroic ideas about his role as a soldier and has little personal investment in clinging to an identity imposed on him by circumstances beyond his control. Left in peace, he would therefore most likely have come through the bizarre period following his return to England relatively unscathed, especially as he seems to have a fairly good sense of the self he would like to shape around closeness to family, marriage and the tranquillity of fishing.

Furthermore, although Kevin, who has waking nightmares about his wounded comrade, Johnny Flodden, is clearly suffering from post traumatic stress disorder, it seems unlikely that his experiences in the Falklands have caused him any irreparable damage. Indeed, on balance, Kevin seems more liberated than troubled by his return from the dead and, soon after their reunion, tells his girlfriend, Julie, 'I can do anything now'.

However, two forces combine to ensure that, far from escaping the box into which circumstances have placed him, Kevin is pushed into tighter and tighter spaces. These are the tabloid press and the army. So far as the newspapers are concerned Kevin is nothing more than good copy. Therefore, when the reborn hero story begins to peter out, as is inevitable given Kevin's lack of charisma, they simply construct new roles for him. One newspaper, for instance, seeks to ginger up Kevin's rather limp heroic image by labelling him, quite inaccurately and implausibly, 'Local Romeo'. Much more promising, though, is the decision of a rival newspaper to remove Kevin's absent body from its original place in a dead hero narrative and to relocate it in an equally sensationalist story of desertion. This new approach proves to be effective not just in adding a twist to a tired story but in catching Kevin within a binary opposition, according the terms of which he must either be a hero, a role for which he is proving increasingly unsuited, or a deserter. The success of this journalistic ploy is immediately evident when Kevin revisits the scene of the village festivities only to be cold shouldered by the same people who had previously lionized him.

The task of dealing with two contradictory identities, neither of which has much relevance to how he sees himself, proves extremely difficult for Kevin. He protests to Julie and to his father that he did not desert and, in a later scene, tries to escape the binary trap in which he has been caught by telling the large crowd of villagers gathered together to celebrate Guy Fawkes' Night that he is neither hero nor deserter. But if he is to go beyond denial Kevin must have an alternative and well-formed version of himself to offer. Before he can develop this self he needs to work through his terrible experiences in the Falklands. Two things prevent Kevin doing this and, ironically, they are both related to the very roles he is so anxious to cast off.

First, like Robert Lawrence, Kevin discovers that not even civilians are willing to listen to a version of war that contradicts heroic mythology. Kevin's father, for instance, is so repulsed by his son's attempt to tell him about the realities of combat that, rather than let him continue with a narrative vital to the process of self redefinition, he dismisses the war in its entirety as 'all in the past now'. Second, once he has been accused of cowardice, it becomes impossible for Kevin to tell the therepeutically import- ant story of how he fled the battlefield in a state of shock after seeing Johnny Flodden's head wound because it is a version of events which makes him sound dangerously like a deserter.

As a result of the impossible situation in which he has become caught up, Kevin's sense of self deteriorates until he begins to take on the role of the unresurrected dead man, the one safe part, if an absence can be called a part, still available in the narra- tives that have been woven around him. Thus, at the end of a day trip to Morecombe, during which he is several times haunted by Johnny Flodden, Kevin tells Julie that he sees himself as a ghost. Three incidents further encourage Kevin to deny his material existence. First, he learns that while he was missing his mother went to a seance during which the medium claimed to be in communication with his spirit; second, he watches the service for the Falklands' dead on television; and third, he discovers that the pages documenting his memorial service have been ripped out of the church records. This obliteration of his dead hero self is particularly significant in that it makes Kevin feel doubly dead. A visual equivalent for Kevin's increasing tendency to withdraw from the world of the living is provided by a night time shot in which he appears as an indistinct lone blue figure blending into a blue background.

The problems of identity facing Kevin Deakin intensify still further when he returns to his regiment. In a milieu obsessed with ideas of glory, the ultimate accolade is to be considered a hero. As Corporal Byker says, 'It's not everyone who will be able to tell his grandchildren he was a hero back in '82'. That this mark of recognition has been accorded to such an unlikely candidate as Kevin Deakin is therefore very threatening to the regiment's sense of identity and it is not surprising that his comrades in arms soon follow the example set by the press and label him a deserter.

However, the suspicion that Kevin deserted is much more serious in a military context than a civilian and, whereas the villagers simply ostracized him, his fellow soldiers embark on a

campaign of active persecution. This persecution is also motivated, ironically enough, by the need of those who served in the
Falklands and who, like Kevin, were traumatized by the experience, to find an outlet for emotions discounted by a military
culture in which they are expected to function like 'high performance machines'. Kevin's chief persecutor, Slaven, for instance,
screams in his sleep and seethes with anger at the Argentinians
who killed his friends. Once again, then, as was the case with
the tabloid press, Kevin's identity as a deserter is a product of
the needs of others and has very little to do with anything integral to him.

Like the newspapers, which achieved their goal through the
use of banner headlines and resounding clichés, Slaven and his
followers need to develop a discourse of sufficient authority to
give legitimacy to the position that they have arbitrarily assigned
to Kevin. As a first step, Kevin's roommates greet him on his
return from leave by placing a newspaper clipping in his locker
and scrawling a yellow stripe across his uniform. Elements from
civilian and military sign systems are also fundamental to the
creation of the rather more complex discourse later employed to
lend an air of dignity to what is essentially a ritual of scapegoating.
A typical example of the crude but effective jumble of regimental rhetoric and legalistic phrases out of which this discourse is
constructed is provided at the beginning of the kangaroo court
when Kevin is forced to swear, 'By the colours of my regiment,
to tell the truth, the whole truth and nothing but the truth'.
Bombarded throughout the proceedings by portentous language
while being physically brutalized, Kevin is helpless to escape
the role assigned him. His one attempt to reshape the discourse
and thus to seize control of the situation by displacing the demand
that he admit to being a deserter with an honest expression of
what he experienced in the moments before he left the battlefield
is simply taken as an admission of guilt. For his soldier accusers
to do otherwise would be to accept the existence of trauma, thereby
calling into question their own fragile military identities.

One soldier does speak in defence of Kevin but the ritual is
preordained to end in a guilty verdict. The punishment immediately meted out takes the form of a particularly cruel custom
called the regimental bath which involves half drowning Kevin
in a tub full of hot water liberally dosed with bleach before
scraping his body with hard bristled brooms. Kevin's punishment

is relevant in two ways to the themes developed in *Resurrected*. First, by scrubbing away at Kevin, the soldiers are tacitly admitting their desire to erase his body because of the problems it has posed and continues to pose as a result of its failure to slot readily into one of the places provided for the body within military discourse. By so doing they are, of course, also inadvertently fulfilling Kevin's wish to escape his own materiality. Second, with this scourging, which leaves a network of bloody lines across his body, Kevin once again becomes identified with Christ. However, the identification is now more ironic than ever because the resurrection promised to him as the dead hero is no longer possible. Victimization has finally transformed Kevin into a ghost and it is therefore appropriate that he should be taken from the Scots Guards' barracks to a military hospital where he is surrounded by the living-dead survivors of the Falklands War. Here he is reunited with that other ghost, the comatose Johnny Flodden, and the film's final shot, which gradually fades to black, is of an almost catatonic Kevin sitting next to Johnny's bed.

Shortly before the end of *Resurrected*, director Paul Greengrass makes use of a tracking shot that moves across beds full of the wrecked bodies of wounded Falklands veterans and ends with the camera focused on a television set tuned to the 1950s war film, *Reach for the Sky*, in order to provide a last reminder of the huge ideological forces against which Kevin Deakin has been pitted. At once we are in the world of heroic myth. Lilting music plays while Douglas Bader's wife pleads with her husband to put off thoughts of returning to action. Bader, however, played in typically cheerful and plucky style by Kenneth More, is not to be swayed by womanly fears and insists that in spite of losing his legs he will fly again. War in this version is, as Bader's wife says, like a cricket match, a game in which the player of character is expected to shrug off injury and return to help the team. The attitudes embodied in this brief clip from *Reach for the Sky* stretch back at least as far as the chivalry and sports ethos of the nineteenth-century public schools and as far forward as the parliamentary debates conducted during the Falklands War. It is a value system that Robert Lawrence endorses and Kevin Deakin rejects. Nevertheless, it is equally destructive of both men.

Tumbledown and *Resurrected* are, then, both stories of individuals, but implicit within these stories is a broader social critique. The chivalric rhetoric that poured forth from the House of Commons and from the pages of the tabloid press in the spring of 1982 may have achieved its large political goals of winning support for the war and enhancing the prestige of the Conservative Party and, more specifically, of its leader, Margaret Thatcher. But, according to *Tumbledown* and *Resurrected*, in winning this support, Thatcher and her Party lost sight of the obligations they owed to young men such as Robert Lawrence and Kevin Deakin whose bodies were co-opted to the service of disembodied ideals. By reframing the war as a typically modern experience of betrayal and alienation, these two films thus make a significant contribution to the critical reassessment of the official myth of the Falklands War that, as we have seen in earlier chapters, has gradually been developing in the written and the visual media since 1982.

Notes

1. Both of these examples are taken from a piece in the *Guardian* that compares the euphemistic and occasionally chivalric language used by the British press to describe the military activities of the allied forces during the Gulf War with the much more explicit terminology employed when writing about the Iraqi army. Thus, 'we neutralize' while 'they kill' ('Mad Dogs and Englishmen', p. 16).
2. See Fussell and Hynes for excellent accounts of the literature and art of the First World War.
3. Once all of the limited newsreel footage of the Falklands War had become available, it was used repeatedly in documentaries about the war. Footage of the aftermath of the Argentinian attack on HMS *Galahad* must have had a particularly sobering effect on a British public caught up in Falklands euphoria. The final episode of the seven-part BBC 1 documentary, *Task Force South: The Battle for the Falklands* (1982), offers some gruesome shots of men burnt and maimed on the *Galahad* and even ITN-Granada's mainly celebratory *Battle for the Falklands* (1982) includes film of badly burned Chinese cooks accompanied by the comment that, 'We saw men with skin dripping from their heads'.
4. *Tumbledown* is based fairly closely on the experiences of the real Robert Lawrence while *Resurrected* offers a rather more heavily fictionalized version of the experiences of Philip Williams. For the two soldiers' first hand accounts of what they went through during and after the Falklands War see Lawrence and Williams, P. For an analysis of the ways in which Wood and Allen have deviated from the historical record, see MacKenzie, pp. 41–61.
5. Wood's screenplay for *Tumbledown* was published a year before the

film was made and differs in a number of respects from the dialogue in the film. However, all the pieces of dialogue quoted from the screenplay in this essay are also included in the film.

6. Rawton is actually Wroughton. See Lawrence, p. 55.

7. Peter Firth, the actor who plays the leading role in *Tumbledown*, is a more imposing and mature looking figure than the real Robert Lawrence, who was rather slight and boyish-looking prior to his wounding. David Thewlis, who plays Kevin Deakin, on the other hand, is an extremely gangling and somewhat ugly actor whose appearance is much more strikingly unheroic than that of the non-descript Phil Williams. For photographs of Lawrence and Williams, see Lawrence, p. 2 ff., and P. Williams, p. 86 ff. ww

6

Ten Years After:
An Ungentlemanly Act

COMMEMORATIVE PIECES

The tenth anniversary of the Falklands War was a curiously muted affair. Because of its new-found sensitivity towards the feelings of former foes become potential allies in oil exploration, the still-ruling Conservatives decided not to use the occasion as an opportunity to 'glamorize' the war. The Party's new leader, John Major, was also presumably less than eager to rekindle memories of the recently deposed Margaret Thatcher's finest moment. Neither, though, did the print or visual media approach the anniversary with much enthusiasm. Thus, the euphoric spirit so widespread in 1982 is seldom to be found in what tend to be rather sombre commemorative pieces.

A good example of the way in which the Falklands War was remembered in 1992 is provided by *'Belgrano*'s Children', an episode in the BBC 2 *War Stories* series that eschews triumphalist recollections of the British victory in favour of a sympathetic treatment of the ill-prepared Argentinian conscripts who suffered and died aboard the *General Belgrano*. Its elegiac tone is echoed in 'Simon's Return', a low keyed BBC 1 documentary in which Simon Weston, a Welsh Guardsman terribly disfigured by burns he received on HMS *Galahad*, returns to the Falklands before moving on to Buenos Aires to meet the pilot responsible for his injuries. Other documentaries provide Nick Barker, the captain of HMS *Endurance*, with an opportunity to speak freely about the Foreign Office's failure to listen when he warned them about an imminent Argentinian invasion ('Nick Barker') and allow Al Haig a chance to offer wittily sour comments about some of the personalities who helped frustrate his attempts to effect a peaceful solution to the Falklands crisis ('Woolly Al').

174

Furthest of all from a celebratory spirit, however, is Denys Blakeway's documentary, *The Falklands War*, broadcast by Channel 4 during January and February, 1992. Based on interviews with many of the war's major figures, including Al Haig, Francis Pym, Brigadier Julian Thompson, Admiral Sir Terence Lewin, Rear Admiral Carlos Busser, and Nicanor Costa Mendez but excluding Margaret Thatcher, who refused to take part, *The Falklands War* develops a view of the conflict in the South Atlantic that runs almost totally counter to the one that dominated in 1982. Thus, in the course of four episodes with the revealing titles, 'The Unnecessary War', 'In Peril at Sea', 'Trusting in Luck' and 'Bloody Choice', Blakeway tells a tale whose tone is set by an opening account of the lengthy history of political and diplomatic bungling responsible for the Argentinian invasion. The mistake upon which Blakeway dwells the longest is the decision to allow the residents of the Falklands an effective veto over a leaseback arrangement that seemed likely to resolve an otherwise intractible dispute. In Blakeway's reading of the Falklands War the rejection of this sensible proposal was probably the single most important factor in Argentina's decision to assert its claims to sovereignty over the Malvinas by force of arms.

Blakeway then goes on to depict the efforts of the task force during the war that followed not as a great triumph but as a series of near disasters averted by remarkable good luck. The operation to recapture South Georgia is thus described as going 'disastrously wrong' and serious doubt is cast on the strategic value of sinking the *Belgrano*. Similarly, considerable emphasis is put on the vulnerability of the British fleet in the absence of air superiority. A lengthy analysis of the events culminating in the sinking of HMS *Sheffield* also suggests a degree of incompetence on the part of the Royal Navy. The climactic land battle is characterized by Blakeway as both 'a reckless gamble' and a remarkable achievement seriously compromised by political pressure for an early victory and by inter-regimental rivalries. *The Falklands War* ends with some comments about the failure of military victory to resolve what Sir Anthony Parsons sees as the 'endless deadlock' over sovereignty.

AN UNGENTLEMANLY ACT: INTRODUCTION

However, the most significant of the 1992 retrospectives is *An Ungentlemanly Act*, a BBC 2 television film in which, rather than simply dousing the remnants of Falklands enthusiasm as Blakeway does, writer–director Stuart Urban pays homage to aspects of the Thatcherite myth of the Falklands War while simultaneously deconstructing it. As such, it is much more effective than other tenth-anniversary works in reflecting the tension that, as I have tried to show in this book, has gradually developed between affirmative and sceptical readings of the Falklands War and its significance in the years since the British victory.

Intentionality of the kind that I am attributing to Urban is, in fact, something that he vigorously denies in a letter written as a response to Philip Kemp's review of his film. In reacting to Kemp's claim that he is making 'explicit play' (p. 65) with the conventions of Ealing comedies such as *Passport to Pimlico*, Urban minimises the artist's role in the creation of *An Ungentlemanly Act* by stressing the film's fidelity to fact. The emphasis placed here on verisimilitude is an echo of the statement that appears at the beginning of the film: 'This film interprets actual events and is based wherever possible on first-hand accounts'. Besides denying that *An Ungentlemanly Act* is an exercise in intertextuality, Urban's letter also dismisses the idea that his film might have political intentions. Indeed, he comes close to conceding the workings of an interpretative hand only in his statement that 'the core of the film is empathy for human beings caught up in this mess' (p. 71). Urban espouses this same limited goal when he tells the *Observer's* Richard Brooks that he 'wanted a human story, not a political one' (Brooks, p. 74).

However, a careful viewing of *An Ungentlemanly Act* reveals a degree of disingenuity in Urban's comments on his authorial role. Certainly no one voice is obviously privileged over any other in this firmly unpolemical film. Nevertheless, a clear, albeit complex, point of view does emerge from Urban's choice of subject matter and from the way in which he organizes and presents the factual components upon which his narrative is based. It is surely significant, for instance, given the wealth of raw material available to him, that Urban should have chosen to limit his tenth-anniversary retrospective view of the Falklands War almost entirely to a delineation of the colonial and rural aspects of island life and to an account of the two days covered by the Argentinian invasion. By limiting his scope in this way, Urban is able to offer an analysis of the impact of a typically twentieth-century war machine on what is presented as a deeply anachronistic society that takes him beyond the personal dimensions of the Falklands War into an examination of some of the major contradictions and points of weakness in the Thatcherite myth of the war.

The tone of Urban's portrayal of life on the Falklands is often made ironic or even gently mocking by the comic juxtaposition of incongruous elements. At the same time, though, the Falklands presented in *An Ungentlemanly Act* bear a close resemblance to the idyllic colonial remnant offered by Thatcher as her model of the authentic Britain. There are, of course, significant differences between the actual and idealized Falklands, and in order to close the gap between them Urban has to ignore some of the harsher realities of the islanders' lives, most notably the difficulties inherent in sheep farming on remote ranches located in the rugged, wet and frequently frigid terrain beyond Port Stanley and the exploitative economic relationship that exists between the serf-like population and its absentee landlord, the Falkland Islands Company.

In the absence of any reference to its grim working conditions or its economic arrangements, colonialism as practised in the Falklands can be presented as a benign system built upon a noblesse oblige relationship between the Governor, Rex Hunt, and the local people over whom he has command. Hunt's authority, as depicted in *An Ungentlemanly Act*, is well received by the inhabitants of the Falklands because his benevolent personal qualities ensure that it is lightly exercised. Even more important, in contrast to the usual colonial experience in which indigenous cultural norms were swept away in favour of alien and frequently offensive British values and customs, Hunt represents a way of life readily accepted by a people who mostly originate from and identify with Britain. Indeed, far from experiencing the problems of difference, the Falklands evoked by Urban, who softens the rough landscape by bathing it in sunlight and who provides frequent shots of the quintessentially English Government House, mirror the idealized England of myth with its great houses, rolling landscapes, kindly squires and happy peasants.

Urban's Falklands have a quality similar to that of the eponymous village in Alan Jay Lerner and Frederick Loewe's musical

play, *Brigadoon* (1947), or Furness, the Scottish fishing village in
Bill Forsyth's film, *Local Hero* (1984), in that all three are presented
as oases where a simpler, rural way of life run in accordance
with traditional practices offers a respite from the grim realities
of the largely urbanized world of the twentieth century. They
are also similar in their fragility and ephemerality. Brigadoon,
of course, appears but once every 100 years while Furness in
Local Hero looms out of the mist like a vision only to become
inaccessible to the film's central character, Mac, once he has made
the mistake of returning to Houston, a noisy, soulless and hence
thoroughly modern place where people devote all their energies
to the pursuit of wealth. The Falklands, in their turn, are made
extremely vulnerable by the commitment of the thoroughly decent
and rather old fashioned governor, Rex Hunt, and the naive and
unworldly islanders, to a kind and gentle style of living poorly
equipped to deal with challenges from the outside.

The potential loss of a way of life portrayed by Urban as comic
yet valuable becomes a stark reality with the Argentinian invasion that provides *An Ungentlemanly Act* with its main narrative
thrust. That the loss is more than temporary is confirmed by the
film's last few minutes during which the sequence of events
culminating in the restoration of British sovereignty is briefly
recapitulated. As presented in this addendum to the main action,
the British forces function not as liberators but as a second wave
of invaders. Thus, the overwhelming visual image of both invasions is of a precious but fragile world smashed by advanced
twentieth-century technology.

With this ending, Urban makes the ironic point that, in
dispatching the task force, it was Margaret Thatcher herself who
guaranteed that the islanders' way of life would be crushed
beneath the same brutal modernity she claimed it would displace.
By so doing he completes an elliptical but powerful critique of
the role played by the Falkland Islands in the myth that Thatcher
wove around the war in the South Atlantic. Earlier stages in
Urban's critique have their roots in the concrete form he gives
to an idyllic conception of the Falklands that could serve Thatcher's purposes only so long as it remained vague and in his emphasis on the fragility and even the absurdity of the very social structures
that were supposed to serve as a model for a revitalized Britain.

While much of his emphasis in *An Ungentlemanly Act* is on
establishing the Falkland Islands as a vantage point from which

to view the deficiencies of Thatcherite ideology, Urban, as I will be arguing in the conclusion to this chapter, finally seeks a position that transcends a concern with a single political figure. Thus, in the end, he neither endorses imperialist nor Thatcherite systems of belief because both provide for a tolerance of war that, from a perspective provided by Mavis Hunt, is irreconcilable with the one value that really counts: a respect for human life. In its most fundamental statement, then, *An Ungentlemanly Act* does valorize the personal but to the detriment rather than, as Urban claims, to the exclusion of the political.

THE FALKLANDS AS FRAGILE IDYLL

The role played by the Falklands in *An Ungentlemanly Act* as a rural, colonial idyll is established by an opening montage during which Urban edits sunlit shots of the landscape in and around Port Stanley into a ceremonial scene replete with visual and aural images of British imperial power. The ceremony's occasion, the laying of a wreath at the war memorial, immediately points up the important part played by the glorification of military valour in an imperialistic understanding of the world. Other images that spring from Britain's imperial tradition include the full dress uniform complete with medals and cockaded hat worn by the Governor, Rex Hunt; the presence of representatives, also in formal attire, of the ecclesiastical, law enforcement and military institutions that once strove to enforce a conformity to British ways amongst the many and diverse cultures that formed the British Empire; and the playing by a Royal Marine band of 'A Life on the Ocean Wave', the anthem of a Royal Navy without which Britain could not have maintained control over its widely disseminated colonies. A final symbol of British imperialism, the Union Jack, which is first shown in a dramatic close up, also serves to reinforce the connection between landscape and system of governance in being a version of the flag adapted for the Falklands by the addition of a sheep at its centre.

    The idyllic quality that what is in reality a rather grim land and seascape assumes in *An Ungentlemanly Act* derives most obviously from Urban's decision to do all his location shooting on some of those rare calm days when the Falklands and their surrounding waters are bathed in sunlight pouring out of a pure

blue sky. It is also a product, however, of the introduction into
the landscape of several evocative images of horses, birds and a
man on a white horse. This final image is particularly important
to Urban's construction of the Falklands as idyll because of its
reoccurance in two paintings. The first, discussed below, offers
an idealized pictorial representation of Empire and the second
is a typically pastoral scene by John Constable featuring woods
and several horses, one of them white.

Shots of the ancient activity of peat digging reinforce the
impression, already created by imperial ritual and images of an
unmechanized landscape, that the Falklands exist in a time warp
where life is more orderly, beautiful and peaceful than is generally the case in the late twentieth century. There is little about
the few glimpses offered of the Falklands' urban centre, Port
Stanley, with its simple wooden houses, archaic phone system
and radio station that plays Jimmy Shand, Frank Sinatra and
Mantovani to contradict a sense of being transported into a somewhat mythic past.

An explanation for the affirmative attitude to imperialism
implicit in the juxtaposition of colonial and idyllic images during
the first few minutes of *An Ungentlemanly Act* is provided by
Urban's sympathetic treatment of a ruling class – comprising the
Hunts and their staff, Chief of Police, Ronnie Lamb, and to a
lesser extent, the Royal Marines' commanding officer, Major
Norman – whose mindset, behaviour and values have been shaped
by a lifetime of service to the Empire. The imperialistic approach
to experience shared by these people is graphically represented
in a painting of a nineteenth-century military officer seated on a
white horse against a tropical background and attended by two
uniformed natives that conjures up a world where the British
have taken on the task of exercising a dignified and paternalistic
authority over suitably deferential and loyal indigenous peoples.
The painting is so evocative for Ronnie Lamb, a veteran of Borneo
that, immediately after he has completed hanging it in the police
station, he expresses a nostalgic intention to greet the 'glorious
weather' by wearing his 'tropical uniform'.

A similarly imperialistic habit of mind underlies the determination of the Hunts' handyman, Don Bonner, to protect the Union
Jack flying outside Government House from seizure by the 'fuzzy
wuzzies', as he calls the Argentinian troops. The military glories
intrinsic to an imperial view of British history are also clearly

much in the minds of Hunt's wife and son when they listen to
the Governor's announcement of the imminent invasion by Argentina. For Mavis, Rex Hunt's stirring words are redolent with the
spirit of Dunkirk while they make Tony think of the Battle of
Britain. Although much too young to have shared in any but
the tail end of the colonial experience, the teenage Tony Hunt,
who always wears a Second World War bomber jacket, is nevertheless clearly steeped in a boys' adventure fiction version of
imperial lore. His response to the prospect of war is, for example, to bring his motor bike spinning to a dramatic halt in front
of Major Norman before volunteering to serve as a dispatch rider.
It is second nature even for Norman who, as we will see later,
does not share all of Hunt's gentlemanly ideas about the conduct
of war, to frame the address that he delivers to his Royal Marines
as they prepare for battle in traditionally patriotic terms. Thus,
he encourages them to act like 'Green Berets and Royals' and
asks them to remember that they are fighting 'for what "Royal"
stands for'.

The influence of an imperial approach to experience on the
behaviour of this group of characters emerges most clearly,
however, from Rex and Mavis Hunt's determination to maintain
old fashioned British standards of good manners, appropriate
dress and refined behaviour even in the most testing of colonial
circumstances. Government House is, for example, furnished
and accoutered in such a way as to allow any situation to be
approached with an appropriate blend of formality and hospitality. Thus, the availability of a spot in the grounds beneath a
fluttering Union Jack and in the midst of carefully laid out gardens
ensures that a proper degree of dignity attends a first meeting
with Major Norman, the new Royal Marines' commander. The
obviously English style of these gardens helps the Hunts to achieve
their secondary goal as hosts by making their recently arrived
guest feel at home. The serving of tea on bone china at the emergency meeting of the Falklands Islands Council called in response
to news of an imminent invasion further exemplifies the importance the Hunts accord to propriety. The same occasion provides
a demonstration of the Governor and his wife's success in instilling
a keen regard for good manners amongst the natives because,
no sooner has Mavis inadvertently blundered into the room, than
the councillors, all formally dressed despite the unscheduled nature
of the meeting, rise to their feet.

A determination to cling to a civilized code of conduct even when the difficulties of life in a remote colony are compounded by the approach of an invasion force also explains why Rex Hunt prefaces his attempts to garner information about the mood in Buenos Aires from the journalist, Simon Winchester, with the serving of tea and chat about cricket. More remarkable still is the Hunts' insistence, despite the absence of guests, that the meal eaten on the evening of the invasion be a formal one served to them as they sit at either end of a grand, candlelit table beneath a portrait of the Queen. Given this abundant evidence of his concern with formality, we are not surprised that Rex Hunt chooses a tie appropriate for his upcoming encounter with the Argentinian military before retiring to bed and that he later makes use of an umbrella purchased at Briggs of Piccadilly as the staff for the white flag carried by Dick Baker during his peace mission.

The self-mocking spirit in which Hunt improvises the formalities of surrender clearly points up an element of comedy in his obsession with propriety that Urban, as we will see later, fully exploits. Nevertheless, while he might gently mock the Hunts and their polite codes, Urban also admires them for their ability to recognize that, far from being mere form, good manners serve a moral function by underpinning an ideal of service to others.[1] Thus, Rex and Mavis Hunt strive consistently throughout *An Ungentlemanly Act* to make the transition from the ritual gestures of concern for others implicit in polite behaviour to genuine acts of noblesse oblige. Mavis is equally capable, for example, of offering hospitality to Simon Winchester of a largely ritual kind and of pausing on her way out of Government House to ensure that the Royal Marines standing guard in the rain are provided with the hot tea and shelter that will be of real use to them. Her understanding of the more-than-ritual function of food and drink is further illustrated when she responds to news of the imminent invasion by offering to make a vat of lasagne 'for everyone'.

Rex Hunt's genuine concern for the people he governs becomes evident several times during the invasion. His priority, for instance, in planning military tactics is to protect the women and children of Port Stanley. This ability to go beyond personal considerations even at moments of great stress is also demonstrated by Hunt's willingness to take the time needed to tactfully dissuade Don Bonner from endangering his life by defending the flag against the Argentinians. A final example of the sense of noblesse oblige upon which Hunt bases his approach to experience occurs when, rather than dwell on the humiliation he has just experienced in the painful ritual of surrender, he turns his thoughts to the situation of the defeated Royal Marines and demands that they be repatriated.

Although the Hunts' code of conduct has its origins in the gentlemanly values of the eighteenth century, Urban makes use of an incident involving the Police Chief, Ronnie Lamb, to ensure that the viewer is aware of its more immediate roots in imperialist ideology. In the midst of the invasion, Lamb is called upon to risk his own life in order to save a foolhardy islander who has decided to walk through the war zone protected only by a white flag. Considerations of personal safety make Lamb unwilling to take on this responsibility and an appeal to his self-proclaimed status as the 'awesome warrior of Borneo' simply prompts him at first to admit an element of exaggeration in his tales of personal heroism. Nevertheless, this reminder of the important part played by the concept of service in the colonial experience is ultimately sufficient to send him racing out of the safe haven of the police station on a life-threatening rescue mission.

Urban's idealized portrayal of the hierarchical social structures around which late colonial life on the Falklands is organized is completed by his depiction of the local population. The islanders, as might be expected of people assigned the role of rustics in a rural idyll ruled by the anachronistically benevolent Hunts, are properly deferential towards their betters. Thus, the women Mavis encounters in the West Store speak to her respectfully, attend to her advice and are obviously honoured that she gives them her attention. The islanders' ready acceptance of their position within the colonial hierarchy is nowhere more evident, however, than in the large number of people, many of them in tears, who turn out to wave their Union Jacks and sing 'Auld Lang Syne' as the exiled Governor and his wife are driven to the airport on their way into exile.

At the same time, though, that Falklands society is organized according to strictly hierarchical principles, authority is exercised with such a light hand that even those at the bottom of the social scale have plenty of scope for exercising the kind of sturdy independence and even eccentricity fundamental to the traditional stereotype of the free born Englishman. The existence of such characterisitics amongst the islanders is first suggested by a shot of a woman walking a sheep on a lead. They become particularly evident, however, during scenes set in the Stanley jail where the one prisoner is so little cowed by the situation in which he has been placed by the workings of a judicial system imported from Britain that he spends his time watching horror videos from the comfort of his bed or wandering outside his unlocked cell. Other examples of the Falkland Islanders' independent stance are provided by the refusal of those living outside Stanley to cooperate with the Governor's attempt to introduce daylight saving time and by the total lack of concern on the part of a drunken sheep farmer whose poorly parked Land Rover has blocked the progress of a jeep occupied by Majors Noot and Norman.

Urban's presentation of life on the Falkland Islands may have, as he claims, a firm basis in fact. Nevertheless, the overall impression created is of a landscape so colourful, tranquil and untouched by industrialization and of a society at once so firmly rooted in traditions of service and deference and yet respectful of individual difference that, far from having the feel of a real place, the Falklands Islands of *An Ungentlemanly Act* emerge as a more substantial version of the mythic Falklands that serve to give a semblance of form to Thatcher's otherwise vague notion of an authentic Britain. The effect, though, of adding flesh to Thatcher's vision of the Falklands is to undercut rather than to reinforce an official reading of the Falklands War because a view of the nation according to which Britain is equally committed to reclaiming an idealized past and to effecting radical change along monetarist lines can retain its credibility only so long as the details remain fuzzy. Once a clear image is created, as in *An Ungentlemanly Act*, of the gentle, unselfish people, the relaxed, eccentric way of life and the unmechanized landscape that would be essential components of any realization of Thatcher's nostalgic vision of nation, the idea that such a society could at the same time be thoroughly competitive, single-mindedly acquisitive and technologically productive becomes very hard to sustain.

Urban further emphasizes the flaws in an ideology that welds together anachronistic and progressive elements by demonstrating how fragile, ludicrous and inadequate the Falklands begin to look when viewed from a late twentieth-century perspective. The fragility of the Falklands as bastion of a largely defunct colonial system is suggested at the very beginning of *An Ungentlemanly Act* when the camera is forced to zoom right in on a Howard

Vincent map of the British Empire before it can locate any places still marked by Union Jacks. And then, all it finds are the Falkland Islands and South Georgia, which between them amount to no more than a scattering of red dots amidst the vast blue of the South Atlantic.

A series of allusions to Rex Hunt's professional past provide further reminders of how close the imperial phase in British history is to its end. As presented in *An Ungentlemanly Act,* Hunt's military and diplomatic careers serve as a mirror of the progressive shrinking of Britain's once magisterial role in the world since the end of the Second World War. Thus, just as he joined the Royal Air Force a little too late to share in the glory of the Battle of Britain, so Hunt's service as a diplomat which, in addition to the highly vulnerable Falklands, has taken him to such soon-to-be-lost colonial outposts as Borneo and the North-West Frontier, has coincided not with the flourishing of British imperial power but with its disappearance. The sense that Hunt is a man fated to be present as some notable phases in twentieth-century history are brought to a close is confirmed by the revelation that he was amongst those evacuated from Saigon at the end of the Vietnam War.

In similar fashion to Hunt's career, physical smallness (with its accompanying sense of fragility), a quality first communicated by the film's opening map image, functions throughout *An Ungentlemanly Act* as a symbol of imperial decline. When the camera tracks back from the initially impressive image of a uniformed and erect Rex Hunt at the war memorial, for instance, it reveals a group of onlookers so few in number that those who are dressed to represent their roles in the structure of imperial authority exercised over the Falklands by her Majesty's Britannic Government come embarassingly close to outnumbering the ordinary citizens with whom they mingle. The following scene in which Dick Baker is shown playing golf is equally suggestive of Britain's shrinking ability to transport its institutions to colonial locations. The course itself is no more than a sheep pasture and the clubhouse is a low portable building that falls well short of the ambitions suggested by the impressive Stanley Golf Club sign behind which it is almost hidden in a low angle shot.

The two most visible symbols of Rex Hunt's authority, besides his dress uniform and cockaded hat, are Government House and the official car. Neither is quite what might be expected, however.

The two-storey brick house with its extensive gardens is impressive enough when viewed in the context of the humble wooden buildings of Port Stanley. Nevertheless, it much more closely resembles the kind of substantial suburban house that a bank manager or a fairly successful solicitor might occupy in Britain than the official residence of a representative of the Queen.[2] Apart from the dining room, where the furnishings include a magnificent table and portraits of the Queen and Margaret Thatcher, the interior of the house is equally lacking in grandeur. The room in which Hunt entertains Simon Winchester, with its fireplace, deep yellow armchair, blue carpets, piano and walls dotted with landscape paintings, might be found, for example, inside hundreds of upper middle class British houses. The most telling detail of all, though, is a clearly improvised nameplate on the door of the Governor's office that not only fails to convey the slightest hint of the importance formerly associated with Hunt's position but also signals the temporary nature of his tenure as imperial overlord.

The shrivelling of British imperialism is figured even more obviously in Hunt's official car, which is a former London taxi cab rather than the expected Rolls Royce. Despite its dark red paintwork and Union Jack pennant, and the provision of an official driver in the shape of Don Bonner transformed from handyman to chauffeur by the addition of an appropriate hat, the taxi remains a relatively humble vehicle that does not look entirely out of place when conveying Mavis Hunt to the West Store in search of tinned fruit. The role played by the Governor's car in communicating Britain's decline as an imperial power is complemented by that of the absurdly small Volkswagen Beetle in which Ronnie Lamb carries out his duties as Police Chief.

Because of the drastically reduced scale on which it is shown to operate in *An Ungentlemanly Act*, the remnant of the British Empire still functioning in the Falklands is not only vulnerable but also absurdly comic. In general, Urban is fairly circumspect about exploiting the comic potential of his material and is content to let his audience perceive for itself the humorous aspects of scenes that are played straight. However, there are several occasions upon which he foregrounds the element of absurdity implicit in his material.

The dignified tone of the impressive imperial ritual performed at the war memorial is undercut, for example, not only by shots of the sparse crowd but also by a cut to a penguin apparently marching in time to what would otherwise be a stirring rendition of the patriotic tune, 'A Life on the Ocean Wave'. A later scene is made even more farcical when Lamb's dachshund, Fritzi, interrupts the serious task of burying important documents beside the Government House flagpole, and hence under the symbolic protection of the Union Jack, by digging up the remains of Lamb's pet parrot, Arthur. The juxtaposition of incompatible elements is also employed to comic effect during the scene in which the radio station's disc jockey follows Hunt's portentous announcement of an impending Argentinian invasion by playing 'Strangers in the Night' while the camera provides a view of the Queen's portrait as it hangs on the studio wall next to a calendar still set to April Fool's Day.

Even more effective, though, in revealing the inadequacies of a colonial system for which Stuart Urban clearly has considerable affection are several scenes in the course of which Rex Hunt, as Commander in Chief of the small force of Royal Marines charged with guarding one of Britain's last imperial outposts, faces up to the challenge posed by Argentina's thoroughly modern war machine. Hunt, whose deep concern for the safety of the women and children under his charge has already been noted, takes his task seriously. Indeed, as we might expect of a man thoroughly steeped in an imperialist culture that values the military virtues over all others, he even anticipates that the impending invasion will provide him with his 'finest hour'. Nevertheless, he fails totally in his task of preventing the Falklands from falling into Argentinian hands.

This failure is due in large part, of course, to the inadequate resources available to a shrunken imperial power. The Royal Marine garrison numbers only 76 men, 42 of whom have been on the Falklands for just over a month, supplemented by nine sailors from HMS *Endurance* and 23 members of the Falkland Islands Defence Force. Besides being few in number, the British forces, as depicted in *An Ungentlemanly Act* at least, seem to possess no weapons more powerful than submachine guns.[3] The Argentinians, by contrast, have 800 men on the ground by the time Hunt calls for a truce and another 2000 about to land. Furthermore, they are able to back up their assault on Government House with rifle-mounted rocket launchers and armoured personnel carriers.

More important, though, in providing an understanding of the inability of a system developed in the nineteenth century to cope with modern reality is Urban's analysis of the part played by anachronistic imperial values in the British defeat. What is particularly apparent from the beginning of *An Ungentlemanly Act* is that, despite the ever-present possibility of an Argentinian invasion, planning for the defence of the Falklands has been conducted according to the muddle-through principles favoured by the gentleman amateurs who were in charge during the great days of the Empire. The incoming Royal Marine commander is immediately struck, for example, by the extent to which the troops about to be relieved have 'gone native', a condition whose main symptoms seem to be long hair, scruffy appearance and a lack of discipline. The tangible effects of this lack of discipline are felt with the discovery that a cracked two-inch mortar, urgently needed for the fight against Argentina, has not been repaired.

Further evidence of the amateurish spirit that characterizes the conduct of military business in the Falklands is provided by Major Norman's comment, made after a cursory scan of the ocean and in direct contradiction of the visual evidence presented to the viewer, that there is 'not so much as a periscope' in sight. Norman and his predecessor, Gary Noot, are also involved in a bungled spying mission that is brought to an ignominious conclusion when their target, Hector Giloberto, the Argentinian State Airline representative, stumbles upon their hiding place. Rex Hunt's limitations as Commander in Chief are highlighted by the scene in which he is shown preparing for the imminent invasion by reading *Battle of the Falklands*, Commander H. Cooper Spencer's account of a British Naval victory during the First World War.

Because of their failure to pay serious attention to advance planning, the British are almost totally unprepared for the invasion when it finally comes. A spirit of desperate improvisation is apparent, for example, in the decision to limit front line defence to the only beach short enough to be mined with the limited equipment available. Such casual behaviour might have been sufficient had the enemy really been, as Don Bonner imagines, the lightly armed natives typically encountered during the colonization process. However, it is hopelessly inadequate when opposition forces emerge from the sea in amphibious armoured cars, instantly putting to flight the three-man British defence force. Given the lack of preparedness of the professionals, it is not surprising that when the moment of crisis arrives the members of the volunteer Falkland Islands Defence Force prove lacking in both the weapons and the training needed to go to war. For one of their number, at least, the principle of readiness amounts to nothing more than making sure he is supplied with sandwiches and a flask of tea.

The negative effects of the casual manner in which the British approach the defence of the Falklands are exacerbated by Rex Hunt's determination, in his capacity as Commander in Chief, to base strategic decisions on the imperial ideals of good sportsmanship, fair play and a concern for honour. His repeated delays in interning Argentine nationals are, for instance, the product of an unwillingness to risk treating them unfairly so long as the invasion remains in doubt. The consequence is a hasty and bungled last minute round up that fails to net their main target, the Argentinian agent, Hector Giloberto.

Of even greater significance is Hunt's refusal to allow Norman to take his Royal Marines into the hills where they could use guerilla warfare tactics against the numerically superior Argentinian forces because he believes that such a course of action would 'look silly' and therefore involve a loss of face. Norman's frustration with the hopelessly outmoded imperialist value system upon which Hunt bases his decision is expressed in his ironic suggestion that he order his men to form a square in imitation of the overmatched British garrison depicted in the film *Zulu*. In reality, since Hunt also refuses to allow street fighting amongst the highly flammable buildings of Port Stanley, the Royal Marines are left with the only slightly better option of engaging in an Alamo-style defence of Government House guaranteed to end in surrender or total annihilation.

The most conclusive evidence of the irrelevance of imperialist values to modern warfare is provided, however, by Hunt's attempts to introduce a standard of good manners into his dealings with the victorious Argentinian commander, Vice Admiral Carlos Busser. When they meet Hunt refuses to shake Busser's hand and insists that he acknowledge the invasion as 'an ungentlemanly act' necessitating an immediate Argentinian withdrawal. While he is kind enough to conform to the genteel style demanded by Hunt, Busser does not, of course, submit to a code of conduct irrelevant to a situation in which superiority is defined entirely by force of arms. Thus, while Hunt may have won the battle of manners, he has nevertheless lost the war, a reality which is fully confirmed

by the arrogant and abusive manner in which Major Patricio
Dowling is able to behave towards the defeated British without
in the least endangering his status as victor.

The people of the Falklands are, if anything, even less well
equipped than their colonial masters to deal with the challenges
posed by the modern world. While their innocence might charm
Urban, he is also well aware that it has a dark side in the form
of a debilitating naiveté, resulting partly from the islanders' anachronistic way of life and partly from their parochial attitudes. This
parochialism is evident both in the suggestion made by a wait-
ress at the Uplands Goose that lasagne, hardly the most exotic
of foreign dishes, will meet the needs of a vegetarian customer
and in the prominence given by the local newspaper to a story
running under the headline 'Artificial Insemination Technique'
and illustrated by a large photograph of a sheep.

The degree to which their parochialism makes the islanders
vulnerable is comically yet chillingly revealed by their inability
to grasp the major implications for their way of life of an invasion by heavily mechanized Argentinian forces. It is perhaps not
entirely surprising that, so long as there is no more than a possibility of becoming caught up in an armed combat, the islanders
have a great deal of difficulty in taking seriously what is to them
a totally alien event. The radio station, for example, is able to
identify as the only tangible consequence of the looming crisis
the need to cancel the annual rugby game between the Stanley
Ladies Rugby Club and the incoming garrison. A similar lack of
awareness is demonstrated by the police constable's ability to
speak of the 'invasion coming tonight' in terms more usually
associated with discussions of the weather.

What is remarkable, though, is the extent to which the residents of Port Stanley seem unable to come to terms with the
fact of war even after its sights and sounds have intruded into
their community. Thus, in one incident, a local woman, dressed
in dressing gown and slippers, emerges from her house to offer
tea to three marines crouched behind her picket fence in order
to conceal themselves from a line of advancing Argentinian
armoured personnel carriers. In another, the local street sweeper,
determined that nothing will prevent him from going to work,
walks through the war zone, the existence of which he acknowledges only by waving a white rag tied to a stick.

The state of denial that characterizes the islanders' response to the violent intrusion of modern technology into their idyllic world is fostered by the partly ironic and partly soothing manner in which the local radio station treats the invasion. Hunt's announcement that the Argentinian forces are about to land, for instance, prompts the disc jockey to play 'Strangers in the Night', followed by the Beatles' gently nostalgic 'Yesterday' and the calming strings of Mantovani. These attempts to obscure the brutal reality of what has descended on the islanders' peaceful community clearly strike a chord with the listener who phones in to describe the deadly combat taking place outside her window as 'colourful really'.

Urban's analysis of the unbridgeable nature of the gap between Falklands society and the modern world represented by the Argentinian invasion force and, more specifically, of the vulnerability of this precious but fragile survivor of nineteenth-century imperialism to the challenge of twentieth-century technology is reinforced by a series of visual contrasts. One is constructed out of cuts between the menacing, dark shapes of Argentinian invasion craft approaching the Falklands and the Hunts, bathed in warm candelight as they eat a gracious meal in their richly decorated formal dining room. Another is created by the introduction of a shot in which a periscope pokes menacingly above the surface of the ocean into an otherwise lyrical montage of the sunlit and placid Falklands' landscape. Later in the film, a particularly dramatic contrast emerges out of the juxtaposition of dark shots of the Argentinian fleet steaming rapidly through rough seas and tranquil images of a moonlit and extremely still Stanley harbour. Finally, while the invasion is taking place, Urban has the opportunity to introduce a number of long shots that capture the incongruous impression created by the incursion of heavily armed Argentinian soldiers in full combat gear into a Port Stanley looking even more peaceable than usual in the early dawn.

JUDGING MARGARET THATCHER

The main action of *An Ungentlemanly Act* is, then, devoted to a portrayal of the Falklands and its inhabitants as an idyllic but fragile survivor of Britain's former Empire that calls into question both the compatibility of the nostalgic and thrustingly monetarist aspects of Thatcherite ideology and the practicality of a plan of national revival based on such a shaky foundation as that provided by one of Britain's last surviving colonies. Urban's critique of Margaret Thatcher and her programme for Britain becomes even more sharp-edged, however, in the final minutes of *An Ungentlemanly Act* which are devoted to a montage of newsreel and staged images summarizing the sequence of events leading to the recapture of the Falklands.

The filming of the montage in eerie black and white, made even stranger by blotches of colour, and the persistence of a howling wind on the accompanying soundtrack make it clear that this addendum to Urban's film is not intended to celebrate the restoration of the Falklands' status quo. On the contrary, although the official taxi is taken out of storage and both Hunt and Norman return to the islands, what Urban seems to be suggesting is that, by bringing even more sophisticated weaponry into play, a point reinforced by images of Harrier jets and the sinking *Belgrano*, Thatcher has simply completed the destruction of an idyllic way of life begun by the Argentinians.

The very brevity of the segment, which gives short shrift to events usually central in dramatizations of the Falklands War, further calls into question any preconceptions viewers might have about the heroic role of the task force as retrievers of history. A similar viewpoint is implicit in the close resemblance between the dark images through which the story of Britain's counter attack is told and those employed earlier in depictions of Argentinian troops and their efficient weapons of destruction. Most significant of all, though, in communicating Urban's position regarding the restoration of British power is a brief news item heard on the soundtrack announcing Thatcher's plans to create a permanent base on the Falklands.

As most of those watching *An Ungentlemanly Act* would have known, this base turned out to be very different from the previous garrison. The 40 or so marines originally stationed at Moody Brook were, according to Urban's presentation of them, easily absorbed into the Falklands' way of life. Thus, Corporal 'Geordie' Gill has not only married a local girl but in defeat feels acute distress at letting down the islanders even though he has fought fiercely in their defence. Fortress Falklands, by contrast, comprises 4000 men and the infrastructure needed to accommodate them, a new runway capable of receiving the largest transport planes, and constant helicopter activity. The result, as one Falklands resident comments in the *Panorama* documentary, 'The Price of Victory', is like living in the centre of London.

Urban never directly states that Thatcher's decision to set in motion a sequence of events that culminated in the destruction of the Falklands' fragile social structure was the result not of unfortunate circumstances but of her inability to recognize the simpler imperial past as anything other than a useful tool for stirring up patriotic sentiment at home. However, a judgement along these lines is clearly implicit in the comparison the viewer is invited to make between Margaret Thatcher and Mavis Hunt.

In general the two women are not at all alike but there is a striking similarity in the roles they assume as mothers to their 'boys', as they both call the British troops, that paradoxically points up their essential moral differences. Mavis, steeped as she is in an ideal of noblesse oblige, interprets the role quite literally and her relationship with the Royal Marines stationed on the Falklands is characterized by a series of caring gestures, including the offer of shelter from the weather and the provision of various forms of food and drink. As a result, the viewer has no doubts about the sincerity of the tears that she sheds at the sight of the defeated Royal Marines, disarmed and placed under Argentinian guard. Thatcher's tearful response on learning that 20 men had been killed in the Exocet attack on HMS *Sheffield* (*Sun*, 6 May 1982, p. 21; Curteis, p. 178) may have been equally genuine. However, because these men died following her orders, there would seem to be considerable justification in viewing the maternal relationship she claimed with them as little more than another cynical tactic for winning public support.

Finally, though, in what is perhaps the most important of the shifts in moral focus around which *An Ungentlemanly Act* is structured, Mavis Hunt serves not just to complete Urban's critique of Margaret Thatcher but to call into question an imperial code otherwise shown in such a favourable light. The implicit debate in which Rex Hunt engages first with the Argentinians and then with Thatcher is focused on the way in which wars should be fought. Mavis, however, introduces a new paradigm by questioning whether they should be fought at all. Thus, in a conversation which takes place as the fighting is about to begin, Mavis sets a concern for the loss of the life of even one man against Major Norman's argument, deeply rooted in imperial codes of heroism and honour, that he must proceed with an obviously hopeless defence of the Falklands because '"surrender" isn't something in our vocabulary' and because he would be betraying his men if he gave up without a strong fight.

Stirring as the view of war shared by Norman and Rex Hunt may be, especially when compared to the expedient reasons that, in Urban's view, prompted Thatcher to dispatch the task force, the consequences of taking up arms are, as Mavis Hunt points out, the same regardless of motive. Her point is graphically illustrated by the close attention paid in *An Ungentlemanly Act* to the lingering and painful death of the invasion's only casualty who is killed not by the ungentlemanly Argentinians but by the gallant defenders of Government House. Ultimately, then, but as his last comment on politics and ideology rather than to their exclusion, Urban does valorize the personal by extracting as the definitive lesson of the Falklands War not that Argentinian and Thatcherite militarism are ungentlemanly acts but that war, with its inevitable assaults on human life, is by its essential nature an ungentlemanly act.

Notes

1. The Hunts' conception of the role of manners derives, of course, from the eighteenth-century code of the gentleman. It is therefore consistent with Edmund Burke's famous statement about the relationship between manners and morals: 'Manners are of more importance than laws. Upon them, in a great measure, the laws depend. The law touches us but here and there, and now and then. Manners are what vex and sooth, corrupt or purify, exalt or debase, barbarize or refine us . . . They give their whole form and colour to our lives. According to their quality, they aid morals, they supply them, or they totally destroy them' (p. 172).
2. At one point in his account of his experiences as Governor of the Falkland Islands, Rex Hunt compares Government House to a vicarage in the Yorkshire Dales (p. 21).
3. In reality the Royal Marines were also armed with an 84mm anti-tank gun positioned to fire at any ship entering Stanley harbour. However, since the Argentinians did not attack by the route Norman anticipated this gun played no part in the battle. See Freedman, p. 111. The other statistics quoted in my discussion of the relative strengths of the combatants are also taken from Freedman, pp. 110–16.

Works Cited

Adams, Valerie. *The Media and the Falklands Campaign*. London: Macmillan, 1986.

Arrivederci Millwall. Screenplay by Nick Perry, directed by Charles MacDougall. BBC 1, 1990.

Aulich, James. 'Wildlife in the South Atlantic: Graphic Satire, Patriotism and the Fourth Estate' in James Aulich (ed.) *Framing the Falklands War: Nationhood, Culture and Identity*. Milton Keynes: Open University Press, 1991, 84–116.

Bairstow, Tom. 'The Fleet Street Warriors Who Turn from Bingo to Jingo in the Battle of Sagging Sales', *Guardian*, 10 May 1982, 8.

Barker, Pat. *Regeneration* (1991). New York: Plume, 1993.

Barnett, Anthony. *Iron Britannia*. London: Busby, 1982.

Barthes, Roland. *Mythologies*. London: Paladin, 1973.

Bate, W. Jackson. *Samuel Johnson*. New York: Harcourt Brace Jovanovich, 1979.

Battle for the Falklands. ITN/Granada, 1982.

'Belgrano's Children', *War Stories*. Directed by Miguel Pereira. BBC 2, 2 April 1992.

Bell, Steve. *Further Down on Maggie's Farm and Other Stories*. Harmondsworth: Penguin, 1982.

——. *The If . . . Chronicles*. London: Methuen, 1993.

Berkoff, Steven. *'Sink the Belgrano!' and 'Massage'*. London: Faber and Faber, 1987.

Bhabha, Homi K. 'DissemiNation: Time, Narrative, and the Margins of the Modern Nation' in Homi K. Bhabha (ed.), *Nation and Narration*. London: Routledge, 1990, 291–322.

Bleaney, Michael. 'Conservative Economic Strategy' in Stuart Hall and Martin Jacques (eds), *The Politics of Thatcherism*. London: Lawrence and Wishart, 1983, 132–47.

Bond, Edward. *Restoration: A Pastoral*. London: Methuen, 1988.

Branfield, John. *The Falklands Summer*. London: Victor Gollancz, 1987.

Brennan, Timothy. 'The National Longing for Form' in Homi K. Bhabha (ed.), *Nation and Narration*. London: Routledge, 1990, 44–70.

Briggs, Raymond. *The Tin-Pot Foreign General and the Old Iron Woman*. London: Hamish Hamilton, 1984.

Brooks, Richard. 'Strangers in the Atlantic Night', *Observer*, 7 June 1992, 74.

Buford, Bill. *Among the Thugs*. London: Mandarin, 1992.

Burke, Edmund. 'First Letter on a Regicide Peace'. *The Works of Edmund Burke*. Vol. 8. London: Rivington, 1803–27.

Burke, John J., Jr. 'When the Falklands First Demanded an Historian: Johnson, Junius and the Making of History in 1771', *The Age of Johnson: A Scholarly Annual*, 2 (1989), 291–310.

Calder, Angus. *The Myth of the Blitz*. London: Jonathan Cape, 1991.

Chambers, Iain. *Border Dialogues: Journeys in Post-Modernism*. London: Routledge/Comedia, 1990.

Collier, Susanne. 'Post-Falklands, Post-Colonial: Contextualizing Branagh as Henry V on Stage and on Film', *Essays in Theatre*, 10 (1992), 143–154.

Conran, Tony. 'Elegy for the Welsh Dead, in the Falkland Islands, 1982' in *Blodeuwedd*. Bridgend: Poetry Wales Press, 1988, 14–15.

Cottrell, Stella. 'The Devil on Two Sticks: Franco-Phobia in 1803' in Raphael Samuel (ed.), *Patriotism: The Making and Unmaking of British National Identity*. London: Routledge, 1989., vol. 1, 260–74.

Curteis, Ian. *The Falklands Play: A Television Play*. London: Century Hutchinson, 1987.

Davidson, Ian. 'A Principle is a Principle', *Financial Times*, 7 April 1982, 7.

Derrida, Jacques. 'Structure, Sign and Play in the Discourse of the Human Sciences' in Philip Rice and Patricia Waugh (ed.), *Modern Literary Theory: A Reader*. London: Edward Arnold, 1989, 149–65.

DeLillo, Don. *White Noise*. London: Picador, 1985.

Dillon, G. M. *The Falklands, Politics and War*. London: Macmillan, 1989.

Dresser, Madge. 'Britannia' in Raphael Samuel (ed.), *Patriotism: The Making and Unmaking of British National Identity*. London: Routledge, 1989, vol. 3, 26–49.

Dr Strangelove: Or How I Learned to Stop Worrying and Love the Bomb. Screenplay by Stanley Kubrick, Terry Southern and Peter George, directed by Stanley Kubrick. Columbia, 1964.

Dunn, Tony. Review of '*Metamorphosis*'/'*Sink the Belgrano!*', *Plays and Players*: 398 (Nov. 1986), 32–3.

Englehardt, Tom. *The End of Victory Culture: Cold War America and the Disillusioning of a Generation*. New York: Basic Books, 1995.

Fairlie, Henry. 'By Jingo, We're All Rooting for You', *The Times*, 17 April 1982, 10.

'Falklands Flurries', *City Limits*, 6 August 1987, 4.

The Falklands Factor. Screenplay by Don Shaw, directed by Colin Bucksey. BBC 1, 26 April 1983.

The Falklands Factor: Representations of a Conflict. Art Show, Manchester City Art Galleries, 10 December 1988 to 22 January 1989.

The Falklands War. Screenplay by Denys Blakeway, produced by Hugh Scully. 4 parts. Channel 4, 13, 20, 27 January and 3 February 1992.

The Falklands War: The Untold Story. Directed by Peter Kosminsky. Yorkshire Television, 1987.

Femenia, Nora. *National Identity in Times of Crisis: The Scripts of the Falklands War*. Commack, NY: Nova Science, 1996.

For Queen and Country. Screenplay by Martin Stellman and Trix Worrell, directed by Martin Stellman. UIP/Zenith/Atlantic/Working Title, 1988.

Francis, Richard. *Swansong*. London: Flamingo, 1986.

Fraser, Antonia. *The Warrior Queens*. New York: Knopf, 1989.

Freedman, Lawrence and Virginia Gamba-Stonehouse. *Signals of War: The Falklands Conflict of 1982*. London: Faber and Faber, 1990.

Fussell, Paul. *The Great War and Modern Memory*. London: Oxford UP, 1977.

Gamble, Andrew. *The Free Economy and the Strong State: The Politics of Thatcherism*. Durham: Duke University Press, 1988.

Gilroy, Paul. *There Ain't No Black in the Union Jack: The Cultural Politics of Race and Nation*. London: Hutchinson, 1987.

Girouard, Mark. *The Return to Camelot: Chivalry and the English Gentleman*. New Haven: Yale University Press, 1981.

Hall, Stuart. 'The Great Moving Right Show' in Stuart Hall and Martin Jacques (eds), *The Politics of Thatcherism*. London: Lawrence and Wishart, 1983, 19–39.

Hardy, Adam. *Strike Force Falklands*. 6 vols. London: Futura, 1984–5.

Harris, Robert. *Gotcha! The Media, the Government and the Falklands Crisis*. London: Faber and Faber, 1985.

Haviland, Julian. '"Rejoice", Says Mrs Thatcher', *The Times*, 26 April 1982, 1.

Herr, Michael. *Dispatches*. New York: Vintage, 1991.

Higgins, Jack. *Exocet*. London: Pan, 1984.

Hobsbawm, Eric. 'Falklands Fallout' in Stuart Hall and Martin Jacques (eds), *The Politics of Thatcherism*. London: Lawrence and Wishart, 1983, 257–70.

Holmes, Colin. *A Tolerant Country? Immigrants, Refugees and Minorities in Britain*. London: Faber and Faber, 1991.

Hope and Glory. Written and directed by John Boorman. Columbia, 1987.

Hunt, Rex. *My Falklands Days*. London: David and Charles, 1992.

Hynes, Samuel. *A War Imagined: The First World War and English Culture*. New York: Atheneum, 1991.

Johnson, Barbara. 'Writing' in Frank Lentricchia and Thomas McLaughlin (eds), *Critical Terms for Literary Study*. 2nd ed. Chigago: University of Chicago Press, 1995.

Johnson, Samuel. 'Thoughts on the Late Transactions Respecting Falkland's Islands, 1771' in Donald Greene (ed.), *Samuel Johnson: Political Writings*. New Haven: Yale University Press, 1977, 346–86.

Kemp, Philip. Review of *An Ungentlemanly Act*, *Sight and Sound*, 2.4 (August 1992), 65.

Langdon, Julia. 'Thatcher's Appeal for Support', *Guardian*, 15 May 1982, 1

Lawrence, John and Robert Lawrence. *When the Fighting is Over: A Personal Story of the Battle for Mount Tumbledown and its Aftermath*. London: Bloomsbury, 1988.

Local Hero. Written and directed by Bill Forsyth. Enigma/Goldcrest, 1983.

Lukowiak, Ken. *A Soldier's Song*. London: Secker and Warburg, 1993.

MacDonald, Robert H. 'A Poetics of War: Militaristic Discourse in the British Empire, 1880–1918', *Mosaic*, 23.3 (1990), 17–35.

MacKenzie, Paul. 'Artistic Truth, Historical Truth: The "Faction" Film and the Falklands War', *War, Literature and the Arts*, 6.1 (1994), 41–61.

'Mad Dogs and Englishmen', *Guardian*, 22 January 1991, 16.

McEwan, Ian. *The Ploughman's Lunch*. London: Methuen, 1985.

Mercer, Derrik, Geoff Mungham and Kevin Williams. *The Fog of War: The Media on the Battlefield*. London: Heinemann, 1987.

Mooney, Bel and Gerald Scarfe. *Father Kissmass and Mother Claws*. London: Hamish Hamilton, 1985.

Morgan, K. S. (ed.). *The Falklands Campaign: A Digest of Debates in the House of Commons, 2 April to 15 June 1982*. London: Her Majesty's Stationary Office, 1982.

Morrison, David E. and Howard Tumber. *Journalists at War: The Dynamics of News Reporting During the Falklands War*. London: Sage, 1988.

Nairn, Tom. *The Break-Up of Britain: Crisis and Neo-Nationalism*. London: New Left Books, 1977

Naughton, John. Review of *The Falklands Factor*, *The Listener*, 109 (28 April 1983), 29.

'Nick Barker – Captain of the HMS *Endurance*', *War Stories*. BBC 2, 12 March 1992.

Noon, Jeff. *Woundings*. Birmingham: Oberon Books, 1986.

Norris, Christopher. *What's Wrong with Postmodernism: Critical Theory and the Ends of Philosophy*. Baltimore: Johns Hopkins Press, 1990.

——. *Uncritical Theory: Postmodernism, Intellectuals and the Gulf War*. London: Lawrence and Wishart, 1992.

Perry, Nick. *'Arrivederci Millwall' and 'Smallholdings'*. London: Faber and Faber, 1987.

The Ploughman's Lunch. Screenplay by Ian McEwan, directed by Richard Eyre. Goldcrest/Greenpoint/AC&D, 1983.

'The Price of Victory', *Panorama*. BBC 1, 14 February 1983.

'The Prime Minister's Interview with Jimmy Young', *The Times*, 20 May 1982, 6.

Raban, Jonathan. *Coasting*. London: Collins Harvill, 1986.

——. *God, Man and Mrs Thatcher: A Critique of Mrs Thatcher's Address to the General Assembly of the Church of Scotland*. London: Chatto and Windus, 1989.

Resurrected. Screenplay by Martin Allen, directed by Paul Greengrass. Hobo/St Pancras/Film Four International/British Screen, 1989.

Samuel, Raphael. 'Introduction: Exciting to be English' in Raphael Samuel (ed.), *Patriotism: The Making and Unmaking of British National Identity*. London: Routledge, 1989, vol. 1, xiii–lxvii.

Scarry, Elaine. *The Body in Pain: The Making and Unmaking of the World*. New York: Oxford UP, 1985.

Seidel, Jill and Renate Gunther. ' "Nation" and "Family" in the British Media Reporting of the Falklands Conflict' in Jill Seidel (ed.), *The Nature of the Right: A Feminist Analysis of Order Patterns*. Amsterdam: John Benjamin, 1988.

'Simon's Return'. *QED*. Directed by Michael Brinkworth. BBC 1, 1 April 1992.

Slattery, Jill. Letter to the Author, 25 May 1995.

Solomos, John. *Race and Racism in Contemporary Britain*. London: Macmillan, 1989.

Stafford, David. 'Spies and Gentleman: The Birth of the British Spy Novel', *Victorian Studies*, 24.2 (Summer 1981), 489–509.

Task Force South: The Battle for the Falklands. Written and produced by Gordon Carr. 7 parts. BBC 1, July–August 1982.

Tendler, Stewart. 'Royal Navy in Action: The Great Ships Sail off to War', *The Times*, 6 April 1982, 2.

Thatcher, Margaret. 'Margaret Thatcher Talks to George Gale', *Daily Express*, 26 July 1982, 15–17.

——. 'To the 52nd Annual Conservative Women's Conference, London, 26 May 1982', in *In Defence of Freedom: Speeches on Britain's Relations with the World, 1976–1986*. London: Aurum Press, 1986, 72–6.

——. 'To the Conservative Party Conference, Blackpool, 10 October 1975', *The Revival of Britain: Speeches on Home and European Affairs*. London: Aurum Press, 1989, 18–28.

——. *The Downing Street Years*. London: Harper Collins, 1993.

Theroux, Paul. *The Kingdom by the Sea*. New York: Washington Square Press, 1984.

Thompson, E. P. 'Why Neither Side is Worth Backing', *The Times*, 29 April 1982, 12.

Thompson, J. *No Picnic: 3 Commando Brigade in the South Atlantic, 1982*. Glasgow: Fontana/Collins, 1985.

Tinker, David. *A Message from the Falklands: The Life and Gallant Death of David Tinker, Lieut. R.N.* Compiled by Hugh Tinker. Harmondsworth: Penguin, 1983.

Tumbledown. Screenplay by Charles Wood, directed by Richard Eyre. BBC 1, June, 1988.

An Ungentlemanly Act. Written and directed by Stuart Urban. BBC 2, 13 June 1992.

Urban, Stuart. 'History as Force', *Sight and Sound*, 2.5 (September 1992), 71.

'We Are All Falklanders Now' (editorial), *The Times*. 5 April 1982, 26.

Webster, Philip. 'Victoria Invoked by Prime Minister', *The Times*. 6 April 1982A, 2.

——. 'Thatcher's "Panorama" Interview: Answering Argentina's Ploy to Stall Military Action', *The Times*, 27 April 1982B, 4.

Williams, John. 'White Riots: The English Football Fan Abroad', in *Off the Ball: The 1986 Football World Cup*. London: Pluto Press, 1986.

Williams, Philip, with M. S. Power. *Summer Soldier: The True Story of the Missing Falklands Guardsman*. London: Bloomsbury, 1990.

Wood, Charles. *Tumbledown*. Harmondsworth: Penguin, 1987.

'Woolly Al Walks the Kitty Back', *Timewatch*. BBC 2. 11 March 1982.

Wright, Patrick. *On Living in an Old Country: The National Past in Contemporary Britain*. London: Verso, 1985.

Young, Hugo. *One of Us: A Biography of Margaret Thatcher*. London: Pan, 1993.

INDEX